ACTIVISM IN JORDAN

ABOUT THE AUTHOR

Pénélope Larzillière is senior research fellow at the Institute for Research on Development (IRD-CEPED, Paris), and associate fellow at the School of Advanced Studies in Social Sciences (CADIS-EHESS). Her research focuses on political commitment, activism and ideologies, specializing in the Middle East. Her previous books include *To Be Young in Palestine* (Balland, 2004). She has also co-edited the journal issues "Révolutions, contestations, indignations" (*Socio*, 2013) and "Faut-il désoccidentaliser l'humanitaire?" (*Humanitaire*, 2010).

ACTIVISM IN JORDAN

PÉNÉLOPE LARZILLIÈRE
TRANSLATED BY CYNTHIA SCHOCH

Zed Books
London

Activism in Jordan was first published in English in 2016 by
Zed Books Ltd, The Foundry, 17 Oval Way,
London SE11 5RR, UK.

www.zedbooks.net

Copyright © Pénélope Larzillière 2016

Originally published in French by Actes Sud.

The right of Pénélope Larzillière to be identified as the
author of this work has been asserted by her in accordance with the
Copyright, Designs and Patents Act, 1988.

The right of Cynthia Schoch to be identified as the translator of this
work has been asserted by her in accordance with the Copyright,
Designs and Patents Act, 1988.

Typeset in Bulmer MT by Swales & Willis Ltd, Exeter, Devon
Index: Rohan Bolton
Cover design: Keith Dodds

All rights reserved. No part of this publication may be reproduced,
stored in a retrieval system or transmitted in any form or by any means,
electronic, mechanical, photocopying or otherwise, without the prior
permission of Zed Books Ltd.

A catalogue record for this book is available from the British Library.

ISBN 978-1-78360-575-0 hb
ISBN 978-1-78360-574-3 pb
ISBN 978-1-78360-576-7 pdf
ISBN 978-1-78360-577-4 epub
ISBN 978-1-78360-578-1 mobi

Contents

	ACKNOWLEDGEMENTS	vii
	INTRODUCTION	1
1	The Jordanian regime	11
2	Becoming an activist	30
3	The student experience	50
4	Activism, a way of life	73
5	Repression and dissidence	96
6	Professional activism as an alternative	110
7	New forms of mobilization	131
8	Disillusioned Islamists	158

CONCLUSION	180
METHODOLOGICAL APPENDIX	189
NOTES	203
BIBLIOGRAPHY	222
INDEX	232

Acknowledgements

This book is the product of extensive field research in Jordan. I wish to express my gratitude to all the men and women who helped me throughout this investigation, although they cannot all be named here. The Institut Français du Proche-Orient in Amman hosted me over a number of years during several stays a number of months long. There I found valuable discussions as well as priceless introductions, and in particular I want to thank Jalal Al Husseini and Fadi Bardawil, as well as Myriam Ababsa, Françoise de Bel-Air and Géraldine Chatelard.

The first phase of this research was presented in the framework of the research programme at the Institut d'études de l'Islam et des sociétés du monde musulman at the École des hautes études en sciences sociales (IISMM-EHESS) in Paris, a programme led by Jalal Al Husseini and Aude Signoles. The observations made during the various programme meetings were extremely useful, and I thank the participants, particularly Philippe Bourmaud, Khadija Fadhel, Stéphanie Latte-Abdallah, Daniel Meier, Falestin Naïli, Daniel Rivet, Vincent Romani, Bernard Rougier and Klaus Schlichte.

I also owe a debt of gratitude to those who read and commented on my work at various stages: Hamit Bozarslan, André Bank, Maher

Charif, Agnès Favier, Elisabeth Longuenesse and Aude Signoles; not forgetting Laurence Proteau, who one morning, when we ran into each other in the metro, gave me precious advice on presenting the activists' trajectories, and Irène Maffi, who wisely encouraged me to add a methodological appendix.

Over the years, in various academic settings both in France and abroad, I also had the opportunity to discuss this research as it matured, which gave rise to profitable exchanges of views. For that I thank Omar Carlier, Hélène Combes, Larry Diamond, Kamel Doraï, Antimo Farro, Wilhelm Heitmeyer, Teresa Koloma Beck, Yvon Le Bot, Sandrine Nicourd, Geoffrey Pleyers, Nicolas Puig, Olivier Roy and Maud Simonet, as well as my colleagues at the Centre d'études populations et développement (CEPED). For discussions about the Arab left, I thank Gilbert Achcar, Mounia Bennani-Chraïbi and Didier Monciaud.

A special mention also goes to the team that helped me transcribe and translate the interviews, which totalled over 600 pages.

Cynthia Schoch, the translator, would like to thank her trainee, Abigail Wahl Genon, for her valuable help with the translation.

Introduction

The waves of protest that swept through the Arab world in 2011 and 2012 and the toppling of the Tunisian and Egyptian regimes have focused attention on the opposition to authoritarian regimes. In Jordan, between censorship, repression and election rigging, political activism is limited despite the democratic opening of 1989. Officially, Jordan is a constitutional monarchy with an elected parliament, but in reality Jordanian politics is an exclusionary system. Many terms, such as "defensive democratization", "paradoxical liberalization" and "authoritarian elections", have been used to describe this ambivalence. Democratic institutions and political opposition do exist, but it remains difficult to address real political issues, and the monarchy as an institution is non-negotiable. Although Jordan does have a constitution, which was adopted in 1952 and has been amended many times since, it accords quasi-full powers to the king, who rules by decree, appoints the prime minister, and can dissolve parliament, which can only draft laws. The official democratic "opening" has not prevented the establishment of a coercive legal framework limiting political participation and expression. The security services remain omnipresent, and repression – although less systematic than before 1989 – continues. The apparent stability of the Jordanian regime is in fact based on complex and changing authoritarian processes that are implemented differently depending on the social and political arena. Against this background, the creation of democratic institutions may be consistent with authoritarian stabilization rather than political liberalization.

However, opposition does exist, and different ways of protesting have emerged. The experience of the opponents sheds light on conditions concerning political commitments in a repressive regime. A field survey conducted over several years has made it possible to chart the paths of longstanding activists of different leanings: Islamists, nationalists and communists. With the exception of the Islamists, who have always been authorized – if sometimes repressed – by the Jordanian monarchy, opposition has shifted from underground movements to a heavily controlled public sphere. A number of activists have also experienced prison. In this book they discuss their motivations, their commitment and the consequences these have had throughout their lives.

These political journeys serve to highlight the general conditions for political activism in a repressive regime, but also the meaning individuals attach to their commitment and their chosen ideologies. How do future activists perceive different points of reference, and how do they decide on their first affiliations? Ideological orientation is linked to loci of secondary socialization, which are often where activists are first politicized. There are few cases of activist families, though the influence of an older brother is sometimes cited. Rather, university and even secondary school are important channels where activist involvement begins. "Mentors", such as teachers or friends, play an important role in this regard, as does the local influence of a particular political movement. While the choice of Islamism by a person attending a predominantly leftwing university may cause surprise, it quickly becomes apparent that this choice was made earlier, in a secondary school where the majority of students were Islamists or under the influence of an older activist brother. In a particular village, the youth centre was predominantly communist, and the young people that attended also became communist. A youth worker who provides books and takes the time to engage in lengthy political discussions acts as a mentor. These local hegemonies tend to persist even if they do not reflect the general context, and activists readily acknowledge the major role they played in their commitment. Some go as far as admitting that, had they gone to a different university, they probably would have chosen a different political persuasion. For the activists, the value of the ideological content chosen is, however, not undermined by this initial indetermination.

While local influences shape the activists' choice of ideology from an early age, once a decision has been made, the majority of them stick with their choice. It is usually sympathizers rather than the activists who switch from one movement to another; for the latter, the impact of militant socialization is very strong. Moreover, for Islamists and communists – much less so for nationalists – the ideological stance relates not only to political position, but becomes a real way of life, often resulting in the creation of a closed circle. This initial engagement has major consequences that are dependent on the regional or international evolution of the ideology adopted, but above all on how it is perceived by the Jordanian regime. Given the semi-secrecy of communists and the integrated opposition of Islamists, the scope of possibilities for the activists is not the same.

The ideological frameworks for political commitment are regional or international: communism, Arab nationalism, Palestinian nationalism or Islamism. The foothold they have is, however, closely dependent on the national context. Palestinian nationalism is a special case. The activists interviewed, whether Palestinian or not, have all been deeply marked by the history of the Palestinian people and the massive influx of Palestinian refugees into Jordan in 1948 and 1967. The Palestinian question in Jordan is twofold. There is consensus concerning opposition to the Israeli occupation of the West Bank and Gaza. However, tensions run high concerning the status and the role of Palestinians in Jordan. For the most part, a distinction has been drawn between "Palestinians" and "Transjordanians". A number of families have branches from both sides of the River Jordan. The Hashemite Kingdom was created relatively recently and the notion of Transjordan did not exist prior to its establishment. However, this is not the point. The opposition between post-1948 Palestinians and Transjordanians is an integral part of the construction of the Jordanian state. After the collapse of the Ottoman Empire, the monarchy began to look for another enemy against which it could build unity. This is how Palestinians and the growing national Palestinian movement were gradually portrayed as figures and influences from abroad in Jordan at the end of the 1950s. The regime, through King Hussein himself, continued to call for unity, while relying specifically on Transjordanians for the public sector. The portrayal of the Palestinian as an "Other"[1] or a foreigner helped to foster the establishment of a specific Transjordanian identity, with Transjordanian tribes being considered as the basis of the regime within a specific legislation. This differentiated treatment of the two populations, in addition to the link to Palestinian exile, led to the gradual establishment of distinct communities. This is not to suggest that the refugee camps – where only a minority of Palestinians live[2] – are hotspots of political activism in Jordan. Young people in the camps tend to be depoliticized, or at least removed from traditional forms of activism.[3] However, the question of "Palestinian" or "Jordanian" origin has become a key political issue. Although the leaders of the political movements generally deny this split, it runs throughout the entire opposition and divides it with respect to the monarchy.

Arenas of activism

Beyond differences relating to identity and ideology, the development of a platform for opposition remains the main issue. The establishment and development of arenas for opposition against authoritarianism constitute a major challenge for the activists. The paths they have taken show the role of university as an important locus of politicization and mobilization, and this is not specific to Jordan. The limited opportunities for political activism in an authoritarian regime can be seen more clearly in the later stages of their involvement. Certainly, at university, student demonstrations are quashed. However, later in an activist's life, loci for activism are lacking and alternative spaces for politicization are sought. Political parties, prohibited for many years and still restricted considerably by legislation after their authorization in 1992, play a limited role. King Abdullah II's accession to the throne after the death of his father Hussein in 1999 undoubtedly changed the social and economic bases of the monarchy. However, it did not put an end to the use of authoritarian methods, since the king retains the right to dissolve parliament and to rule by decree. The main change concerns economic policy, which now falls within a concomitant process of economic liberalization and authoritarian consolidation.

Against this background, the challenge for opposition activists lies more in establishing alternative arenas for mobilization than in participating in a severely limited political scene by way of a compromise. Over the years, professional associations have constituted a place of exception where a certain degree of political activism has been possible despite the monarchy's repeated efforts to restrict activities through numerous draft laws. The red lines not to be crossed are clear. These restrictions and self-imposed limits can be seen in practice: activists tend to favour gatherings in front of the headquarters of professional associations rather than demonstrations, which are more heavily repressed. Likewise in speeches: when pressure from the monarchy increases, members of the associations play down their political role and emphasize the professional nature of their activity.

Professional associations – obvious places in which to pursue activism after university – play a key role in the biographies of almost all activists, and this indicates that the activists must therefore have jobs requiring qualifications. These tend to be professional bodies or corporations, since trade unions are much more closely monitored by the monarchy and do not have the same role. This strengthens the selective nature of activism – at least for the key figures – but it can also accompany a move up the social ladder, since many activists come from poor rural families. Political involvement has consequences for career choice, and in particular restricts fields of employment. For example, leftwing activists are not permitted to hold public service positions, unlike Islamists, who are often teachers. Opposition activists tend to gravitate towards the private sector and in particular towards setting up private clinics or small businesses, which are not as tightly controlled as large businesses, where it is easier for the security services to reject an appointment.

Non-governmental organizations (NGOs) and advocacy groups are other popular arenas among current and former Arab leftwing activists. This mirrors a regional trend, and perhaps the general nature of contemporary activism, and occurs irrespective of government regime. In the Middle East, two elements are at stake, one ideological, the other practical.

The first is the end of the grand narratives: the failure of the ideologies they espoused has led many of these leftwing activists to embrace the broadly accepted notion of human rights in order to maintain their commitment. In so doing, they retain an international foothold, which is crucial for them since their status in their own society is often quite delicate. This does not necessarily mean that they have abandoned their former convictions; some activists prefer to distance themselves from the notion of victimhood (in terms of human rights abuses) in favour of a more politicized self-image.

The second element is that advocacy groups represent a new platform for action. The intent is to become involved in different scenes, from the local to the international level, on the basis of expertise rather than only a moral and political perspective. This approach allows the activists to call into question certain situations, to challenge governments and donors, and to propose a variety of agendas and reforms. They are therefore developing a different type of activism that is both expert and reformist and is based on technical discussion of governmental agendas. This evolution of activism is not specific to Jordan. Although the link with international organizations and their priorities ensures funding and visibility, it also widens the social disconnect, so that the activists can be perceived as an external and internationalized elite.

Recently, a number of leftwing forums have been created with flexible modes of participation that avoid repression by not making the activists "cardholders". They provide for new forms of short-term, project-based mobilization, where the activists agree on a mode of action and a specific demand rather than on a general ideology. In Jordan, NGOs have not been immune to the regime's various attempts to control their activities, whether by legislation, infiltration or co-optation. (New laws implemented in 2008 did spark numerous protests, but these were ineffective.) However, despite repression, the expert and reformist activism of the advocacy groups has taken on particular importance, since the monarchy is heavily dependent on donors and relies on what can be called humanitarian rent; it is therefore difficult for the regime to ignore this type of intervention. Moreover, the so-called "royal NGOs" provide a way for the regime to become involved.

The demonstrations coinciding with the Arab Spring in 2011 and 2012 drew on these alternative arenas and served to strengthen and radicalize them. They were characterized initially by the entry of new, younger actors, who for the most part were not affiliated with political parties, but had been involved in voluntary associations. However, the demonstrations increased in size when activists from established organizations ranging from the left to Islamists joined in, following on from the numerous labour struggles of 2010. Nevertheless, the structural limits of opposition in Jordan have not been radically modified, even if some tribes, generally considered as pillars of the regime, have joined the opposition. The divisions between "native" Jordanians (or Transjordanians) and Jordanian Palestinians continue to cut across the entire political spectrum. However, this movement is experiencing a degree of generational renewal, and its spread across the region has given longstanding activists a new lease of life.

Ideology and commitment

The spread of protests known as the Arab Spring has strengthened longstanding activists in Jordan, and made them more optimistic about the prospects for political change in the medium term. This fresh optimism has in turn given new meaning to their commitment, even as it is accompanied by skepticism toward the monarchy's promises of reform.

The way in which the activists perceive their commitment is closely linked to the successes or failures of the ideologies they support. These have an impact on their political evaluations, but also on their personal ones. Islamists follow a fairly straight path without major doubts, while the ideology they support continues to gain strength. Although they may criticize the strategies of their party or its position regarding the regime, the political vision of Islamism is not called into question. On the contrary, it serves as a reference point for critics of the movement, for example, in the name of greater loyalty to Islamic principles. This relative triumphalism can be seen in biographical interviews, where Islamists express a certain degree of complacency. Intellectual precocity, piety, charitable and political work, and recognition from teachers and classmates are highlighted. Although Islamists are not in power, the social hegemony from which they benefit has a very positive impact on their self-perception. They do not have any real competitors in terms of political ideology or even social paradigm. Irrespective of their success or failure in elections, even the monarchy must be held to account as regards its religious legitimacy and has to adopt a political stance on social issues defined by the Islamists.

The picture is quite different for nationalists and, above all, the left wing and communists. These activists have been greatly affected by the failure of their ideologies. Communists became even more marginalized when they lost international support after the collapse of the Soviet Union. Deprived of social support and heavily repressed, communist solidarity is breaking apart, quarrels and divisions within the Communist Party of Jordan are growing, and disaffection and challenges are on the rise. However, the social trajectories of the communists show that ideological and political failure – a bitter blow to the activists – does not preclude a certain degree of professional success. Activist ties have provided a network and structure that have facilitated their integration into the job market, particularly when they were unable to finish school or university due to crackdowns. However, their attitude towards their own trajectory is fraught with doubts. While their view of the world and their political ideology are largely unchanged, and they remain strongly attached to their principles, they have become rather abstract and have distanced themselves from questioning the conditions that could lead to implementing them. They prefer to reflect on the reasons for past failures; for those who remain engaged, involvement is based more on social issues or human rights. That said, even Islamists are not completely immune from disengagement and rifts; there are also those disappointed in Islamism who have come into conflict with the Muslim Brotherhood, calling into question the organization and the way in which it refers to Islam. They also look for other forms of commitment, becoming involved in associations or even joining leftwing organizations.

As Reinhart Koselleck points out, trajectories of defeat, rifts and changes of allegiance – sometimes a source of great bitterness – are interesting in that the views of the "vanquished" are fraught with doubt, unlike those of the "victors" who remain sure of their choices.[4] This was also observed in the respondents' attitude towards their interviews. The Islamists saw an opportunity to report their successes and did not welcome questions that might challenge this vision, whereas communists used the interview situation as an opportunity to reflect on their journey and to understand what did not work. The stakes are higher for Jordanian communists, who are marginalized in two ways: as "losers" in history, they attract less interest even though they have dedicated a large part of their lives to activism; and as Jordanians, their engagement is somewhat ignored and considered as peripheral, even by their comrades in neighbouring countries such as Lebanon.

These activist trajectories are analysed at different levels. First, the national level, where the link to the regime and repression is played out, shapes the paths. However, ideological flows in the Arab world and beyond also have an impact. Practices are greatly affected by the international development of modalities for political action. Thus, expertise and its corollary, the professionalization of activists, play an increasing role, which is leading to a change in methods of recruitment. Certain transversal elements of the sociology of activism are also confirmed: namely, the importance of mentors, local hegemonies and activist socialization. This review of the paths of longstanding activists also helps to clarify, from within, contemporary developments in activism in the Arab world.

CHAPTER 1

The Jordanian regime

The political image of the Kingdom of Jordan, both peripheral and attractive to the West, is surprising. By way of example, an American journalist describing a day with Abdullah II gave an account full of stereotypes: a king who was pleasant, modern, pro-Western, a supporter of new technologies and a liberal economy with an eminently elegant and active wife. He was working tirelessly to steer his country towards modernity, notwithstanding the struggles of the rear guard of retrograde forces in Jordanian society and tribal elders, the "old dinosaurs" (the phrase used by the king, according to the journalist).[1] Whatever the personality of the current King of Jordan, this image is rooted in the history of the Jordanian monarchy, which has always been seen as an ally of the West in the region, and in particular for the English and Americans, including in regard to the question of Israel. This aspect conceals another: the authoritarian methods of stabilization used by the regime since the beginning, which are a decisive factor for the opposition. This is why, before examining the activists' biographies, a summary of the construction and functioning of the Jordanian state may be useful.

The founding of Jordan was not preceded by a national Jordanian movement, even if anti-colonial Arab nationalist movements were being developed there. Jordan is often considered to be entirely a creation of the British. The majority of activists of all persuasions continue to refer to the artificial nature of Jordan, citing the Sykes-Picot Agreement of May 1916 that divided the Arab provinces of the Ottoman Empire between France and Great Britain.[2] "Southern Syria", the area to the east of the River Jordan, was allocated to Britain. The mandates granted after World War I confirmed the division, but there were some changes. Palestine to the west of the River Jordan fell under a direct British mandate, and the land east of it became the Emirate of Transjordan in 1921. Emir Abdullah, from Hijaz, a region that is now part of the Kingdom of Saudi Arabia, was made leader by the British. He was a proponent of anti-Ottoman nationalism under the banner of the Hashemite family, pro-Western, and opposed a second anti-colonial nationalist movement that sought to build a specific Arab identity that made reference to a great Arab past and technological modernity. Abdullah remained under the supervision of the British and declared himself King of Jordan when the emirate became a kingdom in 1946. An Anglo-Jordanian Treaty continued to give Britain a certain number of rights over the kingdom; it was not until 1957 that those ties were officially broken.

After the assassination of King Abdullah in 1951, the Hashemite power was weakened, despite continued British support, notably financial assistance. The beginnings of political liberalization took hold, firstly under King Talal, the son of Abdullah, and then, after his abdication,[3] by his grandson Hussein in 1953. Arab nationalists then took on greater political importance as a result of elections, but also due to their ability to mobilize large numbers of protesters. Their demands implied a complete overhaul of the Hashemite regime, the questioning of British involvement, and armed opposition to Israeli infiltration in Jordan. The 1950s were characterized by cycles of political openness and repression that mirrored the power struggle between Arab nationalists and King Hussein.[4] Although the Arab nationalists obtained the support of the majority of the population, they lost the power struggle with King Hussein; the liberalization process ended with a coup d'état in 1957 that Hussein was able to use to his own advantage with the support of the Americans and heralded a long period of political repression. In 1953 a law was passed specifically banning communists, and in 1957 political parties were dissolved and martial law was imposed until November 1958.[5] It was reinstated in 1967 and maintained until 1989. Activists were operating in semi-secrecy, with the exception of Islamists, since the Muslim Brotherhood movement was allowed to operate.

However, despite the circumstances in which the monarchy was instituted, even its most determined opponents found themselves within the framework of the Jordanian state, by continually referring to its institutions, even though they did not recognize the monarchy's legitimacy, declaring it to be artificial and totally subjugated to American foreign policy. Here, state institutions played their role in integration. A specific Jordanian identity was created from the ground up, and this is one of the great successes of the Hashemite monarchy.

The Jordanian regime developed specific strategies to build legitimacy and identify national actors on which it could rely in order to determine the political directions of the state: this is a challenge for Jordan – a country that has a subordinate international position and is only partly responsible for determining its own policies and agenda. The strategies for legitimization include the development of a specific Jordanian identity that is based on a policy to differentiate between two categories: "native" Jordanians (or Transjordanians) and Jordanian Palestinians.

In the "native" Jordanian category, the tribe is highly valued, as both an identity and social framework. One of the ways the monarchy tried to build a social base under King Hussein was through the tribalization of political life. This does not mean that tribal networks have automatically supported the monarchy. Hussein sought to ensure their loyalty by handing out posts and resources. This policy was based more specifically on two institutions: the army, with the Bedouins being integrated into special units; and the legal system, with specific legislation for tribes.[6] At the same time, a Transjordanian "memory" was created and passed on by museums[7] and schools.[8]

Transjordanians are therefore a different category from Palestinians, or Jordanian Palestinians, which comprises mainly those who arrived from Palestine after 1948.

The Palestinian question

The Palestinian question is particularly salient in Jordan, since the establishment of the state of Israel and the Arab defeat of 1948 led to an influx of 70,000–100,000 Palestinian refugees into Jordan (600,000 in the West Bank). In 1967, according to official figures, 240,000 displaced persons came to Jordan.[9] The term "displaced persons" rather than "refugees" was used in 1967 because the West Bank was still under the jurisdiction of Jordan, as it had been since 1950. It was occupied by Israel in 1967, but administrative ties with Jordan continued until 1988.

Jordan's population currently comprises 40–60 per cent[10] Palestinians, primarily in the cities of Amman and Zarqa. This range has been given as estimates vary and fuel debates about the political role of Palestinians in Jordan, and in particular about the status to be accorded to Jordan (the transformation of Jordan into a "homeland" for Palestinians was proposed by Ariel Sharon). A census conducted in 2009 by the United Nations Relief and Works Agency for Palestinian Refugees in the Near East (UNWRA) found that there were 1.9 million Palestinian refugees in Jordan. These figures are for Palestinian refugees and their descendants, but do not include the many Palestinians outside these categories. The vast majority have Jordanian citizenship.

Beyond the controversial issue of figures, while the Arab defeat in 1948 allowed earlier forms of anti-colonial nationalism to evolve into pan-Arab socialism, the 1967 defeat helped to forge among Palestinians a specific nationalism that no longer entirely fits in with pan-Arabism. The slogan "the liberation of Palestine leads to Arab unity" replaced that of the Arab nationalists: "Arab unity leads to the liberation of Palestine." In 1970, with the strengthening of Palestinian organizations in Jordan, tensions were heightened towards the Jordanian monarchy, which was fearful of losing control. A decision was made to attack Palestinian groups ideologically as well as militarily. The operation resulted in 3,400–7,000 deaths (some estimates put the figure as high as 20,000). Historically, the Jordanian/Palestinian division is not as clear as it might appear: a large proportion of the country's elite, including Jordanian Palestinians, supported the regime in that attack, whereas opposition groups included Arab nationalist organizations whose members included non-Palestinians. However, this well-known event in the history of Jordan raised the spectre of civil war and marked the climax of Jordanian–Palestinian opposition. It left a lasting mark on the perceptions of Palestinian nationalism and Jordanian Palestinians.

Among the opposition, Palestinian nationalism is currently a key issue – in various forms – for all political factions. However, it is analysed very differently depending on whether the respondents are Palestinian or Transjordanian. Palestinian activists emphasize the importance of the national struggle and the strategies of political organizations in that regard. They also highlight the unity of the region before Jordan was created and the importance of communications between the two banks of Jordan. This reference to age-old ties serves to neutralize true oppositions that jeopardize the unity of the kingdom, to highlight the legitimacy of their presence in Jordan and to reject the systematic association between "Palestinian" and "refugee". Beyond this appeal, they position themselves well within the state of Jordan with its specific characteristics. State institutions have worked their influence. On the other hand, Transjordanians often refer to the control of Palestinian organizations over Jordanian politics and their feeling that the issue of Palestinian nationalism monopolizes Jordanian politics and prevents a focus on issues specifically relating to Jordan.

However, while both Palestinians and Transjordanians routinely mention their differences, they deny that this amounts to conflict. All opposition organizations draw attention to the fact that participation of Palestinians and Jordanians is equal. Reference to a head-on opposition remains a relative taboo within organizations and among activists, since it would have a weakening effect and create divisions within the opposition.

The limits of the 1989 open policy

Although the regime fosters and exploits divisions for political purposes, this does not mean it is assured of support from the Transjordanians. For example, in 1989 the monarchy faced riots in the south because of increases in the price of basic necessities following the implementation of an International Monetary Fund (IMF) structural adjustment programme. The rioters were not Palestinians, so the monarchy was unable to rely on the usual rhetoric of the Other Palestinian, the potential enemy within. These riots were started by unorganized actors (including taxi and lorry drivers), highlighting the weakness of the opposition political movements. Subsequently, nationalists and the left sought to organize these movements to regain some political clout, whereas Islamists attempted to calm the situation.

The strategy of King Hussein was dual, and sheds light on the processes of political containment that are still in evidence today in Jordan. On the one hand, he activated the tribal networks by visiting the south in person and holding a number of meetings. On the other, he authorized the first general legislative elections since 1967 (there had been partial ones in 1984). Political parties were still banned, and it was mainly the movements that were already authorized, namely Islamist ones, that took charge of these elections. Parties were then authorized in 1992.

However, this official "opening" took place at the same time as the establishment of a coercive legal framework limiting freedom of expression and political participation, including a law concerning censorship of the press and publications that punished lèse-majesté with a three-year prison term. Although some restrictions were lifted for activists, who were given back their passports, the security services remain omnipresent, and repression – although less systematic – continues. It is not possible to speak of a democratic transition. The shift has been from no participation to limited participation, and the development of a political arena that has remained in the hands of the monarchy. At this level, the Jordanian regime is showing that the establishment of certain democratic institutions is compatible with authoritarianism – and in fact, many authoritarian regimes have such institutions. Contrary to the expectations of classical theories of democratic transition, democratic opening can simply mean the inclusion of these institutions in an authoritarian system.[11] Albrecht emphasizes the "democracy bias" of theories contending that authoritarian regimes will experience systemic change in the wake of waves of democratization.[12] Rather than being a basis for opposition, authoritarian elections become a way to co-opt individuals.

Furthermore, the demarcation of voting districts has also fostered political tribalization. Rural areas are clearly favoured over urban areas. Depending on the constituency, a member of parliament can represent several thousand or several hundred thousand voters. The one person, one vote (first past the post) voting system encourages a tribal rather than partisan vote, with voters seeking to elect representatives of their tribe from whom they can derive favours and jobs. In this way, greater importance has been given to tribal networks[13] – another strategy that fosters depoliticization. Whatever the political role given to them, tribes do not represent an ideological power. Hitherto, the state has been far more tolerant of tribal violence than it has been of political violence. At university, clashes between tribal groups are tolerated, whereas political demonstrations are repressed.[14] Depoliticization has also been magnified by an economic and political strategy of exporting skilled labour to the Gulf countries – a strategy that has the dual advantage of exporting contention while reducing unemployment among graduates and ensuring overseas remittance income.[15] This strategy was called into question by the second Gulf War in 1990-1991 that led to a huge influx into Jordan of Palestinian refugees who were forced to flee from Gulf countries, notably Kuwait; the strategy has since been resumed.

Towards authoritarian liberalism

The transition from Hussein to Abdullah II in 1999 led to a change in the social and economic foundations of the monarchy, but it did not put an end to the use of authoritarian methods. Abdullah II has continued to implement a policy of tribalization, although he lacks his father's extensive knowledge of tribal networks and his legitimacy, with many emphasizing his education abroad. Rapidly, like his father, he dissolved parliament and ruled by decree. However in 2003, in an attempt to reduce disturbances associated with opposition to Jordan's policy of support for the United States and the Iraq War, he applied the principles of "defensive democratization" and reinstated parliament after a two-year interruption. The war in Iraq had an immediate effect on the demography and economy of Jordan because of the huge influx of Iraqi refugees. The opposition became stronger, however, and in 2005 new repressive legislation specifically targeting the Muslim Brotherhood and the Islamic

Action Front (IAF; the party it spawned in 1992) was passed, banning the use of mosques as political spaces and restricting the activities of professional associations. The same strategy was employed during the protests of 2011 and 2012.

Abdullah II has also steered the country towards economic liberalism, but this is not incompatible with maintaining authoritarian policies in a manner that is not specific to Jordan[16] and that argues against theories viewing economic liberalization as a path towards democratization. Within the framework of this "authoritarian liberalization", the monarchy sought to promote new economic elites. This does not mean that tribal networks were completely marginalized; instead, new leaders were sought within the tribes, and thus a businessman would be preferred to a traditional notable. Authoritarian elections were used for this purpose; one of the outcomes of the 2007 parliamentary elections was that the newly designated "old guard" lost seats to the rich "new guard" supported by the monarchy. Many voters sold their votes to them for 100–200 dinars[17] (they proved this by taking a photo on their mobile phone of their marked ballot paper, or by voting publicly and orally as an illiterate, as permitted under Jordanian law). Electoral promises were made on the basis of these candidates' wealth. The aim was therefore to try to build a new Palestinian elite that could contribute to the marginalization of the Islamists.[18] This new guard won seats, in particular, in poor Palestinian districts that were traditionally Islamist strongholds. The new candidates were seen as rich businessmen who could provide personalized assistance as a result of their wealth. In fact, given the lack of political issues that can be addressed, the role of parliamentarians is increasingly perceived as one of patronage and service provision.[19] While this new guard has formed a parliamentary bloc known as the "national fraternity", it cannot be said to stand for a clear, liberal and ideologically coherent platform.[20] Its electoral success does not mean that the liberal economic reforms have been well received. There were reactions against the privatization policy and opposition to price rises caused by the end of state subsidies. The case of this new guard shows how elections represent a democratic façade for the regime, since parliament has no real political role and the democratic process is heavily biased. Elections are also used to bring out co-opted elites (as has been seen in Morocco[21] and in Egypt[22]). However, as the case of Jordan shows, the success of such an operation is short-lived and limited; the individuals that emerge from this are courted, but do not acquire any real political legitimacy.

The Muslim Brotherhood: a co-opted opposition?

Participation in these fairly toothless political institutions can even cause actors who otherwise have a true social base to be delegitimized. This is evident in the evolution of the Islamists' strategy and the backing they have enjoyed. Present in Jordan since its independence in 1946, the Muslim Brotherhood is the only movement that has always been allowed to operate. On numerous occasions prior to 1989 it proved to be the monarchy's objective ally against the left and Nasserist and Baathist Arab nationalist movements. It backed Iran while the monarchy supported Iraq in the 1970s, but in 1979 it took on board the monarchy's support for the Syrian Muslim Brotherhood against the Syrian regime and again allied with the Jordanian authorities. Since 1989, although Islamists have sometimes boycotted elections, they generally take part in the institutions set up by the regime.

Since the first Intifada, the Muslim Brotherhood has positioned itself in two ways: as a charity network and as a champion of the Palestinian cause redefined in religious terms. These two fields of action have the advantage of not making them enemies of Jordan, unlike the nationalists and the left. In fact, Islamist support for the Palestinian cause has chiefly taken the shape of humanitarian aid combined with a largely incantatory form of nationalism, and the

Muslim Brotherhood does nothing in practical terms to oppose the king's policy in the peace process. In this way, the Muslim Brotherhood has strengthened its position without actually opposing the monarchy. However, once in a stronger position, it added criticism of the Jordanian government's undemocratic practices to its platform, which has won it considerable popular support. Some of its activists have thus suffered government retaliation and sometimes imprisonment. However, there seems to have been no general response to this repression from the Muslim Brotherhood.

Beyond their social network and their function as purveyor of services and aid, the Islamists have real ideological strength. They exercise a sort of social hegemony, in that they define many of the paradigms by which society views and understands itself. Many of their references come from other political currents, but the Muslim Brotherhood has managed to reorganize nationalist religious and even leftist references (that is, the notion of social justice) into a sort of syncretism that sets it apart and gives it strength. It has fought for and virtually obtained a monopoly on religious interpretation. As Gudrun Krämer notes: "The competition to decide who represents the right and true Islam and who is the best guardian of the faith and civil society is in fact one of the main themes of political debate."[23] Emphasis on this aspect also allows the Muslim Brotherhood to position itself with respect to the monarchy, which emphasizes its attachment to the Prophet's lineage and promotes the development of an official version of Islam.[24] This does not mean that the Muslim Brotherhood is unquestioned, but that its opponents tend to argue within a religious paradigm that is highly influenced by the movement's viewpoint. The marginalization of major movements associated with pan-Arab nationalism and Marxism also means that the Muslim Brotherhood no longer faces any real ideological competition, so this movement is predominant by default.

The Muslim Brotherhood maintained a position of conflictual participation, between opposition and co-optation. As the monarchy's only serious challenger, the Islamist movement has thus become a central actor in the game of politics, despite drawing part of its aura from its distance from those in power and its claim to integrity. Above all, it serves as a guarantee that democracy indeed exists by virtue of the fact there is an opposition force. But as the Muslim Brotherhood has become part of the political playing field, it has increasingly appeared an almost too well integrated opposition body,[25] which in a way strengthens the monarchy's position. This shift has had consequences for the perception of the Muslim Brotherhood and its popular support. Its legitimacy has gradually declined because it sometimes appears to approve of government policy. This situation has led to tensions within the movement and the defection, even radicalization, of some activists.

Moreover, under Abdullah II the crackdown on Islamists has become harsher, whatever their position toward the regime, further weakening the most moderate current of the Islamist movement, as its strategy appears to have failed. They were the big losers in the 2007 parliamentary elections, which illustrated the limits of the policy of conflictual participation against a backdrop of growing repression and destabilization. The voting system and the election campaign were criticized. As a result, two factions formed within the Islamist movement, usually referred to as "doves" and "hawks", although the Islamists reject these labels. The former advocated a co-operative attitude, whereas the latter were more in favour of confrontation, some of them calling for a boycott. During the movement's primaries, a majority of party members voted for the hawks. But the party leadership decided not to take the vote into account and chose to field doves as candidates for election. They were accused of co-operating with the government, despite the fact that they were harassed and ended up suffering heavy losses in the elections (with only six seats out of 110). The outcome seriously destabilized the party doves. The Islamists consequently changed tack and boycotted the parliamentary elections in late 2010, then showed their support for the movements in Tunisia and Egypt, calling for a true constitutional monarchy in 2011 and 2012. This evolution in the Islamists' strategy illustrates the dilemmas facing the opposition against a highly controlled but not entirely closed system and the consequences it has for its legitimacy. Organized as a social movement, the Muslim Brotherhood has managed to create a certain sphere of mobilization, unlike the left and the nationalists, who were obliged to remain underground until 1989. Despite this, the Muslim Brotherhood has never managed to give political expression to its social hegemony in an authoritarian system in which its political participation brings about delegitimization and co-optation.

In 2013 the Muslim Brotherhood once again boycotted parliamentary elections, criticizing an election law that, despite certain changes in 2012, still favours the tribal system and under-represents urban districts where the bulk of Muslim Brotherhood voters are found. Most of the opposition forces joined them in this criticism.

These early elections were held after the king decided to dissolve parliament in late 2012. They were supposed to exemplify the implementation of reforms promised by the regime in response to Jordan's Arab Spring. The protest movement expressed a combination of economic demands and demands for political reform such as the election of the prime minister in place of his appointment by the king (see Chapter 7 on new forms of mobilization). Turnout in the elections on 23 January 2013 – 56 per cent of the 2.3 million registered voters – was not as low as the opposition had hoped.[26] But the members of parliament elected were mostly independents who did not defend a precise political line and were mainly backed by tribal networks or economic power. Parliament's patronage role was confirmed, and the newly elected legislative body cannot be said to enjoy any more political legitimacy than the previous one. In accordance with an announcement just before the elections, discussions were held between the Royal Cabinet and parliament regarding formation of the government, but they still resulted in the confirmation of Prime Minister Abdallah Nsour, appointed by the king prior to the elections. Constitutional and electoral reform have thus yet to be fully accomplished.

On his visit in March 2013, Barack Obama congratulated Abdullah II for his handling of Jordan's Arab Spring through promises of reform. The king indeed remains a major ally in the region, and the United States grants the regime massive amounts of aid. Moreover, despite the inadequacy of political reform, and even though political criticism persists and the monarchy and the king himself are no longer spared, demands tend to focus on economic and social aspects. It was the rise in oil, electricity and natural gas prices, which previous governments had managed to avoid, that spurred protests once again, with the largest demonstrations of Jordan's Arab Spring occurring in October and November 2012, now spearheaded by the Muslim Brotherhood. Jordan had raised prices in exchange for a $2.4 billion loan from the IMF at a time when its external debt had reached 22 per cent of gross domestic product (GDP) in 2012. That year Jordan was in the grip of an economic and financial crisis due to the impact of regional strife on various sectors of its economy: an energy crisis following the interruption of deliveries of low-cost natural gas from Egypt, the continuing drop in migrant remittances (a major source of revenue for Jordan which still amounted to 10 per cent of its GDP in 2012),[27] as well as repercussions of the unrest on the tourism industry, including the medical tourism sector – less well known, but essential for Jordan. Subsequently, throughout all of 2013, while movements remained limited, sporadic strikes hit sensitive sectors such as water distribution, and various groups demonstrated against oil, water and electricity price hikes as well as denouncing corruption for its deleterious effects on economic policy.

The regime's ability to meet the population's economic demands is thus essential to its stability. But the Syrian crisis has had a direct effect on this aspect, and today it is the main challenge facing Jordan's monarchy.

The repercussions of the Syrian crisis

The Syrian crisis affects Jordan on the economic, political and humanitarian levels. In February 2015 it hosted 622,000 refugees,[28] partly sheltered in camps where living conditions are precarious, and partly living directly in the urban habitat. The main camp, Zaatari, which in February 2015 sheltered 85,000 refugees, is plagued by water shortages, clashes have occurred over food distribution, and organized crime has taken hold. According to the United Nations Refugee Agency (UNHCR), Jordan currently ranks second in the world in refugees per capita, although the arrival of Syrian refugees started to diminish in October 2014. This population influx weighs heavily on the already ailing Jordanian economy, particularly from the standpoint of energy and water resources, and it has led to a sharp increase in rents – a situation similar to that when a wave of Iraqi refugees began arriving in 2003. This state of affairs heightens tensions within Jordan and increases its need for foreign aid.

More generally speaking, the Syrian crisis once again illustrates Jordan's economic dependence. According to the Organisation for Economic Co-operation and Development (OECD), it receives on average $1 billion in official development assistance each year ($1.4 billion in 2012 and 2013). Beyond the economic aspect, it also has an impact on the country's foreign policy decisions, as it is partly dependent on its two main donor countries, the United States and Saudi Arabia.[29] Due to pressure from these two countries, the evolution of the conflict in Syria and Jordan's failed attempts at a negotiated settlement of the Syrian crisis, Jordan has thus had to alter its position.[30] Indeed, while Jordan has historically opposed the Baathist regime in power in Damascus, prior to 2013 it advocated a diplomatic solution without military involvement. But in 2012 Saudi

Arabia stepped up its insistence and delayed paying out financial aid essential to Amman. In addition to this coercion came pressure from the United States. In April 2013 Jordan altered the course of its policy, consented to a new deployment of military assistance, primarily American (in the form of command and control personnel, staff to train Jordan's armed forces to detect chemical weapons, a Patriot missile battery and F-16 fighter aircraft), to secure its border with Syria, but also to train non-jihadi Syrian insurgents and to supply the rebels with armaments.[31] Subsequently, Saudi Arabia and the United States made several announcements of co-operation and financial support for Amman: Saudi Arabia provided Jordan with $200 million in budget support in 2013, in addition to $5 billion in aid for development projects over five years announced by the Gulf Cooperation Council (GCC). In January 2014 the United States granted Amman $360 million in economic aid and $300 million in military aid, and pledged a loan of $1.25 billion.

While this foreign policy may have provoked opposition within the country, such protest was mild compared to what would have been sparked by an interruption in the flow of aid. Although political rejection of outside interference has been fairly widespread, the opposition in Jordan remains divided over Syria and does not present a united front against the monarchy's policy. A segment of the Baathist left backs the Syrian regime, as do those who are outraged by foreign interference and the militarization of the opposition. However, part of the left has borne the brunt of Syrian repression, while others identify with opposition to an authoritarian regime. Furthermore, the Muslim Brotherhood also backs the Syrian rebellion.

The proclamation of the "caliphate" by the Islamic State in Iraq and the Levant (ISIL) in June 2014 and its expansion toward Jordan's northeast borders has heightened tensions. While at first Jordan refrained from getting involved, it took part in the meeting organized by the United States in Jeddah (with Iraq, Egypt,

Lebanon, and the GCC) and joined the coalition against ISIL in September 2014. It participates in air strikes despite fairly strong opposition to these raids in Jordan, particularly from the Muslim Brotherhood, which criticizes in a foreign war that is not its own. This is not tantamount to support for ISIL, which remains low in the country (the memory of the attacks in 2005 is still fresh),[32] but is again an expression of opposition to alignment with US policy and foreign interference.

While the majority of the population is against ISIL, it nevertheless has support from some Jihadi Salafis. Between 1,500 and 2,000 Jordanians are believed to have left to join ISIL's ranks, particularly from the city of Maan, which has been experiencing a dire economic situation and sporadic rioting. Demonstrations have been held in favour of ISIL. Arrests of sympathizers are growing more frequent. At the same time, the regime temporarily released two Jihadi Salafis who are opposed to ISIL, one of them being Abu Muhammad al-Maqdisi,[33] to drive a wedge into the movement.

In December 2014 the capture of a Jordanian pilot by ISIL, which in February 2015 broadcast a video showing the pilot being burned alive as the names and addresses of other Jordanian pilots were given together with a call to kill them in exchange for rewards, turned the situation around, provoking a burst of patriotism and calls for revenge. Two Iraqi jihadis detained in Jordan and already sentenced to death, one for her participation in the 2005 attacks (ISIL had demanded her release), the other as head of operations for al-Qaeda, both of whom until then had benefited from the moratorium on executions, were hanged. Jordan has stepped up air strikes in Syria as well as in Iraq. It has asked the United States to bolster its support, while the Emirates sent it a squadron of F-16 fighter planes. In February 2015, the United States signed an agreement with Jordan increasing its aid to $1 billion.

The killing of the pilot, a member of a major Jordanian tribe, provoked contrasting reactions. A desire to avenge his death has led to renewed support for the Jordanian army's operations against ISIL, but some, such as the Muslim Brotherhood, view it as an additional reason to desert the US-led coalition.

The Jordan monarchy is thus caught between paradoxical influences: international bodies such as the IMF encourage it to lower public expenditure, but this policy mainly affects Transjordanians and contributes to undermining the support the monarchy enjoys on the domestic front. However, this same support also depends on what Jordan can obtain from its foreign donors and redistribute. The Syrian crisis has accentuated these contradictions by aggravating Jordan's internal situation. However, Jordan's action in favour of refugees also reinforces its position from a diplomatic standpoint and can be used as an argument to secure the renewal of aid. Furthermore, inside the country, the context of destabilization and tension tends to make the king once again appear as a figure of salvation, possibly by default.

The monarchy as a political system was thus not directly challenged during the Jordan Spring, and while criticism persists, the political aspect is no longer the focal point of demands, even if the promised reforms have only very partially materialized and calls for a national salvation government appear periodically. The Muslim Brotherhood movement, which in December 2013 relaunched a campaign on the themes of political reform and the need for economic and social measures, has nevertheless been subject to a backlash as a result of the failure of its counterpart in Egypt, and divisions are growing wider. In April 2014, for instance, the movement excluded the Islamists who drew up a new initiative in late 2013 bringing together opposition figures who demanded reform of the state. Moreover, social and economic demands remain the principal bones of contention. Although in general poverty and economic frustration do not necessarily foster political involvement and protest, in this case economic issues are the main destabilizing factors threatening the monarchy.

This situation illustrates the paradoxes of authoritarian liberalism, as well as its limits and its constraints. Economic liberalism does not necessarily lead to democracy: Jordan provides a counter-example. However, at the heart of the contract that contributes to the relative acceptance of the rulers' independence and authoritarianism (in addition to the Hashemite monarchy's very real supra-citizen legitimacy, by claiming affiliation with the Prophet's lineage) is the regime's more or less direct responsibility for the population's subsistence, which entails strong state involvement. But the shift toward economic liberalism strongly advocated by Abdullah II presents a challenge to this rule. Attempts to rely on the new economic elites that would benefit directly from this policy while posing as models of success for the population have not produced the expected results. Thus, despite IMF pressures, the monarchy has backtracked on this policy and cancelled certain subsidy decreases it had previously announced. Furthermore, the impact of the increase in criminal violence should also be emphasized. Not a single demonstration occurs that does not call for heightened security, broadly defined. The opposition remains divided and society on the whole, worried about the repercussions of conflicts at its borders and identity-based divisions, remains inclined not to challenge the king directly, who still embodies an external reference. This and the monarchy's capacity to honour a tacit subsistence and security contract help to avert potential protest.

CHAPTER 2

Becoming an activist

A political opposition has formed against the Jordanian regime that historically is divided into three main ideological strands: Islamism, nationalism and leftism.[1] Where do the activists in these movements come from, and how did they take their first steps in the various organizations? The paths taken by the Jordanian activists studied show that their convictions stem from their political commitment, and not vice versa. While this statement may seem counterintuitive, it is not specific to the situation in Jordan.[2] Their choices thus cannot be described as ideological, given that ideology permeates the subjects after the commitment is made, during the course of the activist's socialization. How, then, is the initial commitment made?

Activists mention a strong sense of injustice during adolescence, and a desire to combat it. At this stage, neither the precise causes of injustice nor the means to fight against it are clearly identified. The feeling of injustice is rooted in their environment. The Palestinian question is thus central. The sensitivity of the issue is perceptible not only in western Jordan along the Jordan River Valley, but also deep inside the country, where Palestinian refugees and forces are present. But aspects of social inequality also come into play: rural poverty is frequently mentioned. This is a general state of affairs whose effects are not confined to future activists. Moreover, they do not all come from the same social backgrounds. But all of them are characterized by the social significance they attribute to the situation: a combination of certainty of social and national injustice, and a sense of responsibility to help to address them.[3]

The immediate environment plays a decisive role in the second stage: embarking on a structured political commitment and choosing a political orientation. This occurs early on, usually in secondary school, or at the latest at university. Mentors (classmates, teachers, community workers and so on) and local institutions play an essential role, more important than the family, although the influence of an older brother or an uncle is sometimes mentioned. The location of the university is politically significant, and is often chosen in accordance with the individual's political inclination. Unsurprisingly, Arab nationalists attend universities in the Middle East, while communists instead choose Eastern bloc countries. Saudi Arabia only attracts Islamists. Studenthood is an essential period for strengthening commitment and its ideological references. Moreover, some activists only engage in politics during their time at university, and never finish their degrees.

For these long-term activists, their political involvement continues well after leaving university. The commitment then becomes structured around a specific ideology that identifies the causes of the injustice and specifies the type of struggle to be embarked upon.

In the last stage of the commitment process, ideology has become so infused that it orients the person's interpretation of reality and relationship to the world, with major ethical and moral implications. In this regard, ideology is not a consumer product, and activists do not shop around for it. The relationship is far from an external one, because ideology lends meaning to experience, and political involvement is not merely one activity among others. Ideological orientation and the ensuing socialization become truly a way of life, especially for activists who gravitate toward all-encompassing ideologies such as communism and Islamism. This is less true for Arab nationalists. But first let us consider the feeling of injustice as it is described by the activists themselves, even before they make a commitment.

A sense of injustice: poverty and the Palestinian cause

When asked to identify his first political experience, Hamzeh[4] displays "impassioned feelings about the Palestinian question and Arab and Muslim unity". Hamzeh was born in 1944 near Haifa. His family was expelled in 1948 when Israel was created. They fled to Jenin (West Bank), then in 1959 settled in Jordan in the Karameh refugee camp: "That is why I was enthusiastic about any philosophy or authority – be it Islamist or nationalist – that was working in these directions: Palestinian liberation and the value of the *umma*[5] and its honour."[6]

Hamzeh ended up joining the Muslim Brotherhood. But in describing his prior experience, a vocabulary of emotion and indignation toward the injustice of the Palestinian situation is what stands out. As for Ramzi, he was born in 1959 in a rural Jordanian family near Irbid: "I was obsessed with the condition of the poor, and with equality and justice. There were communist students at the youth centre, and that's how I started to associate with the communists."[7]

After long having had contacts with communists at the youth centre and later at university, he ended up secretly joining the Communist Party in 1980 (the party was banned at the time). Members of two very different organizations – one secret and restricted, the other not, and with different agendas – these two activists logically followed very distinct political journeys. However, both of them cite the source of their commitment as being a burning sense of injustice toward situations: one the exile of Palestinians, the other poverty. The strong desire to combat this injustice provoked a desire to right the situation using methods that at first remained very vague. It was only later, through contact with other activists and through their readings, that this feeling of injustice was shaped through ideology, which determined the cause, the aims and the means to pursue them.

Poverty is often mentioned as being at the root of this early sense of injustice, particularly the poverty affecting rural families in small Jordanian villages. This aspect is most frequently mentioned by activists who come from such families, and the link between the activist's individual situation and his preoccupation is quite evident. Returning to Ramzi, he remarks, for instance: "My family was rather poor [...]. I wasn't one of those youths who had free time and could go into town for entertainment, to go to the movies and so on. I didn't belong to the 'golden fun-loving youth'."[8] Ahmed A., another communist activist who had spent time in the same youth centre a few years earlier, also mentions poverty when he talks about his commitment. He comes from a family of poor peasants: his mother owns a small plot of land that she farmed together with his father. Part of the harvest went toward feeding the family, while his grandfather took the rest into town "on his back" to try to sell it.[9] However, the desire to challenge social inequality politically is not only associated with a condition of poverty. Activists from poor backgrounds also emphasize the value of knowledge and education imparted to them by their illiterate parents. Ahmed's mother and grandfather encouraged him to read, which was one of the reasons he attended the youth centre, which doubled as a cultural centre and had a mobile library. Here the activist trajectory is closely tied in with an educational background and is associated with upward social mobility: they would be the first ones in their family to attend university and exercise licensed professions such as medicine or translation.

Even more than poverty, the sense of injustice is primarily related to the Palestinian question – naturally, but not only, among

Palestinian refugees in Jordan. Whether or not they come from the territories occupied by Israel, all the activists feel concerned by what goes on at their borders as well as the impact events have on the political and economic situation in Jordan. They view their indignation about the plight of the Palestinians as a foundational experience whatever their family origin, and all are opposed to Israel's occupation of the West Bank and the Gaza Strip. But regarding the place of Palestinians in Jordan, their positions diverge.

As budding activists, the respondents all shared a gnawing anxiety about the effect the Palestinian presence has had on divisions in Jordan. This concern runs through the all political persuasions, with disagreements restricted to analyses of the causes and the course of action to take. The September 1970 clashes, which occurred while the activists were young – some of them having taken part in them – were traumatic and exacerbated issues of Jordanian–Palestinian division. The Black September conflict is etched on people's minds. Ahmed A., who mentioned poverty above, also emphasizes the decisive role this episode had in making his commitment:

> I'm a native Jordanian. After the civil war, the people were divided between Jordanians and Palestinians [...]. In my case, during and after these events I was a hotheaded youth with the motivation and hope to be able to help change the course of things. I then decided that my path wasn't nationalism, but a party that united all beliefs and all nationalities and that brought people together rather than divided them.[10]

Such divisions have plagued activists since the beginning of their political careers, and still do so today.

The difference between Jordanian Palestinians and Transjordanians is mentioned systematically by both sides, but in terms of denying it exists. They all use the categories of "Palestinian" and "Jordanian", yet challenge their validity. For the political opposition, the idea is to deconstruct a divisive factor and point out the artificial nature of Jordan. For instance, this is the viewpoint of Mahmoud, an Arab national activist born in 1948 in Karak, southern Jordan:

> My family often travelled to Palestine, especially around Jerusalem, for business reasons [...]. I didn't really experience this period, but my family did. It's very important, because it means that the border is not a natural one, and on the contrary it was created by the colonial powers, and of course the regimes that came afterward further consolidated the border.

Likewise, Ibrahim A., born in 1955 in a village near Hebron, stresses these cross-border families:

> I am from a village near Khalil. Our family is a big one, part of it is in Karak. Before the frontiers, people were moving from one place to the other. It is very near. Now someone from Karak will say that they are Jordanian and that I am Palestinian. But that was created by the frontiers, and now people believe in it. This creation had consequences, and now people believe in it, but it is not true.[11]

The categories of "Palestinian" and "Jordanian" are constructed and deconstructed in this way. However, they follow the activists throughout their journeys. Divisions over the Palestinian question create factions within parties, particularly within the Muslim Brotherhood, even if the leaders prefer officially to mask such differences. The degree of importance invested in the Palestinian cause is not solely tied to one's Palestinian or Jordanian "origin"; social status and the degree of integration within the regime also play a role in this regard. But the activists' origin is considered an essential piece of information, as Palestinians are suspected of placing the Palestinian cause before the interests of the Jordan. Palestinian or Jordanian identity is thus clearly assigned even among factions that dispute such labels. Hamzeh, for instance, claimed that activist origins do not matter, yet to prove his point he proceeded to state the Palestinian or Jordanian origin and place of birth of Muslim Brotherhood leaders in Jordan.

Through a combination of assignments of identity and political convictions, the activists' positions are honed over the course of their career. But when activists discuss the moment they joined a movement, they do not directly mention the issue of their origin and the political identity that may be associated with it. Indeed, it is not an issue that activists choose to emphasize. But it is also true that the "Palestinian" or "Jordanian" label is only one feature of their political experience among others, and their positions take shape within political movements.[12] On the other hand, networks and loci of socialization are of prime importance. Ahmed A. points out that he chose the Communist Party in a quest for unity after the events of 1970:

> I was aware that one of the best ways to restore trust between Palestinians and Jordanians was to build a political party on a basis that was poles apart from nationalism, a party that would encompass all religions. At the time there was the Communist Party that expressed my thinking.

But he had become acquainted with communism prior to 1970 at a youth centre through contact with young sympathizers and by reading brochures distributed by the Soviet Union. Such early encounters, in secondary school or later at university, play an essential role. Through them, future activists gravitate towards one organization or another and start to develop their political positions.

Mentors

Indeed, secondary socialization has a strong influence on activist trajectories. Two elements emerge here: the presence of a mentor, a person who serves as a reference for the future activist, performing the junction with the political movement he turns to and an organization; and a place, the youth centre, scout troop and so on, where such ties are formed and develop. The step toward political commitment occurs on a continuum from informal to formal sociability: introduced by a friend or classmate, the young person attends his first meetings, perhaps his first demonstrations. The activist usually clearly identifies the mentor figure when retracing his itinerary. It can be a figure in a supervisory position, such as a teacher, a popular activist or the leader of an organization. Nader, a former communist, was born in 1955 into a farming family near Hebron in the West Bank, which he describes as "neither rich nor poor". He describes his experience at university in Cairo:

> We had a very important professor [...]; there were political debates at the Palestinian Student Union, and there was an Egyptian poet who described Islam as a backward religion, and I stood up for the religion [...]. The next day I met the professor in the cafeteria and he said to me, "Islam is your father's doctrine." We talked for a while after that, and I said, "What you're saying is communist!" [...] He asked me, "What is communism? You're entitled to think what you like [...]; but you came here to learn." I started thinking about it. And the student union was made up mostly of leftists [...]; I finally decided that those ideas were the most important. By the end of the year I had joined the Communist Party.

The affiliation process thus described involves both the mentor figure and the structure of socialization, in this case the student union (as well as the relationship to knowledge, which will be discussed later). Nader hid his membership from his family in Hebron, who believed communists were infidels.

One nationalist activist also highlights the mentorship role of one of his teachers. Azmi was born in 1950 in Jenin of parents expelled from Haifa in 1948. His father was a professor of Arabic. They came to Jordan in 1967 because of the war. He emphasizes his hostility toward Israeli occupation and the influence family stories had on him: "My parents [...] often talked to us about Haifa and the way the Israelis took over and what they did there. That's why I had a preconceived idea, which mainly came from the family. But strictly speaking, my family wasn't into politics." This indignation was channelled into political involvement through an organization suggested to him by a secondary school teacher:

> He always talked to us about nationalist thought. I enjoyed listening to him. He often recommended books to us, and we often conversed together. I was studying the works of Antun Saadeh.[13] He asked me what I thought about his books. I later agreed to join the Front [of National Sacrifice], which was a branch of the Syrian Social Nationalist Party.

With the Front, Azmi went back to Palestine to conduct operations against the Israeli army without his family knowing about his activities.

In other cases, peers such as classmates and fellow students fulfil this role. Thus, for Ramzi and Ahmed, encounters with communist students at the youth centre were decisive. More infrequently, the mentor figure can come from the family circle, an activist older brother or an uncle, as was the case for Mahmoud:

> There was a close family member who had studied in Syria. That uncle had a great influence on me. He was a Baathist[14] [...]. It was thanks to him and his library that I joined the Baath Party, I was often over at his house and read all I wanted. When I joined the party, I was already cultivated, I was aware of the most important issues.

This uncle was also the mayor of Karak and a tribal chief, and beyond the issue of pan-Arab nationalism, Mahmoud also associates his activism with a tradition of opposition within his tribe and in the region[15] (he moreover refers back in history to an early clash with the Turks in 1910, and even a battle between Muslims and Romans):

> Before, we were part peasant and part Bedouin. [...] We don't like the authorities, restrictions, limits and so on. It's part of our upbringing to always be in the opposition, naturally an opposition that demands social justice and defends national issues. It's for these reasons that this area of the south is considered as having always been in the opposition.

Here the tribal network is associated with local identity and a spirit of opposition, not with loyalty to the regime. It is partly connected with party membership.

But in the nuclear family none of the respondents' fathers or mothers appears as a mentor, which may indicate that activism is also a means of escaping the family environment – a question I will return to. There are few activist families, and primary socialization, except through an elder brother figure, does not appear to play a major role. Usually the activist interviewed is the only one in his family. When the parents themselves are politically involved, which is rare, the activist sometimes chooses a different political orientation from his parents. For instance, a militant from a communist family for a while joined Fatah[16] to take part in armed struggle. For Rahil, born in 1957 in a village near Ajloun, there is a certain continuity between having a father who was a respected sheikh in his village and who propounded religious values and the importance of knowledge, and membership in the Muslim Brotherhood. But once again it was his elder brother who really initiated him because he associated with members of the Muslim Brotherhood in secondary school. As for Ahmed, he mentions that his father, although he was not in the opposition or even politicized, was not "loyal" to the regime, which was rare in his circle, and pushed him to take a more critical stance. But other activists are the only members to be part of the opposition in families who unconditionally support the monarchy.

In fact, the parents' political involvement, if any, has less influence than the relationship to knowledge and education that they emphasize. Many activists mention this aspect. This was the case for activists from poor, illiterate families, but it is also true for activists from other backgrounds. For instance, Rahil points out that he learned from his father about "the complementarity between religiosity and the love of science". Furthermore, Palestinians who moved to Jordan after 1948 also stress the importance of earning a degree – the only "transportable" commodity left to these families who had often lost everything in 1948 and/or in 1967. In such a context, a university degree served as a kind of insurance that enabled them to find a job even in situations of forced exile. The desire to excel academically encourages people to invest themselves in a place, secondary school, that is often politicized. And from nationalism to Islamism, all the various political persuasions prize knowledge, whether to enhance the development of Arab nations or as an intrinsic dimension of a Muslim commitment.

The importance of mentor figures and secondary socialization networks in taking the step toward a long-term political commitment is not specific to Jordanian activists. These aspects are recurrent in biographical studies of activism.[17] The question naturally arises as to what extent asking activists to retrace their journey leads to emphasizing this type of figure and initiatory encounter – another form of "biographical bias" that gives a narrative longitudinal coherence and meaning after the fact. But these early political commitments cannot be systematically deduced from the activists' social categories and the positions taken by their families. The social situation creates a sort of "biographical availability"[18] for political involvement, here characterized by the relationship to injustice and academic assiduity. The decision to become politically involved, however, implies a gradual immersion that depends on the type of politicization that exists in loci of secondary socialization. Orientation occurs according to the dominant political currents there and as a result of encounters with mentor figures, which in this case generally involves a relationship to politics combined with a relationship to knowledge. Mentors gradually instil values and references in the activists, especially when they are supervisory figures who embody political and activist experience, and then through socialization with others. But this process also involves readings – often, but not only, recommended by the mentor – that gradually provide the interpretive frameworks that apply to and explain the injustice felt, and identify opponents, the fight to be waged and the means to carry it out. Thus "shared meanings"[19] are gradually constructed, as well as a shared world, with its major figures, its events, its vocabulary, its allies and opponents. While the importance of mentors and local hegemonies is thus not specific to political commitment in Jordan, the political content and the type of organization toward which the activists gravitate naturally fits in with the major ideological trends in the Arab world of the period.

The political currents and their major figures

In the 1960s and 1970s the political playing field in Jordan open to opposition activists overlapped with the division into three main tendencies that exist more or less in conflict in the Arab world: nationalism, Marxism and Islamism. While the activists identify with and define themselves along these lines, this does not mean that certain elements are not found in more than one tendency. Thus nationalism itself is present in the three tendencies, but occupies a different place in each. Moreover, the plural should be used when speaking about nationalist movements, from the Egyptian or Syrian version of pan-Arab currents promoting the unification of the Arab world down to Palestinian nationalism. Furthermore, socialism and nationalism are often combined. The connection between pan-Arab nationalism and Palestinian nationalism is also an issue, because after 1967 a version of Palestinian nationalism developed that no longer considered Arab unity to be the first stage of Palestinian liberation. Palestinian nationalism was also propounded by leftist parties that were primarily made up of Palestinian organizations. Only the communists differ in this regard. The Jordanian Communist Party was founded in 1951 (when Jordan included the West Bank), growing out of the National Liberation League, a communist Palestinian organization.[20] Some of its members were opposed to armed struggle and backed the 1947 UN partition plan. This was a stance that certain communist activists now consider particularly prescient, but at the time it aroused strong opposition among the Arab parties and divisions among the communists. From the 1970s to the 1980s the respective weight of the various movements shifted significantly, which was reflected in the process of activist recruitment. Present in Jordan since it became independent in 1946, the Muslim Brotherhood movement experienced a boom after the failure of Arab nationalism and the death of Egypt's President Nasser and then the collapse of the Soviet Union in 1991, especially when it conducted a campaign in support of the first Palestinian Intifada (1987–1993) with a new slogan: "Islam is the solution."

Beyond the slogans and the various divisions and subdivisions into organizations and factions, how do the activists perceive the political movements at this first step in their commitment? Mentors lay stress on the works of the movement's leaders and intellectuals, and use them as a basis for discussion, as well as magazines and manuals that are circulated widely. Through such literature, the activists become familiar with the ideology and start to adopt its interpretive frameworks. But certain leaders are also charismatic figures who play an essential role by embodying the movement and its values, and bring out emotions. Future activists pay close attention to the fate of these major figures, and are influenced by their destinies, their victories and their defeats.

Abdel Nasser[21] was a particularly central figure in Jordan, as elsewhere in the Arab world. While nationalists mainly hold him up as a leader, his impact extends well beyond this movement alone. The defeat of 1967 and then his death in 1970 weakened the pan-Arab movements. However, as Zeyd's experience shows, having been born in 1962, and thus very young when Abdel Nasser died, the death of a leader tends to bring about a resurgence of fervour surrounding the movement:

> At the time, Abdel Nasser's death really left a mark on me, I remember it. My paternal aunt was originally from Gaza and had to flee to Jordan after the war. Once she arrived in Jordan, she listened to the radio constantly and watched the news, like many Palestinians, to see if they could go home. She was the first in the family to hear that Abdel Nasser had died. [...] She took her black scarf and tore off a piece and asked me to hang it from the terrace roof as a sign of mourning for Abdel Nasser. No one knew about it.[22]

Imbued with this Nasserist fervour shown by some of his family members, Zeyd started to read nationalist literature, which marked the beginning of his political awareness, but he didn't become any more involved. And at university, through contact with Islamist students, he revised his earlier convictions: "The content of nationalism isn't clear. I started researching what the ultimate goal was. Nationalism does not have any precise content. Even the nationalists talked to us about unity and the message. But what is the content of this message? It's Islam."

He then resolutely turned to Islamism. The importance of context and community experiences around the fate of great leaders is clear here, but it is not enough, any more than family background is. It is contact with local mentors that forges activist commitment.

The impact of a leader's death nevertheless remains a recurrent factor, especially if this death is experienced as an injustice. The figure's "martyrdom" lends a face to the sense of injustice, giving it substance and establishing the connection with a specific ideological movement. For Hamzeh, "The really essential factor in my having turned to Islamism was the trial that sentenced martyr Sayyid Qutb[23] to death in 1966." Already in contact with the Muslim Brotherhood without having joined the organization, he experienced this execution by hanging as a profound injustice, and officially joined the movement that same year.

Both of these political experiences fit within a regional Arab space that extends beyond Jordan, where no opposition leadership figure truly stands out. Politically and ideologically, Jordan remains on the periphery. Its models are found elsewhere, and for the communists during this early phase of activism, ideological references and visible figures were clearly regional, even international ones. However, as will be seen, Jordan's institutions and the relationship to the monarchy later gives the activists' trajectories and their perceptions of politics specific national features, despite their rhetoric about Jordan's artificial nature.

Political affiliation is thus a process built up around secondary socialization in secondary school, where a sense of injustice and political emotions are connected with ideologies, leaders and organizations that are visible on the scale of the Arab world, and not only Jordan. However, the socialization that develops around activism is an extension of informal socialization, and does not only hold appeal because it addresses political concerns. When they narrate their biographies, activists also emphasize the appeal of the friendly atmosphere and outings offered by youth organizations.

Opportunities for friendship, leisure activities and emancipation

The youth organizations of the various political movements that secondary school students come into contact with naturally hold public debates and political rallies. But they are also networks and places that offer other activities that can be very appealing, especially in rural areas where opportunities are few. Ibrahim B., born in 1962, talks about Muslim Brotherhood scout troops, weekends and outdoor summer camps that he remembers fondly as much for the people he met there and the friendships he made as for the opening it represented and the possibility of escaping the everyday village routine. Whether in a youth centre or through such weekend excursions or summer camps, political organizations provide a place for socialization among youths of the same age, away from the eyes of the family, the village community or the tribe, and are attractive for these reasons. They are seen as a space in which to become emancipated from family life, a place where allies can be found with whom to develop a new discourse and find other references, away from the family hierarchies. Even within the space of school, they are also a means by which to form positive peer groups apart from the administration and the teaching faculty.

Reputations and atmospheres differ according to the organization. The Muslim Brotherhood lays emphasis on academic excellence, piety and morality. For Ibrahim B.:

> Overall, the most appealing atmosphere was among students who belonged to the Islamic movement, who in fact were the best students. [...] I was preoccupied by existential questions: God, the universe and life. I started looking for answers in Islam. In the mid-1970s most of the youths older than us in school and at university were members of the Muslim Brotherhood. We talked with them. I didn't find satisfactory answers, but I found a lot of psychological peace: a feeling of reassurance and happiness. We prayed, we played and we camped out together – a mixture of religiosity and friendship that offered a certain degree of mental calm.[24]

The hegemonic effect of the locally dominant tendency clearly has an impact here. But it is also apparent that the Islamist movement corresponds to a spiritual and religious quest, and not only a political one.

Emphasis on academic excellence and moral values is a constant among Islamist activists. They portray these features as both a characteristic of their group – which they claim is recognized by their teachers – and a personal characteristic, readily listing their academic achievements as well as their good reputation among their classmates. For them, belonging to such a group also has an emulation effect. This reputation has emerged as the Islamist movement is on the upswing; it shows values that the movement wishes to emphasize.

Nationalists and communists also stress the importance of acquiring skills to work for the development of Arab countries. But this is expressed less in the image of the good student, all the more as their partly underground activism and long periods of being banned worked against them in school. And in reality, due to the importance of political involvement and armed struggle among nationalists, not to mention repression they suffered, some activists never completed their studies – a profile not found among the Islamists.

Furthermore, the communists have a scandalous reputation for immorality that is tied in with suspicions of atheism. While there is a definite gap between the reputation they have among conservative movements and their actual behaviour, Marxists indeed put forward a discourse of personal emancipation. This reputation attracts some youths who expect to find a space of freedom within the organization, a disregard for convention, and to meet women outside their family circle.[25] This was the case for Taysir, who grew up in the West Bank in a village between Jenin and Nablus, while his father was an industrial worker in Kuwait. He was involved in two leftwing organizations, first the Popular Front for the Liberation of Palestine (PFLP) and then the Communist Party, and says:

> The first time I thought about joining a leftwing organization, it was in '67 [...]. I was fifteen years old, and I had read a novel of Naguib Mahfouz, [...] where there were two characters: a communist and a Muslim Brother. And he introduced the communist as a good person. And I liked the character of the communist. Because the Muslim Brother character, he cheated God. He had sexual relations with a girl on the roof of a house. And after that he said, "What have I done?" and so on. But the communist thought, no, it was normal. Communists believe that women should do what they want, to work for the freedom of women. There was that freedom in relationships.[26]

Marxist discourse about personal emancipation is more common in the West Bank than in Jordan. Nader, who also grew up in the West Bank, also discusses the appeal of an apparently freer, more open environment. Nader was a practising Muslim during adolescence:

> But then I stopped when I graduated from secondary school and I had lots of trouble with girls and with society [laughs]. Since I was a teenager, I read a magazine called *Le Rendez-vous* that was full of artists, movie stars and film directors and lots of beautiful women. They really seemed open and liberated to us. I was fascinated by the world of performance, and I went to study theatre.

In the minds of these adolescents, the freedom and non-conformism of the entertainment world is confused with a similar atmosphere among the Marxist left, and there is a continuum between artistic creativity and political commitment. They see a connection with the cultural world that does not appear among activists who grew up in Jordan. Nader and Taysir would both choose creative professions, one becoming a writer, the other a stage director. They would remain affiliated with the Marxist left without ever being directly involved in activist campaigns. The appeal of a freer lifestyle in the process of affiliation is mentioned by these "artist sympathizers" who joined organizations in their youth while remaining on the sidelines. It is never mentioned, however, by card-carrying communists who devote themselves body and soul to the organization. True communist activists, especially in Jordan, where they are far more criticized, rather seek to counter this reputation – which, moreover, does not correspond to their experience within the party. Ahmed B., who came in contact with the Communist Party in the 1970s through a friend from secondary school, even tested the communists when he joined: "I had some concerns, so on the membership application I wrote: 'In the name of God most gracious, most merciful.' And I figured that if they handed it back to me saying that I couldn't write such things, then that would mean they really were infidels!"[27]

From mentors to youth group outings, the ideological choice made thus largely depends on the proximity of activist organizations and the strength of their local presence. The ideological meaning comes later, in the course of the activist's training. Contrary to what one might think, activists are the first to underline their initial ideological indetermination, emphasizing their sense of injustice and their desire to get involved, without reference to a specific political movement. Ahmed B. thus says: "I think that if there had been the Muslim Brotherhood at the time, that they had given me documents and said to me that there was an organization, that they wanted to do things and so on, I would have been prepared to join. I didn't have a preconceived choice."

The fact that local factors rather than ideological ones have been identified in the affiliation process does not for all that indicate a lack of political conviction. Conviction, in fact, is built up gradually over the course of political activity, along with the acquisition of the vocabulary and arguments used by one ideology or another. It is thus not affected by this initial vacillation. The activists could have been convinced to join another organization, but in fact their ideology was the one they were looking for. In cases where an activist later has doubts about his own commitment, it is less due to disappointment with the ideological foundations than with the organization itself and how it functions. Much of the consolidation process takes place at university, where the ideology is mastered and activist skills are acquired, while ties are created and experience is gained in Jordan and abroad that leave a lasting mark on the activists.

CHAPTER 3

The student experience

Activism gathers momentum at university. Indeed, the respondents point out the importance of the debates that took place during their time there and the ensuing politicization they experienced. In that regard, Jordanians are no different from their counterparts in other countries for whom university – when they attend – is an essential moment in the joining process. Furthermore, these activists, who enrolled in university between the late 1960s and the early 1980s, were often the first ones in their families to attend university, sometimes even secondary school. New public universities with lower tuition rates broadened access to higher education, particularly at Nasser's instigation.[1] Licensed professions were no longer reserved for the families of notables. Trajectories of upward social mobility became concomitant with a high demand for these new graduates, essential for the country's economic development. Jordan's universities were set up relatively recently. The two main state universities, the University of Jordan and Yarmouk University, were founded in 1962 and 1976 respectively,[2] but it was not until much later that all disciplines were taught, and they still award few PhDs. Many activists thus went to foreign universities, except the Islamists. Indeed, most Islamists interviewed went to university later, and thus were able to take advantage of the development of Jordan's universities. Unlike the nationalists and communists, few have studied abroad, except for some who followed a curriculum in Saudi Arabia or in Europe. While some of them never graduated, all of the respondents attended university at some point. Attaining positions in the movement leadership implies early membership, but also socially selective admission that reinforces the scarcity of arenas of opposition under an authoritarian regime, mainly represented in Jordan by the universities and professional associations.[3] The Palestinians who attain such positions thus rarely came from the camps; those with such a trajectory are victims of informal discrimination in terms of access to university.[4] Among the respondents, post-1948 Palestinians generally come from families with connections in Jordan or enough income not to have to go through the camps on arrival (with the notable exception of Hamzeh, mentioned in Chapter 2). Palestinians from the camps are less active in these organizations, and rarely attain cadre positions. No matter how Palestinian identity is politically construed, social origin seems to play a more decisive role in advancement within party ranks.

How does orientation toward a university and a given course of study occur? In the activists' narratives, the choice of university is rarely the product of reasoned reflection, and is generally made in haste. Families have little information at their disposal, and rely on advice from a neighbour or an uncle whose son is already at university. Tuition fees are an essential criterion. This is why Syrian and Egyptian universities are primary destinations. For Nader, the first in a family of thirteen children to earn a secondary school diploma, the family took up a collection to send him to study in Egypt: while fairly low, tuition and the cost of living are heavy burdens to bear. Grades received on the equivalent to the baccalaureate exam determine what disciplines are open to students in Arab universities: medicine and engineering are at the top of the hierarchy, and the human sciences way at the bottom. In practice, most students go into the most prestigious field open to them. Nader, however, who had enough points to go into engineering, let himself be guided by his attraction to the movies and the image of a more liberated artistic world. It is true that his father is a film buff and took them to Bethlehem every Friday. They were the only family in their village to travel there: "I went off to study filmmaking, to become a film director, which had a relationship with artists, but at the film institute all the courses were full, so they told me to go to the theatre institute […]. I liked it so I forgot about the movies."

Khaled, whose father – in prison – and uncle were communists, went off to study in Romania in 1975 thanks to a contact his uncle had with the Jordanian cultural attaché in Romania who got him enrolled in the university:

> I wanted to study architecture, because I was used to working with my uncle who was an office architect. […] When I went to sign up for architecture, they said it was $450, so I asked if they had anything cheaper, and they said geology. I was still $100 short, so I borrowed from a fellow student, but meanwhile my uncle had written to me to say that geology wasn't recognized in Jordan, so I registered for stomatology because the curriculum was the shortest, but my mother told me I should sign up for general medicine. You know, a mother's dream […] and when I went in to register, the secretary said the same thing, so I signed up for general medicine.

Zeyd, whose shift from nationalism to Islamism at university was mentioned in Chapter 2, did not have the number of points required to matriculate at the University of Jordan, so he went to study in Italy. His family was unaware of enrolment procedures and the range of choices offered, but the Italian Embassy was next door to their home, and Zeyd had friends already studying there who could plan his arrival. He chose the first university that accepted him, and studied architecture. He stayed for two years without earning a degree, then went home and enrolled in first-year Islamic law at the University of Jordan.

But while orientation toward one university or another primarily depends on grades on the baccalaureate, family income and information gleaned from the local set, the political movement that is predominant there largely determines the direction of the future activist's career. There are two scenarios: when the activist is already highly involved in a specific movement in secondary school, he continues in the same vein at university, whatever tendency dominates at that particular university. In the opposite case, he tends to join the dominant current at university. Thus, in the case of Arab universities, Jordanian students in Syria and in Egypt in the 1960s and 1970s tended to gravitate toward the various currents of Arab nationalism, whereas in Saudi Arabia they sympathized with the Muslim Brotherhood. As regards European universities, it was for the most part their first exposure to Western society, for better or for worse. Isolated in Italian society, Zeyd and his friends, for instance, became involved with a network of Arab students and practising Muslims who organized debates and study groups. This would be decisive in his move away from pan-Arab nationalism and his involvement in an Islamic philosophical society. The situation was somewhat different as regards the universities of Eastern Europe, where the choice was more obvious. Students who attended them often had a grant from the Communist Party and were already members or sympathizers of the communist movement.

Local hegemonies and waves of membership

New memberships thus highly depend on local hegemonies, the majority tendency at university, or in secondary school prior to that. These hegemonies need to be replaced in the context of the historic political evolutions in Jordan and throughout the region. The 1960s were characterized by the rise of Nasserist and Baathist Arab nationalism, then by the Arab defeat of 1967 and the subsequent promotion of Palestinian nationalism with the rise of Fatah. The Marxist left and the communists for a long time held an important place, but the collapse of the Soviet Union in 1991 ended up effectively sidelining them. Islamism and the Muslim Brotherhood experienced a gradual rise, and finally achieved a majority in Jordan in the late 1980s. The evolution in membership trends reflects the power of the various currents. There is in fact an age gap between Islamists and the other respondents: most of the Islamists with a long history of activism were born between 1955 and 1965, whereas the birthdates of adherents of the other types of movement are between 1945 and 1955. Ibrahim describes similar patterns of membership within his own twelve siblings:

> My older brothers, who were born in 1940 and 1945, were Baathists and nationalists. The second group of brothers, born in the 1950s, belonged to the Muslim Brotherhood. Personally, I started out with the Muslim Brotherhood, but I didn't identify with their cause. That's why I left. It was a time of change and chaos. My younger brothers don't belong to any political creed or party, but they're religious.

While the general trend in membership thus matches the historic evolution of the movements, there are "staggered" memberships on the margin: early membership in the Muslim Brotherhood, or affiliation with a leftist movement later in life. These new memberships reflect local hegemonies, themselves out of step with the majority current at the local level. Before becoming the leading political force, the Muslim Brotherhood thus already exercised a degree of influence in some secondary schools during the era of pan-Arabism and the Arab left. For instance, the decision of a member of an Islamist movement to join the movement in a predominantly leftist university can actually be traced back to an earlier orientation from a secondary school with a strong Islamist movement and with a militant older brother. Local hegemonies have a certain inertia with respect to the general context. The youth centre that Ahmed A., and later Ramzi, attended remained communist for a long time after the left began to lose influence and funding from the Soviet Union had dried up. The ongoing existence of such loci and their associated social networks produces new memberships on the left despite the general context of the movement's decline.

But beyond the historic evolutions and certain local distinctions, universities map out a geography of activism, with different currents as well as repertoires of action, and an activist's destination abroad has particular influence on his or her subsequent path.

Arab universities, curricula and armed struggle

In the 1960s Arab universities, especially in Damascus and Cairo, but also in Baghdad and Beirut, were intense loci of politicization where students from all Arab countries met and where awareness of Arab unity was forged. In addition to the need to leave Jordan to study due to the very sparse academic offerings, there was a sense of moving in a common Arab space to which the various Arab universities in the Middle East belong, despite there being different currents of pan-Arabism, from Nasserism to the Syrian and Iraqi Baath parties. Many students already belonged to organizations when they reached university. But they were particularly influenced by the unique atmosphere and intense discussions among students who came from the various Arab countries and had the feeling they were in the process of building a great Arab nation.

Ahmed C. was twenty years old when he left Amman and arrived at the University of Damascus in late 1968. He hails from a modest Jordanian family, his father being a grocer. Unlike many others, he had no former political experience, which he attributes to the ban on political parties in Jordan at that time (until 1989). This ban did not prevent other activists from joining organizations, but as it was, Ahmed C. went through secondary school in an environment that was not particularly politicized. He points out:

> I went to Syria to study medicine, not to engage in political activity. In Syria and in Egypt, you didn't have to pay tuition, unlike in Jordan, after the unification between Egypt and Syria.[5] So in Syrian universities young people from all over the Arab world mixed. That influenced me to move toward the nationalist vein, it was the foundation of my Nasserist experience.[6]

After meetings and discussions with students from the Nasserist General Union of Arab Students, he joined the organization and gradually became an important figure. They criticized Syria's policies, "[which] weren't positive for Syria and we were against the [political] apparatus in Syria". Ahmed C. also appreciated the organization's international footing, having a presence not only in Arab countries, "but in Europe and Yugoslavia as well – all of them Nasserists!" The 1967 defeat did not immediately demobilize the pan-Arabists. On the contrary, the struggle was now entirely up to them. Politicized later than the others, Ahmed C. was less affected by the events of 1967. He continued medical school without interruption before returning to Jordan in 1976. But for the others, armed struggle became central to their activism and caused a hiatus in their academic career. A pivotal year for them was 1968, with various consequences depending on the stage they found themselves in. Jawad, for instance, studied law in Syria and took part in pan-Arabist political awareness campaigns, such as debates, meetings and so on. He returned to Bethlehem in 1964, and lived through the 1967 defeat. That was the breaking point; he went over to armed struggle and began to advocate Palestinian nationalism, which he believed had become necessary due to the split between Egypt and Syria and the end of Arab unity. His trajectory is characteristic of the shift to armed struggle and the reorientation toward Palestinian nationalism after 1967. But, being older, he had time to finish his degree prior to 1967, and did not experience a hiatus in his academic career, unlike Riyad and Mahmoud. Both of them went to school in the same village near Karak. Mahmoud describes the poverty there: "It was a simple life, with no complications. Even if life was tough, it was cold, there was poverty and so on. When I was in school, I had only one pair of pants and one shirt for a whole year." But he also described the nationalist atmosphere. They belonged to the same tribe, of which Mahmoud's grandfather and then one of his uncles were chiefs, who left his mark on him. Riyad and Mahmoud both joined the Baath Party early on. This movement corresponded to the general inclination of their tribe, even if no one in their immediate families was an activist. In 1968 Mahmoud was twenty years old. He had just received his secondary school degree and had already been active in the party for several years. He enlisted in the armed wing of the Baath Party and "became part of the Palestinian resistance". For three years he devoted his energies entirely to the struggle. He played an important role during the clashes in 1970 with the Jordanian army as he was chief of a Palestinian camp in Amman. He was jailed in Jordan for one year, and upon his release went directly to Syria, and later Lebanon. There he continued to fight as a *fidâ'i*, but at the same time he began his university studies, graduating with a bachelor's degree in political economy, and later a master's degree in history.

As for Riyad, two years older than Mahmoud, at the age of eighteen he was imprisoned for seven months in 1965 and banned from university for two years. In 1967 and 1968 he also joined the Arab Liberation Front struggle for Palestine in Jordan.[7] Already at that time he regretted the divergences among the various nationalist and Marxist movements. In 1969 he was admitted to the University of Baghdad, and went to Iraq to study medicine and later specialize in surgery while pursuing his activities in the Baath Party. In both of these men's cases, participation in the struggle and the ensuing crackdown interrupted their academic careers. Fairly quickly, however, they returned to university while pursuing their political activities, even though Riyad and Mahmoud were from families of farmers and were the first to have access to higher education. The acquisition of skills and university degrees to further the development of Arab nations is an integral part of the pan-Arab nationalist discourse. Their activism in the Baath Party eventually led them to pursue academic achievement as another facet of their activism.

In these two cases the hiatus was fairly short compared to those imprisoned in Israel, like Azmi, who was among the persons displaced in 1967. He joined the armed struggle for Palestine in 1968 at the age of eighteen, and was arrested by the Israeli army. He wasn't released until eighteen years later, in a prisoner exchange. However, like Riyad and Mahmoud, he began studying sociology as soon as he was released, working all the while to pay for his studies. Azmi finished his master's in Jordan, and then got his doctorate in Lebanon. Jordan's universities were by that time well established and offered several courses of study, but still did not award PhDs.

Activists born after the 1950s less frequently went abroad to universities in the region, tending to study in Jordanian universities, mainly the University of Jordan in Amman and Yarmouk University in Irbid. They met fewer Arab students from other countries throughout the region, but the atmosphere was just as politicized, Palestinian nationalists and leftist organizations being predominant. Most students were of Palestinian origin, despite the institution of a quota system in the 1970s and scholarships that gave preference to Transjordanians, particularly members of the army.[8]

Ibrahim A. left the West Bank in 1976 and began to study mathematics at Yarmouk University. He describes the political atmosphere, focused on defending the Palestinian cause, as well as the coexistence of different ideological currents at a time when the Muslim Brotherhood's influence was on the rise:

We competed over who was reading which books. We had political and ideological orientations, but sometimes they were just labels [...]. At university, at first the Muslim Brotherhood thought I was a good Muslim because of my lifestyle. On top of it, they found that I had a good, strong influence over the students, during discussions for instance, and they wanted me on their side. But when we started talking, we got into arguments because they weren't on the side of the national cause, they were with the Americans at that time, and sided with the worst Arab regimes.

For Ibrahim A., it was clear that the Islamists enjoyed preferential treatment from the university administration and the Jordanian regime to counter the influence of the left, nationalists and Palestinian Liberation Organization.[9] For him the main goal was Palestinian liberation, and he joined Fatah in 1977 for this reason, even if ideologically he considered himself a Marxist:

I didn't consider the leftists true Marxists. They were entirely under the influence of Soviet ideology. In Fatah, they figured I could be a Marxist if I wanted, as long as I didn't try to convince the others. Fatah wasn't a place for ideology, but for combating the occupation.

Gradually activism took up all his time. Ibrahim A. became head of Fatah's relations with other groups. He also took part in communication and recruitment. In particular, he participated in organizing demonstrations, sending two busfuls of volunteers to South Lebanon after the Israeli offensive in 1978. He was imprisoned for the first time in Jordan in 1980, and was released after demonstrations supporting him at the university. Ibrahim A. exemplifies the promotion of specifically Palestinian nationalism in the 1970s. As he points out, Fatah took a stance "beyond ideologies" that was not rooted in a more general representation of society and the forces driving it. Its aim was to bring the struggle for Palestine to the fore and be in a position to unite activists from various backgrounds. Emphasis on armed struggle caused a hiatus in the academic trajectories of its activists, as it had done for the Arab nationalists a few years earlier. But unlike them, Ibrahim A. did not return to education afterward. Fatah militant discourse did not place emphasis on education and earning a degree. Its objective was not to form an educated elite to advance the development of Arab nations, but to combat the Israeli occupation in the present with weapons and words. Universities were above all a space for mobilization. Ibrahim A. finally abandoned his studies altogether and worked full-time for Fatah.

Crackdowns on the communists, and internal divisions

In this environment that was mobilizing for armed struggle, communist militants followed a very different trajectory, the Jordanian-Palestinian Communist Party having become divided over the issue as of 1968. The headquarters in Amman as well as a segment of communist activists in the West Bank, followers of al-Salfiti,[10] were against guerrilla action and advocated other means of struggle as well as co-operation with the Hashemite monarchy. Communist leader Fouad Nassar, on the other hand, who went into exile after being jailed for five years, founded the armed wing al-Ansar ("The Partisans") in 1970 and encouraged communists to take part in the struggle for Palestinian national liberation. Divisions over the Palestinian cause also led to a territorial division. In 1982 the West Bank branch of the Jordanian-Palestinian Communist Party claimed its independence and merged with Gaza to form the Palestinian Communist Party (which later adopted the name the Palestinian People's Party).

These divisions had a number of consequences for sympathizers and activists. First of all, youths who nevertheless sympathized with the communist movement decided to join Fatah and other organizations to take part in the armed struggle, which emerged in the 1970s as one of the central repertoires of action for the Palestinian cause. This was the case for Khaled, whose studies in Romania as of 1975 were mentioned above: "When I was about fifteen or sixteen I joined Fatah, because I wanted to take up arms, but the Communist Party did not fight, otherwise I would have joined the Communist Party because I come from a communist family. [...] But I joined the Communist Party in '74."

In the context of the period, the Communist Party's position was controversial because of its perceived lack of support for the Palestinian cause. Tarek comes from a Palestinian family which had to flee Jaffa in 1948. He joined the communists in secondary school in the early 1960s, but distanced himself from it in the 1970s, putting forth the same argument:

> In secondary school I sided with the communists with the aim of asking them when we were going to take up arms and fight for Palestine. And then I saw that an answer wasn't forthcoming, or at least not clearly. [...] The communists did not back the Palestinian cause.[11]

For communist students in Jordan, however, this non-participation in armed struggle caused less of a hiatus in their academic careers. The communists, moreover, like their nationalist counterparts, placed emphasis on earning degrees, although the communist organization maintained greater control over its activists. Joining the communists required total commitment as well as toeing the party line in all areas of life, not only politics. This aspect was particularly evident in the handling of students sent to Eastern bloc countries. Khaled refers to this with regard to his stay in Romania:

> I was very active politically; I was part of the student union bureau, where all the leaders were communists. After seven years of school I went back, in 1982. There had been the Israeli attack

in Lebanon, and there were a lot of students who wanted to fight. I was one of them. Our final exams were in September, but I left in June. I would be a fighter, and not a doctor! I wanted to join a group of combatants [in Damascus], but then the Communist Party told us to go back and take our exams, that we'd be more useful that way.

So Khaled went back to Romania.

But even if fewer activists interrupted their studies to take part in armed struggle, crackdowns on communists were particularly harsh, and still prevented a number of them from finishing their education, either because of imprisonment or because they were banned from university. While all political parties were banned in Jordan up until 1992, the communists came under a specific law in effect up until 1989 according to which membership in the Communist Party was punishable by fifteen years in prison. Anyone found in possession of the newspaper published by the Communist Party was liable to a prison sentence. Communist activity at university was thus twofold. The visible side pertained to participation in student life, topical debates on Israel, Lebanon and so on, and political struggles, without explicitly claiming an affiliation with communism. However, anything to do with the communist organization was carried out underground.

In 1984, then especially in 1986, students at Yarmouk University in Irbid staged strikes and demonstrations. They were protesting against a rise in tuition fees and demanding the creation of an independent (and cross-disciplinary) student union. Ramzi, whose affiliation with communism was mentioned previously, was one of the movement's leaders:

> I was jailed for two years, until the end of 1985, first for three months by the secret police [Mukhabarat][12] in Irbid, then for sixteen months in Irbid prison without trial. Then I went on a twelve-day hunger strike, and at the same time there were

student demonstrations in the city of Irbid. Then, [I was held] for three months by the Mukhabarat in Amman, and then I was released. When I was in Mukhabarat custody, I was in solitary confinement. They beat me, but [...] I never agreed to sign the official retraction.[13] When I got out, I went back to university. My family had registered me each year so that I would be granted an extension. One month later, the events of 1986 began.

This time, security forces stormed the campus and killed three students. Ramzi adds: "The security forces that came on campus had been trained to be particularly harsh. They weren't told that the students were fighting for their rights but that they were leading decadent lives. That's why they were so violent, especially the Bedouin forces."

This account reflects the growing antagonism between Bedouin forces – a pillar of the monarchy – and "Palestinians" (even though in this case Ramzi's family is Jordanian). Palestinian nationalist organizations were involved in the mobilization. Savagely beaten, Ramzi nevertheless managed to escape from campus: "Other students helped me, given the shape I was in. Then party members came and took care of me. They hid me for six months."

Ramzi then escaped to Syria, but he suffered the consequences of divisions in the Jordanian Communist Party. Indeed, notwithstanding the question of armed struggle, the Irbid protests intensified internal tensions in the Communist Party over its position with regard to the Hashemite monarchy. For the secretary-general in Amman, the protest was decided locally, against the directives of headquarters. Ramzi in fact worked in co-ordination with a local cadre from the Muslim Brotherhood who experienced similar difficulties with his own leadership, even though the Muslim Brotherhood, unlike the Communist Party, was not banned. At the national level, Communist Party influence declined, and after the above-mentioned spate of repression, the leadership's strategy was to reposition itself away from head-on opposition, especially after its split with the Palestinian branch. Moreover, the Jordanian regime had identified national leadership cells, and communist leaders could be subject to "preventive" arrests. Ramzi describes their activism as "routine", contrasting it with the dynamism found in the areas of Irbid and Karak, where the communists continued to recruit and took more revolutionary stands. In fact, the division also affected the more or less orthodox relationship with the Soviet Union and the party's monolithic structure. As an example, Ramzi relayed a joke that was commonly told among activists critical of the party: "When it rains in Moscow, they open an umbrella in Amman." Such divisions finally resulted in the creation of an independent committee in Irbid that refused to align itself with the Soviet Union. They sought to move closer to what they considered the new European left, independent of the Soviet Union, that came out of the 1968 movements.[14]

As Ramzi points out, these oppositions had a very real effect on his student career:

> In the end, what was strange was to run into the same behaviour from the Yarmouk University administration and the party. Yarmouk stopped me from pursuing my studies because of my political activities, and the party also stopped me from going on with my studies because of my political activities.

Yarmouk University indeed refused to issue a transcript for his years of study, which would have enabled him to register at a university in Syria. Retaliatory measures regarding the awarding of degrees or registration in upper years were fairly frequent, and were a decisive factor in limiting student activism, given the cost of university. University doors in Eastern bloc countries were also closed to him due to the Jordanian Communist Party's opposition to his activities in Irbid. With unofficial papers from Yarmouk University, he ended up studying Arab literature for two years in Syria, for which he could not get official credit. It was two brothers in Australia "who were financially well off" who supported him during that period. But for Ramzi, in any event, "at the time, my primary goal wasn't school, but political action".

Between underground activities and prison time, communist activism in Jordan's universities made it difficult for members to continue their studies, though this was offset by the ideological emphasis – as for Arab nationalists – on earning degrees and the possibility of continuing their studies in Eastern bloc countries. As an internal Communist Party dissident, however, the injunction to earn a degree was not applied to Ramzi, and the party, on the contrary, thwarted his efforts. But through his political activities he acquired other skills that he would later manage to convert into a professional career.

The same emphasis on the acquisition of knowledge is found among Muslim Brotherhood Islamists, even if the preferred disciplines are not the same. But most of all, the organization was never banned, and during this time it was backed rather than repressed by the Jordanian monarchy, except for certain specific actions. This is reflected in more linear academic trajectories among its activists than for the nationalists and the communists.

Islamist mobilization in universities

The Islamists' experience in Jordan's universities is first of all one of a minority trend, then in full expansion as of the mid-1970s, ending up as a majority in the late 1980s. Most long-time activists have been members or sympathizers since secondary school. Others, from non-politicized backgrounds but defining themselves as conservatives and practising Muslims, were also attracted to the movement. Such is the case of Badi', born in Shobak in southern Jordan, in the Maan area, who came to the University of Jordan in

1983 at the age of eighteen. He enrolled in mechanical engineering with a small army scholarship because his father was a soldier:

> At university, as a practising conservative Muslim, Islamic activism was for me the most preponderant. And the image I had of the other side wasn't good. Ever since childhood, I had heard people say communism wasn't good, Baathism wasn't good, the nationalist movements weren't good. I read a lot [...] to stay true to myself and the idea that it was important to practise religion and to be involved. That was the idea at first. But today my convictions have gained greater consciousness.[15]

At university, the Muslim Brotherhood primarily focused its activities on student issues and providing services to students. The same strategy was adopted in professional organizations, based on the defence of professional interests much more than on political issues. This approach falls in line with the social history of the Muslim Brotherhood movement and the scope of its charity network. In 1973 the movement was involved in the strike against the tuition hike, organized by the student union founded in 1969 at the University of Jordan. Having arrived at the University of Jordan a few years before Badi', Rahil, whose involvement with the Muslim Brotherhood in secondary school was mentioned in Chapter 2, registered at the Faculty of Islamic Law. He became a student representative following the 1975 elections in which the Muslim Brotherhood achieved notable support in the Faculty of Sciences and the Faculty of Islamic Law, even though the left and the nationalists remained in the lead. But the student union was disbanded by decree in 1975,[16] and the student elections were cancelled in the context of the general crackdown on political activity by the Jordanian authorities. Rahil then talked about the new strategy implemented after this, which focused efforts on hitherto neglected student associations.

On the model of what the Muslim Brotherhood had done in other faculties, Badi', together with fellow Muslim Brotherhood members, formed an association for mechanical engineering students in 1983:

> I talked to the teachers, to the dean and to the head of the faculty about the students' needs. We could sell them items, school supplies and books. In engineering, there were specific tools that we bought and sold as a service dedicated to the students. For a while I was president of this association. We also worked on articles that we posted.

More political activities, defence of the Palestinian cause in particular, were built up on this foundation, especially after 1987, with the beginning of the first Intifada and the creation of Hamas. Badi' thus explains:

> We organized lots of activities and events [...] which led to conflicts with the university administration [...] [which] wanted us to do less of it. [...] There were problems, but not as much as at Yarmouk [...]. We organized events in support of Hamas as soon as it began. We showed pictures of what was going on.

The Muslim Brotherhood suffered less severe measures than the other groups, but when its activities joined those of the opposition, as was the case in Yarmouk, arrests were also made in its ranks. The reprehensible activities were not so much support for the Palestinian cause as the degree to which student political activism had turned into opposition to the Jordanian regime and the university administration.

Badi' was not troubled by the authorities. Rahil, on the other hand, who was still at university and working on his master's degree, was apprehended by the General Intelligence Department and held for seven months in the wake of the Yarmouk events mentioned above, in which the communist Ramzi was one of the leaders. Rahil recounts: "There were a lot of arrests, not only of students, but also of members of the Islamist movement, among them academics and civil servants [...]. Some of them still today have not got their jobs back."

Indeed, the Jordanian regime also went after the national headquarters of the various organizations, pressuring them, successfully, to exert authority over their more militant local sections. When Rahil got out of prison, the University of Jordan gave him his master's degree, but his passport was confiscated. As there was no doctorate of Islamic Law in Jordan, at first he was unable to continue his studies. He was also banned from holding a public sector job. Paradoxically, this situation allowed him more freedom to engage in political activity with the Muslim Brotherhood. Such pressures on his professional career had the opposite effect, and reinforced his activism, which became his main activity, given that other outlets were blocked. Rahil makes the connection very clear:

> I was not allowed to travel abroad, [...] and I was also banned from holding a state job and that's why I couldn't finish my degree until 1990 [...]. And I couldn't work in the private sector. So at the time I was available to do political canvassing for the Muslim Brotherhood.

He thus devoted himself to full-time campaigning until a doctorate of Islamic Law opened up at the University of Jordan in 1990, enabling him to finish his studies and earn his PhD in 1995.

As for Badi', he had no trouble finishing his master's in five years, like most Islamist activists interviewed, except for Rahil. Badi' nevertheless mentions the problem of striking a balance between his voluntary work and his studies, to the detriment of his education. This echoes a typical concern among activists regarding the impact of the time spent on political activities on their studies and their jobs. However, there is no clear line drawn among these various areas because the Islamist commitment goes beyond politics to encompass everyday behaviour.

Social leaders

One of the specific features of the Islamist commitment is the adoption of a personal ideal that incorporates morality, piety, academic achievement and social leadership. In this regard, it is not merely a political stance, but is echoed in the very notion of commitment, *iltizâm*, for the Islamists, which includes the idea of obligation and, in the broad sense, a religious dimension as well.[17] The activists clearly integrate these various dimensions, which are very present in the interviews.

The relationship to knowledge and academic excellence fits into this framework. The most prized disciplines have to do with the construction of an Arab and Muslim identity: Islamic law, the Arabic language, and especially the sciences, attention regularly being drawn to the Arabs' historic contribution to these disciplines during the Middle Ages. The titles of engineer and PhD have gradually become more valued than that of sheikh. Islamists were particularly involved in engineering, the desire to reclaim possession of the sciences, which is also another way of challenging Western technological domination.

While in education, it thus becomes an integral part of the commitment process to be a good student, well ranked and recognized as such. Such behaviour is perceived as a sign of moral superiority and leadership, not only an indication of the acquisition of knowledge. For the respondents involved, this is reflected in the emphasis they place on their scholarly achievements. They call attention to their scores on the baccalaureate, and later at university, always claiming to be at the top of their class, and highlight their intellectual precocity. Nawal joined the Muslim Brotherhood in secondary school, mentored by one of her teachers. She recounts:

> Already at a very young age I didn't think that people were put on earth just to eat, drink, sleep, travel and have fun [...]. I wondered, "Why did the Lord of the universe create us as Muslims, and why did he create us at all?" [...] So I started looking in books. Although in the Arab world reading isn't considered a priority, I did my research at a very early age [...]. I continued with my PhD studies even though I was married, I had children and a lot of responsibility – and, thank God, I succeeded and did very well.[18]

Rahil recounts that at school he started a discussion group to talk about the philosophy of the Muslim Brotherhood, and that this group "was considered to be the smartest". He boasts of his good grades in scientific subjects and Arabic language, and associates this scholastic achievement with the three pillars of the Islamist commitment he advocates: piety, intelligence and moral righteousness. Badiʿ, who, unlike the others, mentioned the negative impact of activism on his studies, points out his honourable ranking on the baccalaureate and the academic excellence of his wife, also an activist, "who is a gynaecologist, and who was always at the top of the class at university and in school". These activists emphasize their academic achievements, whatever contradictions they might encounter elsewhere. The Islamists are eager to promote themselves as bearers of knowledge, and not only in the religious domain. Moreover, their political success has a positive influence on the activists' perceptions of their academic itinerary.

But it is not only important to have good grades; the goal is also to become a *qaïd* ("leader"). The term is used often, its legitimacy being based on the importance of previously mentioned qualities: academic excellence, piety and moral righteousness. Rahil thus mentions "the moral examples and authenticity" he has observed among the Muslim Brotherhood, which encouraged him to back them. Thus legitimized, the goal of leadership is then clearly stated and placed in the framework of a religious duty. Rahil describes how student activities serve as training and an access route for Muslim Brotherhood students to become leaders in society.

In this context, the notion of service promoted by student associations takes on a broader meaning. The activists embrace it on a personal level as a moral quality that enhances them and is an integral part of their religious commitment. Badi' thus describes what prompted him to get involved:

> A sort of inner desire to live for others, not for myself alone. That led me to devote myself to the service of others. [...] If, later on, you're elected, then you have responsibilities and duties to fulfil. Thus you feel the need to do something, to be a leader. Today, I feel that it's a responsibility and a duty that the Almighty asked us to fulfil [...]. Everyone likes to become a leader, and someone who does this job can [...] thus assert himself [...]. When I work for the Muslim Brotherhood, I'm not working to make a name for myself [...]. That's proscribed![19] But naturally, someone who does such a job becomes known, and that is more important than any personal pride one might feel deep down.

Furthermore, the rise of the Islamists also coincided with a new generation of engineering graduates who have had difficulty finding jobs. Following the increasing availability of higher education, they no longer form an elite, as was the case for the previous generation, and the Jordanian economy, long based on indirect income from oil,[20] is having trouble accommodating them. They are attracted to the Islamist movement, where their studies are valued and they find a social role despite unemployment. In addition to the legitimacy drawn from a religious affiliation, activism offers them social recognition. This is clear among the Islamists, as their movement has experienced growing success, which they attribute in retrospect to their first steps in politics and their self-assessment. For the nationalists and the communists, the opposite has occurred. The defeats suffered by their parties have led them to give a more nuanced assessment of the moment they became involved in politics, and they evade the question of personal success. In fact, among the various groups, activism has had varying impacts on academic trajectories depending on the role attributed to knowledge in the chosen political orientation, the repertoire of action used – armed struggle is the principal issue – and the type of repressive measures applied by the regime. This differentiation continues beyond university, when for many the ideology espoused turns into a true way of life with its specific socialization patterns.

CHAPTER 4

Activism, a way of life

Ideologies take shape over the course of the activist's career. They are not simply a matter of political doctrine; ideologies also have specific consequences for activists' lives, depending not only on their content, but also, and above all, on the extent to which they convey an overall worldview. Two different ideological aims can be distinguished. In the case of nationalism, the cause is limited to a specific political goal. It does not represent an overall doctrine or a particular lifestyle, and moreover seems to be assimilated easily by the other two currents, Marxism and Islamism. Activists from either tendency generally talk less about true opposition to pan-Arabists than differences in opinion as to the primary goals. For the communists, nationalism is merely a stage, whereas for the pan-Arabists it is an end in itself. But in the second case ideology goes further and builds a truly global and structured worldview. Thus, for the communists Marxism offers an overall framework of interpretation. This all-embracing aspect of ideology is also found among the Islamists. The activists' very lifestyle is affected, because a human ideal is included that they are urged to put into practice in their daily lives, in their family, at work and in their social relations in general. This is also reflected in the building of social networks among people sharing similar practices, the activists thus literally developing a closed circle and a counter-society.

Communist marginality

The content of an ideology has an influence not only on activists' lives, but also on the way their political orientation connects with their social environment, either in harmony or in conflict with it. For communist activists, the relative marginality of their trajectory has put them rather at odds with their social milieu – a fact they must deal with throughout their careers. The first confrontation is with the family. Rare are those who come from a communist family, and the initial reactions to them tend to be refusal, rejection or concern. Atheism, and especially the link seen between atheism and immorality, poses a particular problem for the activists' associates. However, they often end up receiving support from their immediate family,[1] and it is rather the more distant family, the tribe or the community, that puts pressure on them. When Nader's uncle went to visit him in Cairo, where he was studying drama, and realized he had joined the communists, he went home to see Nader's mother and told her: "And do you know who communists are? They're the ones who sleep with their sisters!" But his mother stood by him. Ahmed A., whose affiliation with the Communist Party at Yarmouk University was mentioned previously, received support from his parents, who defended him against the others and helped out his wife while he was in prison. Atheism, however, was a problem for them, especially with regard to their community: people came to tell them their son was against religion. There were also government campaigns on the issue.

This matter was crucial for the Jordanian communists. It sidelined them within their own society despite the efforts made, as pointed out by Ramzi, another communist activist at Yarmouk University:

> There was the question of religion, it was the main point for the communists. We were considered atheists, irreligious and so on. Our policy was never to take part in discussions about religion, it wasn't at all the main issue for us. [...] We made sure never to behave outrageously. We didn't drink in public, for instance. Our idea was that we were part of this society, and we did not want to shock it profoundly.

Faced with a particularly conservative environment in Jordan, the communists did not advertise atheism. Within the party, the position was secular rather than atheist, refusing to base its policy on religious factors and Islam. In this way, the Communist Party, and more generally the Marxist left, offered a prime space for mobilization for minority Christians.[2] But some activists continued to worship, and political meetings could be suspended for prayer:

> We even had communist comrades who held important positions even though they were religious. [...] At one time, there was little political openness. So instead of meeting separately with the cells, I called all the comrades to a single meeting. We were in the middle of deliberating when we heard the call to prayer [...]. All the comrades went, except for the head of the party organization and myself. [...] We had respect for religion, but there was government propaganda in those years. [...] They presented the communists as infidels who knew no father or mother or sister – a pack of lies![3]

A communist stance can thus be the source of rumours and sometimes exclusion from rituals. Ahmed A. recounts:

> I had a comrade in Irbid. His wife had died. The day of her funeral, his wife's family was there [...]. Here, you know, we put the body directly in the grave and the gravedigger lowers the body with the help of a family member. When her husband went to do it, his wife's family made a scene because he was ungodly,

an atheist, and they didn't want him to touch their daughter. Just imagine: the husband's wife is dead, and he isn't allowed to carry her and help with her burial.

Beyond issues of morality and atheism, "there were people who respected us but who kept their distance because they were afraid. They knew we were going to prison," Ramzi recounts. Indeed, the communists' political activities, their involvement in local struggles or for the Palestinian cause, earned them a certain degree of respect, tinged with fear of punishment. Ahmed B. tells a similar story: "The Communist Party could not act like a party that had positions that were completely accepted, but people appreciated its qualities of resistance, tenacity, opposition and sacrifice."

Often the support received from friends and family is more personal than political, the family being primarily concerned about the danger the activists may have to face and to which they may expose their family. Deep down, Ahmed's parents would have preferred him not to associate with the communists and place himself in danger, even if they stood up for him in the face of others. Ramzi blames himself for the negative consequences of his activism on his family:

> My father had diabetes, and I'm convinced that the worry I caused him hastened his death. [...] After '86, I hid out for six months. My family didn't know where I was. And the secret police frequently went to the house to ask them about my whereabouts. They finally took my brother and my father away to interrogate them. I feel responsible for that.

The communist commitment can also create a maladjustment or marginality that tends to weaken activism and can result in withdrawal from the movement.[4] However, the activists discussed here have all had long-term commitments, even if some have changed track or switched affiliation toward the end of the road. Such difficulties are offset by the development of a closed circle among communists, an alternative network of socialization that provides activists with support, but also exercises control.

Communist circles: an alternative form of socialization

The commitment to communism is associated with a specific socialization context. Communist activists develop a common lifestyle, and a closed circle that is strengthened by the need for mutual solidarity to counterweigh the harsh measures they have been subjected to and the ambivalent relations they have with the rest of society. Communist families support each other when an activist among them is in prison or has gone underground. The communist commitment thus not only implies becoming part of networks of activists, which would mean additional opportunities for socialization, but because of social rejection and general doctrine, it also penetrates the private sphere. The party issues guidelines in this regard, as Khaled recounts, having gone to study in Romania: "In Romania, I was living with a Romanian woman. But the Jordanian Communist Party didn't want us to marry foreigners because they wanted us to spread through Jordanian society. They told me: […] you come home, and either you bring her over or you don't." His passport was immediately confiscated by the Jordanian authorities when he returned in late 1982, he was not allowed to travel, and he lost contact with her.

Communists are aware that it is difficult to change their societies from within. In such a situation, marriage is perceived as a political issue, and founding a family is viewed as a potential lever for change. Taysir, whose involvement in communism was discussed earlier with respect to artistic circles, discusses this awareness:

> There were people in the party who got married to Eastern European women rather than marrying Palestinians and working hard with these women to make things change. But that's what I did. I fought alongside a woman from Gaza. Her father was an underground communist. And I urged her to sign up.

Most marriages take place between activists, because people meet within the party, or at least within the Marxist left, because one person convinces the other to join, and because the harshness of measures against them also induces those who are not affiliated to give up associating with them. Several activists mention the break-up of relationships during their incarceration.

Kinda is an activist who joined the Democratic Front for the Liberation of Palestine (DFLP) and then the Union of Jordanian Women, a leftwing organization that was officially shut down by the Jordanian government in 1978 for its opposition to the Camp David Accords, but which reformed in 1989: "It was hard for me when I wanted to get married, because I absolutely wanted someone who could respect my commitment. That's why I married late and I could consider marrying Ahmed, because he had respect for my activities."[5]

The couple supported each other's political commitment. Female activists are less severely punished than men, and are not imprisoned, although they are sometimes placed under house arrest.[6] During the times Ahmed A. was in prison, it was important to Kinda to save face and prove to the rest of the village that they nevertheless led a normal life and could cope. According to her, this was essential to preserve her life in the village, and in that regard she received support from her family and from other women in the same situation. She spoke of long bus trips to the prison with other political prisoners' wives, during which they sang songs and picnicked. The aim was also to lighten up the situation for their children. As one of their daughters says: "For me, I was just on a normal visit to my father. I didn't realize what imprisonment was." When reality dawned on her, her mother explained at length the difference between political prisoners and common criminals, and her daughter remained proud of her father. These activist networks, which thus double as activist family networks, have a central role; they create an ordinary space with common expectations and references. They also serve as professional networks. They provide support to preserve, as much as possible, a semblance of normality despite repression; but also when activists go underground.

The Soviet Union: a foundational experience

In this context, the collapse of the Soviet Union was all the more traumatic for the communists as it meant the beginning of the disintegration of their closed circle. In Jordan it was virtually concomitant with the end of communists' having to live in secrecy that came along with the country's "democratic opening". The collapse of the Soviet Union was also experienced as an ideological defeat that deeply destabilized the activists. This was true throughout the Arab world, but it especially affected the majority Communist Party faction in Jordan, deeply infused with orthodox Soviet communism. In fact, "the orphans of the Gorbachev era"[7] essentially had access to Marxist theory through brochures circulated by the Soviet Union, to the dismay of Ahmed B., a communist dissident in Irbid:

> When we [communists] arrived in the 1970s, there was no tradition. Everything was possible before we saw the Soviets. We could have acknowledged other Arab sources. As for me personally, […] I didn't like the Soviet publications. But generally speaking, the Communist Party had opted for cultural enrichment through Soviet publications.

According to Maher Sharif,[8] Arab communist submission to the political and ideological authority of the Soviet Communist Party explains that they were never able to devise a more accommodating theory that was better adapted to their situation and have not recovered from the collapse of the Soviet Union. Added to this feeling of defeat were also the years of persecution and the experience of prison and torture for the most militant among them. These experiences have been the source of all the more bitterness among Jordanian communists as they feel that their comrades in the

Middle East have not acknowledged the difficulty of their struggle. As Stéphanie Latte-Abdallah points out: "their confinement to the Jordanian national arena isolated them from their regional networks and financial backers, their long stint underground moreover cutting most of them off from a broad social base".[9]

Just when the communists were losing a large segment of their funding due to the demise of the Soviet Union, their emergence from underground revealed their small numbers and their divisions. Ahmed B., whose commitment had not wavered even after a year and a half in prison in 1981, left the Communist Party at that time:

> For us the situation was a new one, […] nothing was hidden any longer; the issue was, "Let's assess our political ideas," which had just taken a big blow […]. And it was devastating […]. During the period of underground activity, internal divisions were stimulating […]; but now this was no longer the case because every disagreement was aired in public.

And yet, like Ramzi, Ahmed B. was at the heart of the Irbid split that had challenged orthodox and Stalinist communism. Already, during a break in his studies in the Soviet Union, he did not like "the gap between rhetoric and reality". The Jordanian Communist Party did not take kindly to his sudden return: "They almost punished me […]. But when I came home, I went back to doing my political canvassing at Yarmouk University and I regained trust." In retrospect, communists who had travelled to Eastern bloc countries are clear that they already had doubts about the survival of the communist system. However, in their experience, there was a huge difference between their advocating a more activist and revolutionary direction within the Communist Party and the sudden growth of divisions and subdivisions that became plain to see after 1989, just when they were realizing their political weakness.

The divisions and the ideological defeat, emergence from underground and growing social rejection concomitant with the rise of the Islamists spelt the end of communist solidarities. The trauma caused by these rifts is on a par with the degree of involvement the activists invested in the party. As Ahmed B. says: "My whole life was wrapped up with the party [...]. The party this, the party that, all the time, in all my thoughts." Divisions affected couples, families and friendships. Taysir compares the break-up of his marriage with a "Stalinist" to the failure of the Soviet Union. He also lost his closest friends, a communist couple. He stresses the political disengagement and social isolation:

> Before, when the state arrested someone, people hid him and helped him flee. Now sometimes they grab him and turn him in to the police, even if the government didn't say he was wanted. They say, "Take this communist [...] because he's against Islam [...]." There used to be 300 people in the audience, now only thirty come to see each show. Now very few of us get together. [...] Why be involved in politics? To free Palestine, develop society? There's no longer any horizon for developing this society through socialism.

After the fall of the Soviet Union, activists generally retained their Marxist convictions through which they interpreted the world, particularly in terms of matters of injustice. But they lost the networks through which they had structured their convictions, and the social and political foundation for this ideology has collapsed. The closed circle of activists, the close interweaving of social and political networks, no longer compensates for social marginality, producing isolation and bitterness among many of them. Disengagement is one result, but there are also changes of allegiance and realignments that are based in international events and considerations of human rights. The new forms of mobilization involved will be discussed in Chapter 6.

The Islamist foothold

Among Islamists there is also an all-embracing ideology that does not only apply to politics, but also a view of humanity and a moral doctrine that maps out a lifestyle. It provides a general line of reasoning and conduct. Hamzeh, a party cadre in the IAF,[10] thus talks about a "complete Islam, that applies to all matters in life, devotion, thought, belief and line of conduct". Another activist in a meeting speaks of a "holistic concept".[11] And when it comes to illustrating their commitment, activists have been known to invite an investigator to come and observe their family's everyday way of life and the importance of religious practice in the home.

Marriage and family also become a matter of religion and politics, as the case of Hikmat shows. Hikmat was born in Karak in 1956, and joined the Muslim Brotherhood during secondary school after the war of 1973. He later became a senior cadre, like Hamzeh:

> My life, my work and my political affiliation are in harmony because at home we all are part of the same movement. My wife, my sons and my daughters all share my orientation […]. My sons at university are active with other youths in the Islamic movement. […] Many of us marry a woman from the Muslim Brotherhood. I initiated my wife into political involvement, and some time later she joined the Muslim Brotherhood […]. I chose her right from the start because she was religious and committed.[12]

In this case, Hikmat's wife joined the party after her marriage, but she was already sympathetic to the movement. But there are also marriages between activists. Badi', whose involvement in the Muslim Brotherhood at university was described in Chapter 3, also considers that his wife's support and his family's ideological cohesion are essential. He emphasizes the notion of sacrifice, which enables him to underscore the scope and the value of his commitment:

When we decided to marry, I told her I was a member of the Muslim Brotherhood. Why? Because the Muslim Brotherhood was subject to pressure [...]. It was my duty to inform her that the man she was going to marry might be exposed to sacrifices that she had to accept and assume. [...] It is important for everyone in the family to have the same orientation, because it makes it easier to accomplish the work at hand, the political actions and the necessary sacrifices.

Passing on their sense of commitment and their political orientation to their children also appears to be self-evident (whereas the communists, on the contrary, do not wish to see their children choose the same path, feeling that such a choice is too difficult and demands too great a sacrifice). Badi' also points this out: "We urge young people to join the party. It is thus only natural for my children to do the same. [...] I bring up all my children this way, that is why they always come with me to all the various events, even the youngest of them."

Creating a specific socialization in political networks enables likeminded people to get together, sharing the same ideals and promoting the same way of life, whereas the time invested in activism limits opportunities for other types of sociability. Reference to a global doctrine and the desire to reform both people and society are evident in the establishment of an Islamist counter-society, as is the case in other countries, Egypt in particular.[13] The Muslim Brotherhood has its own sources of funding, not least the collection of *zakat*,[14] and in Jordan it has full latitude to develop charity organizations, unlike the other tendencies. As one activist points out: "As a current of Islam, our action fits in with the social service. We have penetrated society with the conviction that it will adopt Islamic ideas."

In keeping with its overall approach, the Muslim Brotherhood organizes activities in a wide range of areas – an essential aspect, according to Badi':

> I wanted to act in several different areas [...]. The Muslim Brotherhood was present in parliament, in unions, in student organizations, in social work and so on. There are teachers whose mission it is to preach or give children lessons at the mosque, undertake social work and collect donations to hand out to orphans and widows. A member of the Muslim Brotherhood can be a shopkeeper and at the same time work for the city government, [...] serving the entire population.

Employment at the municipal level has often been chosen by the Islamists as it provides a space for opposition that has enabled them to reinforce their support by proving to be expert and pragmatic administrators – far from the image they tend to have in the West.[15] They have also become involved in the education and health sectors, even founding hospitals. These Islamized spaces are specific loci where activists have access to services that are consistent with their principles. But far from being at odds with the rest of society, these spaces on the contrary permeate it and mark the start of true social hegemony. Not only are Islamists not forced to go underground,[16] but they have been experiencing greater social continuity.

From social work to politics

> Being a Muslim means you have a role in society.[17]

For the activists, that involves belonging to a relational network strengthened by a common commitment, not as protection from or an alternative in the face of social rejection, but as providing leadership for society as a whole. They stress the respect they are shown, which is not due to their position as an opposition force, unlike the communists, but is instead related to the values they represent. Tribal ties, for instance, are not adversely affected by their commitment. According to Hikmat, even though various currents exist within his clan: "everyone there respects me and appreciates me because I'm part of the Islamic movement". This is partly an expression of the consistently positive assessment Islamists tend to have of their own trajectory and the way they are perceived by others – an assessment based in the internalization of their political success. But the "self-evidence" of the Islamist commitment that stresses Arab and Muslim authenticity (a term used recurrently by the respondents), unaffected by any foreign influence, is indeed one of the movement's achievements. A young activist from the IAF thus mentions the natural aspect of Islamism: "Politics is part of a Muslim's nature. [...] Many youths don't have a political framework, but at election time [they vote] according to their nature: Islamic civilization [...]. Prayer and fasting have a prolongation in society, in political action or thought."[18]

The continuity between religion and politics was for him a positive determining factor: "I was looking for a link between politics and the faith I grew up with and the respect I have for religion [...]. I thus attempted to bring the two together, which naturally directed me from the start toward the Islamic movement."

The argument is twofold: first, the primary characteristic of society is to be Muslim, and second, politics is necessarily in continuity with religion: "The separation between religion and the state was a decision made by the various regimes in order to weaken the former. That does not suit our countries, because for a person who is part of Islam, this separation prevents him from thinking and acting." Islamism here is presented as a sort of reverse orientalism, in that it also essentializes the reference to Islam, although this time it is with a view to magnifying it.[19]

The Islamists fight on the political front in part to promote reference to religion, but mainly to ensure a monopoly over religious interpretation, as Badi''s statement illustrates in claiming to be committed to "serving my mission, that of Islam in general, as the Muslim Brotherhood views it". In fact, the importance of religion is agreed upon, whereas the sources can always be interpreted in different ways. The political issue is indeed at the level of interpretation, and the struggle to determine who holds the keys to such interpretation and can thus draw political legitimacy from it.

Integrity, justice and ambition

Reference to religion lends a certain legitimacy to the presentation of programmes to moralize political life. The Islamic Action Front thus set up an anti-corruption commission, of which Badi' is a member, that focuses on the workings of parliament and the government, but with fairly slim means. It promotes integrity and justice, and Islamism is credited with paying considerable attention to these matters, which seem all the more crucial as economic development in Jordanian society is highly inegalitarian. The moral aspect associated with religion has enabled the Islamists to place its services, including the fight against corruption and in favour of social justice, at the top of their agenda, ahead of their positions on the Palestinian cause. Hikmat finishes the presentation of his action within the Muslim Brotherhood by saying: "as a brotherhood, as a movement, we must move forward to guide people and serve them. All this in a perspective of equality and justice without any corruption." On the other hand, opponents to the Islamist movement and those who leave it focus their attacks on this point in particular, pointing out the discrepancy between their claims and what really goes on inside the movement and in the charity networks.

In accordance with the rationale of an ideological continuity between the political sphere and the personal sphere, Islamist activists highlight the notion of integrity at both levels: that of their personal moral code and that of their political network. Another aspect that flows from the appeal to religious references is the moral character that thus tends to be associated with the activist's personal ambitions. Individual success in this context in fact becomes an extension of one's religious commitment, a sign of one's chosenness and the righteousness of one's principles. The desire for success and self-fulfilment can thus be expressed unabashedly: "I found that this political avenue gave concrete expression to my convictions, my ambitions and my aspirations and that it reflected my personality. So I joined. What's more, it could also help me fulfil my personal desire to attain a position of power."[20]

The Islamists' quite positive assessment of their trajectory and their academic achievements, as well as their openly expressed desire to lead, have been discussed previously. These aspects clearly fall in line with the continuity sought between religious commitment, the movement's political and social success and personal achievement. But the movement continues to gather strength, and it is not by chance that a young activist from the Islamic Action Front mentions this fact explicitly. The status of leader in society not only offers personal rewards – network, respectability, and so on, which, as Badiʿ indicates, should be side effects, and not the primary objective. One can note here a shift from politics to personal development and the economic sphere, which, according to Patrick Haenni, has occurred through the Islamists' assimilation of management literature.[21] This has accompanied the professionalization of activism and the acquisition of expertise by organizations, an international trend that is not confined to Islamists. In economic terms, the Islamists are not against liberalism. However, the notion of social justice still remains very prominent within the Muslim Brotherhood, even if it tends to be equated with fairness, and it is rather in certain Salafi currents that there is an ongoing shift toward a "theology of prosperity" in which piety and wealth are linked.[22] The promotion of personal success, the emphasis on economic matters and the professionalization of activism further reinforce the link between activism and work, although these all-embracing ideologies already incorporate the professional sphere.

Work and activism

From closed circles and secrecy to social integration, the way in which activism accompanies, enhances, replaces or hampers a professional career varies considerably. First, in the course of a political commitment, skills and networks are developed that can be transferred to the world of work. In an authoritarian regime, however, opportunities to thus acquire political capital and possibly positions of power that can influence hiring practices are scarce: activists are by definition in the opposition, and have little to offer at this level other than conflict with the powers that be. In Jordan the situation is different, however, between the left and the nationalists on one hand and the Islamists on the other, the latter being better integrated, more tolerated and more numerous. The communists are thus less able to transfer their virtually non-existent political capital than their activist capital[23] in the form of skills acquired through activism. Ramzi, who was unable to finish his studies due to his intense activism and his expulsion from university for political reasons, returned to Jordan in the wake of the 1989 liberalization after a period underground, living in exile in Syria. He was finally granted a job interview by a chemical company, a field of which he had no knowledge:

> During the interview he mainly talked to me about politics. [...] He was aware that I knew nothing about chemistry, but he was banking on my communication skills. [...] Political activity did a lot to hone my communication skills, and that helped me succeed [...]. My former comrades help me, now they are my customers, and also because they know the price I've paid, having not finished my degree and so on.

Activist networks turn out to be networks of potential clients, and help offset the lack of patronage from the government. Thus a former member of the PFLP who became a prosthodontist fits out leftist militants; an entrepreneur opens a big café where former comrades gather and where the air conditioning was installed by a leftist technician, and so on. It is often thanks to such links that these small private companies manage to survive.

Professional sectors exist for the Islamists in Saudi Arabia. This is, for instance, where Hikmat went to work once he got his anaesthesiology degree (before changing track and becoming an attorney); it is also where Badi''s son went to work after having been turned down for a job in a refinery due to his father's political activities and his own political orientation at university. Badi' himself was denied the necessary security clearance to work at a refinery he applied to in Jordan – one way of putting pressure on activists. But there are alternatives in Jordan, particularly at the private al Zarqa University where many Islamists teach. Rahil was given a position there after being expelled from Al al-Bayt University:[24]

> Things didn't last at Al al-Bayt University. The king [Hussein] died, and there was a change in policy. [...] The security forces were not pleased with my being hired; they were against my staying at the university in 1999 [...]. I went to al Zarqa University,[25] where I still am today. There's no problem there because it's a private university and it's dominated by the Islamists.

As for Badi''s son, here the immediate impact of the policy change toward Islamists begun by Abdullah II is apparent when he succeeded Hussein. Now Islamists have trouble entering the public sector, a restriction that previously only affected the communists and the nationalists.

Limited career choices

Activist networks are thus mobilized particularly to offset the effects of punitive actions on activists' professional lives, and their professional orientations are largely a result of taking into account such measures. The state is the main employer in Jordan, and would be a natural career prospect for these graduates, but as in large corporations, state jobs are not open to communists. Ahmed A., who holds a degree in English, worked as a teacher for a year until the school principal received orders to dismiss him: "Then I found a job with a big Yugoslavian company, but the security forces also requested I be dismissed. They call the director or ask to be sent a list of employees for approval."

Ahmed B. encountered similar difficulties, and turned toward the private small business sector:

> When I got out of prison, I was known as a political opponent. I worked in drafting and cartography. I chose that sector because there are small offices. When you work for a big company, you're harassed. They arrested me twice at my workplace. But if you work in a small office with only one boss and one employee, it's hard to say, "He goes." It causes problems, whereas if it's a big company, they officially get the message across, "We don't want this person to work here."[26]

Similarly, Ahmed C., whose studies in medicine and his affiliation with Nasserism at the University of Damascus were discussed earlier, lost his job at the Jordanian Ministry of Health after he was imprisoned for holding political meetings in 1985. When he was released from prison, he opened up a private practice. Countless other examples could be cited. In Jordan, professionals in the small private sector thus have greater political room to manoeuvre than in the public sector or in large companies or major industries. On his return from Romania, Khaled worked for years in a private hospital run by members of the Baath Party before opening up his own practice:

> I couldn't work in the public sector [...].[27] X Hospital called me because I'd done my residency there. The private sector also hired people like us, despite pressures, because they paid us less. I'm a hard worker. In my case, this is how they applied

pressure: they [the security forces] called me during work hours and said: "We know you do very good work, that your superiors are happy with you, but we're going to bring you in when you're on night call between 2 and 4 a.m. and we're going to give them trouble." But they [his employers] were very understanding. When I was jailed for five months, they paid my salary to my mother. Both of them were communists in the Baath Party, they didn't back the government.

Their hospital had been funded by private donations, which made them independent, but the private sector also finds other advantages in hiring employees subject to pressure: they tend to accept longer hours and lower salaries.

However, some communist activists were able to turn this exclusion from the public sector into real professional successes, which may seem paradoxical with respect to their political marginalization. But remuneration is higher in the private than in the public sector. Khaled thus pointed out that as an arthroscopic surgeon, he now earns more than a minister. As for Ahmed A., he now works as a translator for an international organization. As first-generation graduates of the early years of the increased availability of higher education, they had skills that were still fairly rare in Jordan. These individual professional success stories are often overlooked during interviews, overshadowed by remarks and concerns expressed about their political defeat, but the fact remains that these activists or former activists are far from being marginalized from an economic standpoint. Their political organizations' emphasis on engineering or medical training, activist networks – and paradoxically, their exclusion from the public sector – have served them rather well, encouraging them to turn their energies toward more lucrative growth sectors.

On the other hand, the Islamists, who have more options, have in the end been less successful professionally, or at least some of them, despite the extent of their networks and their political foothold. First, the generation gap between Islamist activists and nationalist and Marxist activists means that Islamist activists arrived on the job market just as the phenomenon of unemployed graduates began to appear. Second, while Islamists also prized the training of engineers, another current of activists specialized in Islamic law or Arabic, fields for which the main career opportunities are in teaching. They therefore have a strong presence in public education. In the long run, however, this choice has proven to be problematic, because since Abdullah II came to power he has sought to sideline them from it, and switching to a career in the private sector is more difficult. The Islamists have partly overcome this problem by fostering the development of a private Islamic education system from the primary level to university.

Ethics, work and recognition

Even though they retain roles in the public sector and big business, Islamist activists also point out that they enjoy more independence in small companies, and praise entrepreneurship over wage-earning jobs, as in the case of Badi':

> This is one of the reasons for [political] success: you can make your own hours. The work day is flexible compared to an employee's. There is also a lot less pressure than on employees, whether in the public or the private sector. Besides, employees are sometimes obliged to have a given [political] orientation, or on the contrary, to abstain from politics altogether.

There is, of course, the issue of repression, which is exercised differently depending on the sector. But independence and flexible schedules enable them to devote themselves to their political activities.

However, for activists subscribing to all-encompassing ideologies, one's occupation should fit, rhetorically at least, into a more general ethical and political worldview. For the Islamists, commerce fits in perfectly, which explains the compatibility between Islamism and economic liberalism. Badi' thus invokes Hassan Al-Banna, the founder of the Muslim Brotherhood in 1929:

> In one of his commandments, imam Hassan Al-Banna says: "Do not attach importance to wage-earning!" That means that you should always work in commerce. The Prophet says that four-fifths of God's gifts are in commerce. Hassan Al-Banna urges us not to settle for being an employee.

These activists see a connection between professional independence and political independence, and associate both with entrepreneurship and the professions. They also underscore the compatibility between such professions and their principles. Thus, Hikmat, a lawyer with his own firm, explains:

> You're not subject to external pressure, either from the government or an employer. [...] A person who defends a political stance does not live in fear of being dismissed at the end of the month and being prevented from working. [...] Besides, the very essence of a lawyer's profession is to defend freedoms and political stances, and that is perfectly coherent with my political orientation.

Things are different for the communists. The fact that some of them have become entrepreneurs as a consequence of their being barred politically from other jobs can give rise to ideological qualms, especially with regard to profit. In these cases, their activism is framed in terms of doing business differently and ethically. Ramzi, who is now head of a chemical products company, thus explains: "I try to work differently. I do business honestly. I don't make unjustified profits, I respect my customers and my employees. So there is no contradiction with my convictions."

Through such rhetoric, one's professional activity can be reincorporated into the overall view conveyed by one's activism. And Ramzi also finds himself on the winning side in business because he ascribes his company's success to this ethical image, in addition to his activist network. Once again, there is convertible capital – in this case, a reputation – that largely overshadows considerations of success in the political sphere.

Activism thus influences professional orientations and job opportunities, but conversely, when faced with unemployment and therefore a lack of recognition in the workplace, developing a self-image of being morally and politically committed can also be an alternative. One unemployed IAF activist from Zarka constantly emphasized his total religious commitment, and the way his family experienced it, each time he was asked questions about his academic and professional career.[28] Activism in this case serves to ground and provide self-esteem for those with only minimal social and financial resources who do not have access to other types of social recognition. Such occupational failures can be offset by activist involvement, whereas, on the other hand, political defeat does not rule out professional success that draws on the experience of activism. The connections between work and activism are thus all the more numerous and diverse when they are backed up by activist experience that is also multidimensional.

Here, activism is thus not merely one activity among others, but affects all of the activists' fields of activity. This influence is reinforced by the all-encompassing nature of the ideologies discussed above, which are not limited to taking a political stand. Such a broad impact is, of course, hardly surprising among activists who got involved early and who have had a longstanding commitment. In fact, the evolution is striking. These activists have gone from affiliation with the closest available movement and its networks, with a certain ideological imprecision, to a solid political conviction that can withstand a degree of social hostility as long as an alternative closed circle is formed. But becoming an activist in an authoritarian regime also means facing repression throughout the entire affiliation process. From going underground to prison or exile, repression affects the very heart of activists' lives and dramatizes the consequences of activism. For this reason, perhaps paradoxically, repression further reinforces the central role political commitment has for these activists.

CHAPTER 5

Repression and dissidence

How did the activists deal with daily repression and confrontation with the Jordanian regime? Although, despite appearances, the political opening up in 1989 did not modify the coercive foundations of the regime, the methods of repression evolved. This led to major changes in the lives of semi-underground nationalist and communist activists, who were able to come out into the open.

Nationalists and communists: impossible and necessary underground activity

> What do they mean by secret activity? It's true that the Communist Party was underground, but the leaders were known and openly called themselves the Communist Party [...]. Certain activities were secret, but even when we wrote a secret document, it would go to the intelligence service, they knew about it and what it said, so it is not really underground work the way it is in Latin America.

This is how Ahmed B. sums up the stakes of this particular semi-underground activism in the face of an extremely well-informed authoritarian regime that nevertheless does not completely crush all types of activism. The security apparatus, made up of the various intelligence services, military and police corps, is omnipresent, and none of the nationalist and communist activists interviewed really slipped through the cracks. The dense socialization of the small Jordanian society also makes belonging to a political group very difficult to hide. The older communist leaders were particularly affected, the vast majority of them having been arrested between 1957 and the end of the 1960s. Repression continued throughout the 1970s and 1980s. The activists risked brutal arrests, interrogations and torture.[1] The length of incarceration ranged from a few weeks to several years, either in collective cells reserved for political prisoners or in solitary confinement for some. Indeed, the activists, especially the leaders, were well known to the security forces and intelligence agencies. What was crucial during these periods in prison was to avoid admitting belonging to a banned political party and not being found in possession of any propaganda material. Lack of evidence (documents, denunciations or confessions) did not prevent incarceration, but it could shorten its duration. The policy of repression in place maintained certain legal frameworks, namely the courts, where such evidence played a role.

Between 1977 and 1996 Ahmed A, a regional communist leader, was arrested several times. He was jailed for a year and a half the first time, and for shorter periods thereafter. He sustained several injuries in the course of these brutal arrests:

> We know that if you have documents on you when you are arrested, you will go to jail for five to fifteen years. It's a sort of provocation for them. For me and others, these regular arrests continued [...]. The party was outlawed, but if I was arrested once again, that didn't matter. The main thing was not to admit anything in front of the intelligence services. I denied everything. I did not admit to anything, they could not find any proof about the party.

This position was confirmed by Ibrahim, a member of Fatah-Intifada who was imprisoned for six months in 1986: "We would never admit that we were members. We would always say: 'We believe in what they say, but we are not members.'" During an umpteenth arrest, Ahmed's wife managed to grab his coat at the last minute, as it contained compromising documents. When he tried to go into hiding in 1986 after the events at Yarmouk University, Ahmed A., who was too well known, was quickly arrested after being denounced. However, he was not tried as a member of the Communist Party because "very few people would agree to testify against someone in court".

Tarek, a member of the Communist Party mentioned earlier, did not escape being tried as a communist because he was arrested while still in secondary school in possession of communist literature. He was sentenced to fifteen years in prison for communism, possession of illegal documents and lèse-majesté. Tarek wanted to fight for the Palestinian cause, and had recently made contact with the communist group in his secondary school. He is from a Palestinian family that arrived in Amman in 1948 during his childhood.[2] However, the "bourgeois family", as Tarek described it – his father was a fabric merchant and his maternal grandfather had been a senior official in the Turkish administration and a landowner – had sufficient funds to avoid going to a refugee camp even though their situation deteriorated greatly afterwards. Tarek remained in prison for several years before his father, "who had contacts in the government", was able to get him out. His family, which was also subjected to pressure and interrogations, tried above all to keep him away from politics. Tarek, who was deeply affected psychologically by prison and the pressure to co-operate and betray his comrades, says he was literally saved by his father's intervention. He went to Czechoslovakia on a scholarship from the communist student union, and went to medical school, like his older brother, who was already in Europe, although he would have preferred to study political science. He spent close to ten years in Czechoslovakia, and got married there.

After the Arab defeat in 1967 and the new wave of Palestinian refugees that ensued, Tarek agreed less and less with the communist position against armed struggle, so he joined Fatah. A year before finishing his specialization in gynaecology, he returned to Jordan to visit family. As soon as he arrived at the airport, his passport was confiscated. Stuck in Jordan, he looked for work as a doctor with the United Nations Relief and Works Agency, which accepted him even though he could not provide the certificate from the intelligence service, which generally vets any candidate for a job in any institution or large company. This shows, moreover, that the agency had some leeway in this regard: "During the interview, I told them: I can't provide it, [...] because to give it to me, they [the intelligence service] want to make me pay the price, they want me to act the way they want, and I am not willing to do that." In 1974 he thus started working as a doctor in Palestinian refugee camps in Jordan, where day in and day out he was confronted with suffering and hardship that reinforced his political determination. He became increasingly active in Fatah.

But along with others, he also became increasingly critical of Fatah's decisions under the leadership of Yasser Arafat and his followers, "conservatives close to the Muslim Brotherhood who prevented Marxists and progressives from taking part in decision-making". Tarek felt the movement was becoming institutionalized and less revolutionary, that "it was becoming a place to find a job". He was against accepting what he called a mini-Palestinian state, and most of all he felt that in 1982 Fatah should not have left Beirut, but should have continued the resistance there. This critical faction was at the root of the split that spawned Fatah-Intifada in 1983. But in 1983 Tarek was arrested once again, and for him it was due just as much to Jordanian political repression as it was to a betrayal by Fatah, which wanted to get rid of its dissenters.

Tarek was in prison for six months on this occasion, and endured solitary confinement and torture:

> When I think of it, it makes me crazy and sick. Being tortured in prison, all alone in a cell, it is suffering that makes you wonder if morals even exist [...]. I remember how the police would come and begin hitting us all over with sticks and insulting us; and they enjoyed what they were doing. [...] The degree of humiliation ... it truly scarred me. You have surely heard things about torture, but in reality it is much harder and much more atrocious. There was a lieutenant who told the soldiers to hit us really hard, and if a soldier didn't do it, he was the one who got hit. I also remember that I refused to yell or cry or to show any weakness. Several times they sent me to the hospital because of the torture. But once, they came in the middle of the night, and one soldier told me, "You have to cry out." I said it was impossible, so he crushed my fingernail, and I yelled. It was terrible, but yelling made me feel better, and as a doctor I became interested in that. From that day on, when I was hurt, I would yell. I yelled because it made me feel better when I did. I used to think it was bad if I yelled. They would hit me in front of my friends: it was psychological torture for me and for them.

His Czechoslovakian wife is a lawyer. She contacted the Red Cross in her country and got it to intervene. The Red Cross was able to put an end to the torture, and the conditions in the prison improved a bit. Tarek was allowed to have visits, but he refused to let his children see him that way: "Having them see me in that condition would have been the worst thing for me." The violence of political repression is apparent in his experience, but so are its limits in a system that seeks to maintain a certain internal legitimacy and its international standing. Thus the government actively maintains patronage networks, and international pressure is taken into account.

Activists are rarely specific about the torture they endured and its psychological impact, even though they talk more freely about the physical scars. Tarek is an exception, probably because it put an end to his career as an activist. However, others who were imprisoned for shorter periods came out of jail with their political determination reinforced. For them, ideology gave meaning to their experience in prison and helped them endure it, so giving up or questioning their engagement was inconceivable, even if, like Ahmed A., they found the cost of their commitment too high and they did not want their children to follow the same path. This profile is common among long-term activists. Activists who break under the pressure of imprisonment, solitary confinement and torture do not return to activism afterwards. Special treatment was reserved for communists who were induced to denounce communism, and their denunciations might be published in the newspapers. This made public their renunciation and the fact that they had yielded to get out of prison, thus cutting them off from activist circles once and for all.

Tarek was not a member of the Communist Party at the time of his second imprisonment, though he was still influenced by Marxism. But for him, his arrest was also the result of political betrayal by Fatah. After this experience, he felt deceived and humiliated and put an end to his involvement. He was deeply affected by the divisions in the political organizations, and no longer believed in the possibility of group activism or the ideal of pan-Arab unification. He also questioned the heroic vision of imprisonment: "I have a communist background, and the communists nourish the mind until people become resistant, strong as a rock [...]. But you know, wasting away in prison for a hundred years advocating resistance is not heroic – making progress is!"

Political activism in Jordan now seems impossible to him. Political action can only be underground since it was outlawed. But secrecy is impossible, and according to him, infiltration of political groups by the secret police is all-pervasive, and so is betrayal. In the absence of a feasible repertoire of action, and faced with violent repression and the experience of betrayal, the perspective of political change vanished for him. However, in 1989 he was contacted by former acquaintances from the Baath Party, the Popular Front for the Liberation of Palestine, the Democratic Front for the Liberation of Palestine[3] and Fatah, among others, to create a political opposition front based on nationalism. Tarek eventually joined the group, at first with little conviction, on the strict condition that there would be no underground activity.

The year 1989 was a time for activists to emerge from underground. But the strong coherence of the organization, the discipline imposed on the activists and ideological dogmatism had made particular sense in the face of repression. This was even the only context in which communist activists such as Ahmed B., who were critical of the orthodoxy and the lack of reflection, defended this type of organization:

> We were more involved in mobilization and internal cohesion. And when a member found himself before the security forces, that was the most important thing – that he stood firm and loyal, did not speak, did not admit to anything. And that is better than being wrapped up in theory, books, highly educated, knowing about philosophy, and then arriving in front of the security forces and spilling everything.

The consequences were even more momentous for the communists, since the Soviet Union was to collapse just two years later. With the loss of the Soviet Union as a reference and justification for underground struggle, the years of opening up turned out to be a period of major upheaval for the communists. Paradoxically, repression – which indeed made the growth of their base difficult because activism proved extremely costly – produced a repertoire of action, one of semi-underground activism, where adversity itself managed to reinforce party cohesion.

The policy of repression tried to crack activist solidarity by specifically targeting certain categories. Thus, native-born Jordanian Muslims were particularly targeted, as their engagement in the

Communist Party challenged the political structure of the monarchy whereby the tribes, especially Muslim tribes, were considered natural allies, while Palestinians were seen as the opposition. Ahmed A., who came from a large Muslim tribe in the north of Jordan, explains:

> It drew attention: "You belong to XXX [the name of the tribe], what are you doing in the Communist Party?" For the government, it changed things because the secret police spread the lie that all Jordanian Muslims were loyal to the regime, that the Communist Party was Christian, and that the opposition was Palestinian. So they couldn't figure me out. However, I wasn't alone. Jordanian Muslims were the specific target of my activism.

Ahmed B., also a Jordanian Muslim, shared this experience, and insists on the intensification of repression:

> The security apparatus believed that you had strayed among the communists, [...] and that is why they considered [Jordanian Muslims] to be weak links for breaking into the Communist Party. [...] For example, in 1981, among the ten students arrested there were two communists and members of other organizations. The other communist was held for three months, and the others one month, but I was in jail for a year and a half! And the guys from the security forces would say to me: "How is it possible? There are people from Nablus who have told us everything and you, you're from XXX [a village in Jordan] and you don't!" They didn't want the party's actions to spread throughout Jordanian society, whereas they considered that among Palestinians, everyone was politically active anyway.

Furthermore, although the 1989 opening up put an end to communist and nationalist underground activism, it did not actually mean the end of repression, even if it became less systematic. Activists did not gain any real freedom of action, yet they did lose the cohesion and working in tight-knit cells which semi-underground activism had made necessary and which had masked their ideological decline. After 1989, being an activist remained difficult and costly for activists as well as for their associates. Pressure in the workplace and periods of imprisonment continued, as did preventive arrests. Leaders of different movements were arrested right at the beginning of any political agitation, no matter what their real involvement was, in order to deter other activists. That is what happened regularly up until 1996 to Ahmed A., the local communist leader mentioned earlier: "We can get into people's heads," his interrogator said. "You haven't done anything, but if we had left you on the outside, you definitely would have done something." Ahmed A. concluded: "A person is supposed to be innocent until proven guilty. But here it's the opposite: you are guilty until proven innocent!"

Authoritarian elections

Although parliamentary elections have been organized regularly from 1989 onward, running for office is not easy, and these authoritarian elections have not really opened up new opportunities for action. Ahmed A. was a candidate for office twice, in 1989[4] and 1993, under the slogan "Democracy and Social Justice". The notion of social justice was first put forth by the left, but it was later taken up by the Islamists, who significantly modified it by linking it to the notion of fairness rather than to equality. In any event, the electoral campaigns did not focus on this issue. Ahmed underlined the obstacles and intimidations during the electoral process, which targeted his supporters more than himself:

> Regarding my own campaigns, the pressure [from the security forces] was directed at my associates and my support committee and so on, not directly at me, because I had already been imprisoned five or six times. They knew that they could not pressure or intimidate me. However, for my associates there were threats to their jobs, for example. And it often worked, there were people who gave up.

The monarchy promoted certain candidates while brushing others aside. Ahmed A. was not elected, though according to him, his share of the vote was respectable. Belonging to a large tribe did not act in his favour here; in fact, quite the opposite. The majority of his tribe did not support him because of his ties to the communists, and in 1993 his tribe fielded another candidate, with the government's support, to run against him. Ahmed got his best results in urban areas. In any case, even if he had been elected to office, the margin for manoeuvre of members of parliament is extremely limited and the parliament cannot draft laws.

In fact, neither the elections nor the parliament have opened up a true space for real opposition, and certainly not the possibility of political change. In this context, participating in elections has turned out to be a mixed blessing for the opposition. Although they gained a platform for expression, at the same time the limits of their action quickly discredited them. This was particularly visible among the Islamists who were elected. This did not mean, however, that there was nothing at stake in the elections. In fact, they were about confirming or renewing certain elites. The parliament came to be seen primarily as a locus for clientelism, patronage and distribution of favours and jobs. Ahmed A. came up against this aspect, and it was what finally disappointed him the most in his campaign experience:

> While I was presenting my platform, especially the problem of unemployment, people would say to me: "We don't need to solve everyone's problems or find a general solution for unemployment, but we want a solution for our sons." I don't think the population wants to fight on the political front. [...] They are only interested in finding a job for someone in their family, and that's it. They go to a minister or a deputy because they're looking for someone who can pull strings for them.

In a difficult economic context, this is how parliament is perceived by voters, who are looking to elect representatives who can help them out. Islamists play on this culture of favours and patronage as well.

Repression and legitimacy

The trajectory of the Muslim Brotherhood Islamists was relatively the opposite, since they had never experienced intense repression or had to go underground, and 1989 simply provided an opportunity to create a party out of a strong, thriving social movement. However, when Abdullah II came to power, it brought about the loss of their special status. It became much more difficult for them to work in the public sector, especially in education, where they had been particularly present, and they also experienced periods of imprisonment (from a few days to several months), depending on the demonstrations staged. Activists who were opposed to what they called the normalization of relations with Israel were especially targeted. Rahil, an Islamist party cadre, explained:

> We had participated in the government, but now the state apparatus has completely gotten rid of us. [...] There is not a single director. We can't work in radio, television or newspapers, obviously not in the security forces and the army, [...] and it is illegal for a member of the Brotherhood to teach law. There were members in education, but their careers have stalled. They cannot be school principals. The Ministry of Awqaf [5] gave us trouble; it is forbidden for a member of the Muslim Brotherhood to preach on Fridays.[6]

Although the most militant members had already experienced repression, this marked a clear change in its scale. Discrimination consisted mostly of pressure in the workplace and limiting jobs accessible to activists. That is why Islamists, who up until then had been very well represented in the public sector, developed an alternative sector with private schools, which allowed them to return to teaching. Furthermore, for some of them there was a sort of ratchet effect: career limitations turned activism into a form of compensation, rather than discouraging them from it.

Another paradoxical effect, which the Islamists admit themselves, was the legitimacy that repression gave them in an authoritarian context. In interviews, Islamists thus emphasized the incidents of repression they suffered, and often denied being treated differently from the leftists and nationalists prior to 1989. That established them as members of the opposition and underlined the sacrifices they endured for their engagement, thereby enhancing its worth. While their position as an integrated (even co-opted) opposition gradually chipped away at their legitimacy, repression had the opposite effect. This is what Badi', whose experiences as an engineer turned Islamist activist at university were mentioned earlier, pointed out:

> In 2002 I was imprisoned again because I was against normalization [...]. The government imprisoned dissenters, sent them before the courts, sentenced them, and had articles published to drag their names through the mud. [...] This pressure had a positive aspect: it brought increased respect.

The trials against the Islamists and being sentenced in the State Security Court gave them renewed publicity as members of the opposition. Hikmat, a cadre in the Islamic Action Front mentioned earlier, became a human rights lawyer at the State Security Court and took part in the Islamists' trials that were transferred there: "These were cases that interested public opinion. I became well-known because I defended in these cases." Both Islamist and nationalist lawyer-activists denounced the arbitrary nature of the convictions and the interference of the executive branch and the army. Hikmat explained:

> Despite all our efforts, in the end the judgment followed the government's will, especially when there was interference between the judiciary and the State Security Court. [...] Sometimes, even when everything was clearly in favour of the case being dismissed, the defendant could still be found guilty.

Jawad, an Arab nationalist expelled to Jordan in 1970 after spending three years in Israeli prisons, became a lawyer and defends dissidents of all persuasions in the State Security Court:

> Military courts, like the State Security Courts, are true courts of shame. [...] They have nothing to do with justice. [...] Justice is supposed to be independent, while the army merely executes the orders it receives and has no decision-making power. [...] Over the last dozen years the state has been reorganized and has taken control of the judiciary in Jordan, and today I don't believe it is possible to re-establish the rule of law in public affairs.

Even though these lawyer-activists are skeptical about their ability to influence the outcome of a trial, the courts nevertheless serve as a platform for militant action. This points up the ambiguity of the various types of action that can be deployed under an authoritarian regime, such as participating in elections. It is possible to express some degree of opposition, as the criticisms voiced in these interviews prove, but despite assurances about the protection of anonymity, they still have grounds for concern. It is possible to invoke human rights, for example, and the legal framework has been preserved. Thus lawyers combine activism and professional activity while opening up another militant category path for the opposition. However, the possibility for expression does not mean there is possibility for action, and it does not constitute an opposition force to counter the policy of repression. Nonetheless, during the trials, lawyers as well as the defendants retain their positions as part of the opposition, and make this known. This does not have the same impact as participating in elections, which can undermine the opposition's legitimacy by its being associated with the exercise of authoritarian power over which it has no influence. Here, the result is the opposite, and Islamists have regained legitimacy and appeared once again to be a true force of protest.

From martial law and bans on political activity to authoritarian elections, the various methods of repression have evolved. For activists, this has been reflected in the move from underground activity to the dilemmas of political participation under an authoritarian regime: Should they try to use the political space available to them as a platform for expression, or should they avoid it since it does not prevent the muzzling of political expression? In this context, how can the opposition maintain or regain a legitimate position? Finally, how can channels of mobilization be found and converted into potential for protest against authoritarian methods? In fact, it is more by investing in alternative arenas that mobilization and politicization have been pursued. This has been the case for professional associations, whose important role has been maintained regardless of the evolution of repression.

CHAPTER 6

Professional activism as an alternative

When political parties are outlawed or strictly controlled, professional organizations represent one of the rare areas, along with universities, where collective action and mobilization are possible.[1] The importance of their professional role guarantees an institutional existence even in the face of authoritarian regimes. Their possible politicization is thus a major issue, and these organizations are subject to intense pressure from the state, especially during professional elections. In the Arab world their positioning in relation to the government falls into two categories: in one, which reflects "corporatism",[2] professional organizations are used by the state as a channel for communication; in the other they use their professional aspect and their recognized economic utility as a way of retaining some leeway and becoming a locus of opposition,[3] a true alternative to political parties.

In Jordan both categories exist. There are labour unions (*niqabat al ummal*), in which membership is not compulsory, these unions being somewhat similar to the American definition. There are also professional associations[4] (*niqabat mihaniyya*), which are reserved for the licensed professions. Membership of them to exercise the profession is compulsory, such as for engineers, architects, doctors and dentists – even though today, members who do not pay their dues are rarely excluded from these professions. In addition to services that are specifically reserved for their members (such as pension funds, healthcare and professional training) and their role in defining the profession, professional associations are involved in political activity (discussions about the government's agenda, calls for democratization and rallies in support of Palestinians, and so on). Moreover, they were formed as a result of the professionals' own desire to organize collectively. Some of them, such as engineers, had already formed a group that was then converted into a professional association following a law officially regulating the profession.

The situation is entirely different as regards labour unions. In 1953 workers gained the right to form union organizations, but they were created from the top down by virtue of decrees that could be revoked by the government.[5] This particular legislation reveals the Jordanian regime's mistrust of working-class trade unions, which were largely influenced by the left, whereas the authorities considered professional associations an elite that could be on their side. Although labour union leaders participated for a time in political mobilizations, since 1990 they have been widely co-opted by the Jordanian regime, on which they are entirely dependent financially. They have therefore never really played a political role or organized protests or negotiations over labour laws (in particular about the absence of a minimum wage),[6] although they have taken a new approach since the Arab Spring.[7] For Elisabeth Longuenesse, this "corporatist" logic, the most common model in the Arab world,[8] reflects the absence of a strong socio-professional identity that is a driving force for mobilization and unification.[9] Nilüfer Göle gives the same analysis for Turkey: "Politicization or even radicalization went hand in hand with the creation of engineers as a socio-professional category."[10] In his analysis of judges in Egypt, Bernard Botiveau also underlines a link between the creation of a profession, the appearance of a true *esprit de corps* and politicization.[11]

Here the professional dimension was built as a resource, and later we will examine how the engineers' association was able to establish a balance of power with the authorities by playing on its professional expertise, which was indispensable for the Jordanian economy and the realization of government projects. In return, this professional anchoring had a strong impact on the politicization and the methods of mobilization – which, as it happened, were less about professional and social issues than about adopting a position on the domestic political agenda (essentially on the subject of political participation), and especially on foreign policy (first and foremost, on the Palestinian question).

Research on the production of politics currently focuses on battles to include new issues that have generally been excluded from traditional institutional politics. However, confronted with authoritarian practices that aim to suppress any possibility of questioning the authorities and their agenda (which is not incompatible with the official existence of a parliament and political parties), the challenge of politicization is, on the contrary, the very creation of a political arena.

Thus, focusing on professional associations as a locus of politicization and an alternative arena for mobilization raises another question: that of the impact on activism when these associations become the only locus (and not just one of the loci) for possible political opposition. The very nature of these organizations, whose leaders are often also company managers and whose members are necessarily highly educated, results in an activism that is necessarily rather limited and selective. It also, for the most part, averts class struggle. Professionalization conceived in this way allows a certain questioning of the intense policy limits imposed by a coercive regime, but it also adds another, linked to the organization's membership and their social profiles.

An alternative political arena

Political parties were completely outlawed from 1957, when martial law was first instituted, until 1992. Since then their activities have been strictly regulated and they have had a hard time finding activists. Party activities are extremely limited by law, so political parties have remained weak and their restoration has not lessened the role of professional associations. On the subject of professional associations, Egbert Harmsen describes them as an "oasis of opposition in a desert of authoritarianism".[12] They have more leeway than parties, and most of all, their impact differs. Aside from the Islamist movement, a leader of a professional association is much better known than a member of parliament, for example.

The economic importance of professional associations

The twelve professional associations that exist in Jordan nowadays had about 130,000 members in 2011.[13] Professional and political aspects were present right from their creation in the 1950s and 1960s.[14] Each association sought to regulate its profession by limiting membership to those who had the required qualifications.[15] This requirement was matched by the implementation of professional and social services. Certain professions make it mandatory for members to sign up for pension funds and healthcare schemes. Professional associations are financed by members' dues, returns on investments in their projects, donations, and in some cases, by state subsidies. Their professional vocation gives the associations specific legitimacy based on the possession of knowledge: engineers, lawyers and doctors represent an established technocratic elite whose opinions cannot be easily ignored and are essential for the implementation of policies to modernize the country. These professionals also make up an invaluable pool of highly skilled labour which it is Jordan's policy to export.[16] Politically, the six professional associations that originally founded the Union of Professional Associations predominate: doctors, engineers, pharmacists, agricultural engineers, lawyers and dentists. With its 70,000 members,[17] the engineers' association is the largest of these, and has vast resources at its disposal, making it financially independent from the state (unlike the journalists' association, for example).[18] Ali is a civil engineer and an independent leftist activist (he left Fatah in 1993). His comments illustrate the dynamics of the power struggle between the professional associations and the state:

> The state cannot organize the profession without us, that's what gives us our strength, and if we bowed out, the country would be completely disorganized. For example, we engineers inspect the plans for each building; [...] the government cannot do that in our stead. There was an incident where a floor collapsed in June, and it is because each year four or five buildings are built without the association's approval. It's due to corruption among people close to the government, [...] who build without permission because it goes faster, but also to put pressure on the associations and the leaders, who won't give in.[19]

In addition to professional expertise, the professional associations have another source of public legitimacy: they are the only institutions that follow truly democratic election procedures.

Highly legitimate elections

The electoral system adopted by the associations limits the possibilities of co-optation and gives its leaders a high level of legitimacy. Each profession holds its elections and appoints a council by voting for a list of members. On the same day it elects a president directly for a two-year term, which can be renewed once. Since 1966 a joint council has existed, made up of the presidents of the professional associations, and it is headed in turn, for four months, by the president of one of the associations present at the Professional Associations Complex. The council and the Professional Associations Complex have played an important part in reinforcing the role of the associations by presenting a united front.

The political evolution of the professional associations reflects that of the various partisan currents: in the 1970s and 1980s most of them were run by the left. Now, however, the majority are presided over by Islamists, particularly in the various association councils. For the engineers' association, this change took place as early as 1988,[20] when the Islamists first won the presidency of the association and then a majority on the council. The Islamist predominance is clear, yet it should not be overestimated. As the Islamists campaigned in favour of the re-professionalization of the associations, the political nature of their stronger presence within these organizations must be qualified. The electoral process is a long one, and mobilizes professionals, but rising unemployment among professionals in recent times has led to a decrease in the payment of dues and voter participation, which means that the base upon which the Islamists were elected is not as broad as it might seem. Furthermore, the direct election of presidents favours prominent personalities regardless of their political leaning, which may be different from the majority of their council. Some nationalist and leftwing professional figures enjoy a strong personal reputation, which meant that the Islamists lost the presidency of the medical association in 2009.

The professions mobilize for the Palestinian cause

No matter what political orientation is dominant, the strong public legitimacy of the professional associations and their social utility have allowed them to establish a certain balance of power with the monarchy and prevented them from being outlawed, though some of their leaders have been imprisoned from time to time. The main focus for mobilization has been support for the Palestinian cause, which has been the remit of several inter-association political committees: the Palestine committee, the committee for prisoners and the Anti-Normalization Committee (concerning relations with Israel). However, professional associations have also addressed internal issues such as democratization, freedom of expression and denouncing martial law. Supporting the Palestinian cause and Palestinians in the West Bank and in the Gaza Strip – a subject where a consensus exists among the different political currents – obviously raises fewer problems *vis-à-vis* the regime than domestic freedoms, as long as Jordan's foreign policy regarding Israel is not called into question. In this respect, the Anti-Normalization Committee, one of the best-known and most active, was particularly repressed (for example, it was declared illegal, intimidation was used, its members were imprisoned and meetings were cancelled).[21] Islamists served on the committee (in particular a well-known independent Islamist dissident, Layth Shubeilat, who was several times president of the engineers' association)[22] as well as leftist activists. During the general campaign against normalization launched at the end of 1994, unable to influence the government's agenda directly, the professional associations decided to expel any professionals from their ranks who did not respect the boycott of relations with Israel. This measure was strongly denounced by the monarchy, which, in reaction, continued to employ expelled engineers while accusing the associations of being anti-democratic since they denied their members freedom of decision.[23]

The political mobilization of the professional associations was essentially built around Palestinian nationalism. In the 1960s and 1970s the associations worked with Palestinian organizations present in Jordan and supported them during clashes with the Jordanian army in 1969 and 1970.[24] It should be remembered that the West Bank was annexed by Jordan from 1949 until 1967 – which marks the beginning of Israeli occupation – and that Palestinian engineers in the West Bank constituted a branch of the Jordanian engineers' association. The associations in the West Bank are now under Palestinian jurisdiction;[25] however, despite the official break-off of administrative relations between Jordan and the West Bank since 1988, strong ties have been maintained up to the present. In accordance with the archetypical figure of the engineer in developing countries, which associates socio-professional identity and the country's construction, the Jordanian professional associations embody a sort of incomplete nationalism, since Jordanian nationalism by default always refers to Palestinian nationalism.[26] This situation could explain their mobilization.

The actions carried out by the professional associations in reaction to the Israeli attack on the Gaza Strip in December 2008 and January 2009 show not only the importance of the Palestinian issue within the associations, but also the associations' general role as political standard bearers. Nevertheless, during the mobilization, the clear demarcation of their action was once again evident, both spatially and in substance. Political activism was debated within the associations while relations with the regime were becoming increasingly tense. Insistence on the professional role of the associations neutralized the crisis, but also limited the action undertaken, which was redefined as humanitarian in nature.

Right from the first day of the Israeli offensive, the federation of professional associations, and in particular the engineers' association, mobilized and issued the first opposition communiqué calling for a rally in front of the association headquarters. Even before the statement was released, the switchboard was flooded with calls from people who were shocked by images broadcast on Arab television channels, and they naturally turned toward the Professional Associations Complex,[27] identified as one of the rare loci for potential mobilization. A first joint demonstration was quickly organized, bringing together a variety of political parties and professional associations, leftist, pan-Arab nationalist and Islamist. The first march went through central Amman and headed toward the Israeli embassy. In the face of the overwhelming reaction of the people,[28] the Jordanian regime gave the impression of opening up the political field somewhat by allowing space for an organized expression of these reactions. However, the movement very quickly divided into three separate currents of various sizes, each occupying different areas of the city of Amman: the largest demonstrations were organized by the Islamists (the Islamist Action Front, the Muslim Brotherhood and the engineers' association, predominantly Islamist), who held their gatherings in places far from the city centre and barely marched after the first demonstration. In doing so, the Islamists maintained their ambivalent position of loyal opposition, which is their specific stance in Jordan. They proved their ability to mobilize massively while avoiding confrontations with the police which would have taken place if they had marched on the city centre or near the Israeli embassy; other highly supervised gatherings were organized by the government in the city centre; finally, segments of the leftist and nationalist currents continued trying to organize demonstrations – declared illegal – close to the Israeli embassy. Their mobilization was much weaker, and was repressed.

The agitation continued for three weeks, and the associations issued numerous communiqués. They organized actions in direct support of the Gaza Strip (collecting funds, sending doctors and engineers) while delegations gave the international community eyewitness accounts of the extent of the damage, in particular through a documentary film made by the engineers' association. However, once the offensive had stopped and the strongest wave of indignation had passed, the Jordanian regime had no intention of letting the agitation take root. In February 2009 delegations, in particular representing the dentists, were blocked in Egypt. For their part, the Islamists and the associations were careful not to express open opposition. To avoid losing their political gains by continuing to mobilize, which had been declared illegal, association leaders put an end to the gatherings and the communiqués, and focused on the strictly humanitarian aspect of their support for the Gaza Strip, agreeing to participate in meetings with the interior minister to "maintain good relations".[29] It is striking to note the evolution in the position of the president of the medical association, who before his election spoke about political mobilization, but thereafter strictly humanitarian mobilization.[30] In fact, the Islamists and the professional associations – predominantly run by Islamists – emerged stronger from the mobilization campaign. The Islamist Action Front was able to regain the central role it had lost after its defeat in the legislative elections and the internal dissent that ensued. The mobilization for Gaza provided evidence of its popular support, giving it more leeway in relation to the Jordanian regime. Furthermore, the professional associations, which a short time before had to confront multiple questions about their professionalism and had barely avoided electoral reform, were now in a better position to oppose any new measures in this direction. This reinforced position, however, did not modify the tacit limits of their action.

A limited space

Professional associations therefore represent an alternative space for mobilization that benefits from the involvement of activists who have no other arena at their disposal. Thus a number of political struggles in Jordan involve the creation of professional associations. A good example is the long battle to form the teachers' association. Civil servants are not allowed to belong to employee labour unions, so professional associations offer them a way to circumvent this interdict.[31] In 1975 the monarchy prohibited the creation of a teachers' association and imprisoned the activists responsible for the initiative. The activists in question, who secretly belonged to the Communist Party, had started a petition that gathered thousands of signatures. The quest continued to be promoted regularly by teachers, who organized demonstrations and sit-ins in Jordan's main cities. In the context of the wave of Arab protests in 2011 and 2012, a law was finally passed that allowed the creation of the teachers' association, but prohibited it from engaging in any type of political activity. Labour unions have also been campaigning for more independence.

This political space remains sharply circumscribed in terms of possibilities for action and mobilization. The monarchy has often modified or threatened to modify the laws governing professional associations, and in particular their electoral laws in order to impose a single-round uninominal voting system.[32] Each time the regime has attempted to outlaw or restrict them, the professional associations have nevertheless managed to maintain their ability to take action by focusing on their professional roles and using their ties to the regime's elite, even though their political activities are, for the most part, what lends them their strong popular legitimacy. The limits are as much due to direct injunctions by the monarchy as self-censorship on the part of the associations, which, being aware of the red lines not to cross, avoid direct confrontation with the authorities. Thus the balance of power tends to shift depending on the political situation, but also remains clearly delimited. The comparison with the Moroccan situation is striking, as analysed by Frédéric Vairel, who points out the way institutionalization creates boundaries.[33] As in Morocco, the boundaries and their limitations are also visible in spatial terms: the types of action predominantly chosen by professional associations are rallies in front of their headquarters rather than street demonstrations, for example. The associations allow some public expression of political opinions, but not much else.

Another limitation on the subjects and types of mobilization stems from the class heterogeneity that is specific to these professional associations. Thus it is possible for a well-known political dissenter to have an extremely negative reputation as the boss of a company due to his particularly strict management style, and this can limit his ability to mobilize members within the professional association. In return, his position, politically or at the head of the association, prevents social conflict being directed against him:

> Imagine that I am an oppressed engineer, I work with my oppressor in the same association. X, whom I worked for and with whom I had problems, was the president of the association! There is one case in which the association defends its members, and that is during a conflict with the government, otherwise within companies that is not possible.[34]

This heterogeneity is also evident in relations with the state. Professionals have different interests depending on their position in the rentier economy and neopatrimonial redistribution circles, which determine the degree to which they are inclined to question the economic system.[35]

Furthermore, when professional associations become not only a locus for political opposition, but *the* locus for opposition, that limits the social base for political engagement as well as the notion of elite or avant-garde which is used as a key element for negotiating their right to political expression, as a former president of the engineers' association explains:

> As an association, we clashed with the former interior minister on this subject, and we claimed that the professional associations are part of the country, their members are the society's avant-garde, and therefore they have the right to express their opinions on national and Arab questions as well as on questions of freedom.[36]

The members of professional associations must have specific degrees, although in the 1980s the changing trend of association leadership from the leftists and nationalists to the Islamists brought about a social evolution. The leftist and nationalist leaders were prominent citizens from a traditional elite, but in the 1970s and 1980s the granting of scholarships and the opportunities offered by socialist countries to attend university for little cost transformed the social make-up of these circles.[37] The rise of the Islamists coincided with the emergence of an educated middle class that had an increasingly hard time gaining access to the job market in a difficult economic context.[38] Although there have been some Jordanian Palestinians among the association leaders, they have almost never been Palestinians from the refugee camps,[39] but rather activists from Palestinian families that were wealthy enough and had enough contacts to avoid the camps when they went into exile in Jordan. The social broadening of the professional associations therefore remains relative, especially at the top of the hierarchy.

Union engagement

The specific nature of what is almost the only locus for political mobilization other than the universities is reflected in the educated activists' paths of engagement. Those who belong to professions that have politically active associations – engineers, doctors, dentists and lawyers – are all involved and carry out the majority of their political activities through the associations. Most of them are association leaders who run for election or are active in various committees (the anti-normalization committee, the freedoms committee, the prisoners' committee and the women's committee). The case of one of the activists interviewed shows that the administration of a professional association can also be an outlet for a well-known activist, even if he does not have the qualifications required by the association.[40]

From university to professional association

Whether they are Islamists, nationalists or communists, educated activists join the association circles, which are seen as an accessible space for mobilization, after a hiatus in activism to complete their military service (during which they are often deployed within their skill area, thereby gaining their first professional experience). But these associations are much more a space for pursuing political engagement started at university than a space for politicization, at least for the leaders. As was shown in Chapter 1, initial political orientation takes place at university, or even in secondary school. Among the professional association activists interviewed, almost all of them had already been activists in student associations. Many of them had participated in student elections (by discipline).[41] The university thus represents the fundamental locus for acquiring activist capital – political language and mobilization techniques – as well as political capital, both of which will be useful in the professional associations and will allow them to gain access to key positions.

The path followed by Wael, an architect born in 1956 in Amman, is highly representative in this respect. His family illustrates the ambiguity of the distinction made between Jordanians and Palestinians and the multitude of migration flows in the region. His grandfather, who was born in Nablus, settled in Jordan long before the wave of refugees in 1948. His father, born in Salt, ran a road transportation business between Jordan and Syria. Wael became interested in the Islamist movement in secondary school – a process that for him was linked to an ethic and an evolution in his family. Veiled criticism of his elders and a certain moral posture emerge in his description, but it also mirrors political change in the country: "In my family, the elders were not very religious, and the younger generation was more so. When we went to the mosque, the elders went to the movie theatre and smoked. While we did community service, they pursued personal activities."[42]

Wael became an active member in Islamist associations at university. Like many Islamist activists, he insisted on his role as a social leader. He was successful several times in elections for the engineering students' union (to which architects belong). After university, he opened an architecture firm and became very active in the engineers' association. At the age of forty-seven he was elected president for a first term, followed by a second (the president of the association can only serve two terms). Although a long career as an activist is not a sufficient condition for gaining access to such positions – Wael also benefited from a political shift in favour of the Islamists – it is, however, a necessary condition. Outsiders rarely achieve this level unless they are backed by the government (they are generally referred to as "governmentals" within the associations, and "independents" in the media).

Only one activist was an exception in this respect. For Maysarat, a civil engineer born in 1961 in Amman, his politicization took place after university. Although he was still at university during the events in Yarmouk in 1986, he did not get involved in the protest, which he did not understand. But as a young graduate and newlywed in 1989, he and his wife followed the first election campaign with great interest, and it was the independent Islamist dissenter Layth Shubeilat who initiated him into the movement:

> His statements caught my attention. […] Instead of going out to parties, my wife and I went from one place to another following him to hear him speak. He spoke well in an engaging way, and what he was saying was new. That is what made me get involved in politics.[43]

It was through Layth Shubeilat that Maysarat started becoming active in the association, and especially in the Anti-Normalization Committee of which Layth Shubeilat was one of the leaders. Afterwards, Maysarat was also actively involved in the issue of freedoms in Jordan. However, he did not run for election, and he attributes his refusal to join a party to being a latecomer to political commitment:

> Despite the advantages of being in a political party and in an active group with whom you can work, the party forces you to

adopt particular politics, and sometimes you may have a different opinion. Therefore you must adopt an opinion that is different from yours [...]. In general, people join the party early, when they are young, but I started collective work late. I was twenty-seven years old, and I did not want to join a party.

Maysarat thus indirectly underlines the defining characteristic of early ideological and partisan immersion.

Professional activism/political activism

The activists' different types of involvement within their professional associations underline a dual tension between corporatist engagement and a general political engagement, and between a political stance as the opposition and the desire to gain recognition by being co-opted into the official Jordanian political system, regardless of its limits. While leadership positions in the associations give their leaders a great deal of visibility, they also involve maintaining relations with the government. An example of this has been described earlier concerning the mobilization for the Gaza Strip, but Wael also illustrates this in his own way when he underlines the associations' capacity for mobilization and opposition (strikes and demonstrations) and, on a positive note, how members of the associations have become ministers and won parliamentary elections. Committee members more systematically adopt a posture of opposition than the leaders, although some have held both types of posts. Moreover, Maysarat makes a clear distinction between activism on the committees and what he calls political activities, which for him involve governmental ambitions. He rejects participation in elections, considering them fundamentally skewed. The full ambiguity of the professional associations' position can thus be seen with regard to the types of commitment themselves; the associations are a rare authorized arena of opposition, but also allow the state to integrate an elite.

Furthermore, professional commitment also includes defending vested interests, which the activists generally combine with their political activism. In this way, they continue the types of actions implemented at university, where providing services for students and mobilization about curricula and tuition fees were central parts of their activities. A general desire for social and political involvement is highlighted and the distinction between professional activism and political activism is blurred when association activists talk about the content of their engagement. Mixing politics with social and professional services is a way of giving legitimacy to professional activism. For beyond the limits imposed by the monarchy, there are debates within the professional associations about the appropriateness of political action. In 2000, only 20 per cent of association leaders declared an affiliation with a party.[44] Moreover, at the Professional Associations Complex, career events as well as job forums attract many more people than political demonstrations, not least because the latter may be risky.

Women professional activists

Women activists are a small minority in the professional associations, and they are particularly involved in the professional and social aspects.[45] Officially their status in professional associations is the same as men's; however, in practice things differ: for example, women do not have the same access to pension funds and social security as men do.[46] Following a classic model, although women are present (as a minority) on the list of candidates for election, they do not attain senior positions (even the presidency of the nurses' and midwives' association – in which women are a large majority – is generally held by a man). In association meetings organized by Islamists, women sit together at the back of the room. Women's field of activity is focused on the women's committees in each association and in the inter-association women's committee, where Islamists are very largely predominant.

The secondary nature of their engagement evident in the gender-oriented space they are allotted through activities that address women specifically appeared only marginally in interviews. Women insist on their desire to serve – a subject which is also very apparent in interviews with men. Like men, their activism in professional associations is influenced by their previous involvement at university. However, political subjects are much less prominent, and the professional aspects are strongly emphasized. Women engineers have specific difficulties gaining access to the job market appropriate to their level of skill, which is a particular preoccupation for them. They emphasize training and internships and are very active during forums involving businesses and young women graduates organized by the associations. Many have part-time jobs or do shift work. It is not uncommon for them to leave the workforce after the birth of their second or third child. Unemployment is therefore their foremost concern, and their engagement in the associations is particularly oriented in this direction. Linda, a chemical engineer born in 1975, ran as an Islamist in the branch-level elections when the director of the first company she worked for asked her to – evidence of the corporatist perspective. Her main goal is "reducing the unemployment rate and developing the profession".[47]

Although women are particularly aware of the professional support associations can provide, the nature of their involvement in this field can also be explained by the specific problems linked to political involvement. For Rima, born in 1976 and also a chemical engineer and an Islamist, religion and the desire to serve others motivate her commitment. She says that it was especially hard to get her family to accept it, "because the hours of volunteer work were late and because of widespread ideas about the links between professional associations and politics". Socially, it is easier for these professional women activists to gain acceptance for their service activities, and especially activities specifically dedicated to women. Furthermore, women Islamists insist on the morals and ethics that stem from the link between religion and involvement as it is understood in Islam. Iman was born in 1962 in Jerusalem, and her family went into exile in Jordan in 1967. She stopped working after the birth of her fourth child, dedicating part of her newfound free time to the engineers' association's women's committee, where she ran for election:

> Since I am on the white list [the Islamist list], I know that the participants are religious, devout and of good moral character. They are not pursuing their personal interests, but the general public's interest. Relationships between men and women respect religious boundaries. [...] Men and women avoid persistent eye contact. [...] I know that when I work in this way, I am satisfying God; it is not sinful, and there are no problems.

Involvement in this movement is thus a sure way of being able to represent oneself as morally respectable even when their activities and their travelling may be considered inappropriate in their social environment. The majority of these women professionals run as Islamists; class and generational trends are perceptible here. They are younger and quite representative of the new generations of educated women from the middle class who have shaped the core of Islamist mobilization. They are participating in the professionalization of the associations promoted by the Islamists. However, they are not necessarily involved in the Muslim Brotherhood outside the professional association.

Nevertheless, these educated women's commitment raises problems concerning their availability – even more so than for men. The little free time women have is mentioned both by men, in order to justify the low level of women's participation in professional associations, and by women, who underline how difficult it is to reconcile the demands on their time. The fragile balance between professional time, involvement time and family time is emphasized by the insistence by both male and female Islamists on women's central role in child-rearing. This is a classic issue in Islamist women's commitment. Also, especially among Islamists, women who hold the most active positions in professional associations are often those who do not work or do not have a family of their own. This concurs with common observations about how the roles assigned to women in society[48] and their difficulties in gaining access to high-level jobs[49] carry over into activism. Nonetheless, these women activists highlight the personal satisfaction they receive from their engagement in terms of self-growth, socialization and giving meaning to their lives.

The women engineers and activists emphasize on the professional activities of the associations without contrasting them with the political role of the organizations. Indeed, internal debates regarding the role of professional associations are not restricted to their difficult positioning within a more or less repressive national context. They are also linked to a general evolution of activist techniques towards greater expertise. In the case of these organizations, there is a threefold dynamic at work. First of all, there is the direct influence of international donors,[50] in particular through the idea of "good governance" that emphasizes standardized management practices and aims to undermine the legitimacy of openly axiological messages. Second, even the Jordanian regime promotes this aspect and seeks to comply with international organizational norms. Indeed, Jordan is directly linked to donors, which are among its main resources: Jordan is one of the highest per capita recipients of aid in the world, to the extent that the phenomenon is referred to as "humanitarian rent". Lastly, opposition activism is moving increasingly toward militant counter-expertise that is looking to advise or reform the state's action. A whole NGO sector is developing in this field, but the professional associations, whose statutes promote the relation to knowledge and skill, are also well positioned. The reorganization of political practices is, however, in line with a general evolution that is not limited to "peripheral" countries, even though it is particularly visible there.[51]

CHAPTER 7

New forms of mobilization

Political opposition in Jordan has changed tack in the face of repression, entering new arenas for political expression and altering its methods of action. While a given group's relationship to the Jordanian regime remains a decisive aspect of activism, it is important not to disregard how regional and international influences factor in as well. Repertoires of action used elsewhere and international evolutions in forms of political action have repercussions. The most violent methods, particularly suicide attacks, are the ones that have drawn the greatest attention and media coverage. But the real change has come about in an entirely different arena of activist involvement, different in both form and substance: expertise and project-oriented mobilizations. These fit within what may at first appear to be a post-ideological context, although this does not mean that there is no ideology underlying this evolution. However, activists explicitly claim to have gone beyond ideology. They no longer put forward charismatic leadership figures except when referring to the past. They look to the international scene in seeking an effective repertoire of action, adapting it to different watchwords and objectives. Vincent Geisser, Karam Karam and Frédéric Vairel have observed "the gradual decline of hegemonic mobilization methods based on a strong congruence between ideological watchword (radicality of demands) and protest methods (radicality of forms of action)".[1]

Expert activism and project-oriented mobilization

This evolution is reflected by the shift in partisan commitments to no longer being the activists' principle focus. Above and beyond involvement in Islamism, nationalism and/or leftwing politics, an entire sector of advocacy groups and NGOs has developed since the 1990s. This is the much-touted civil society placed high on international organization agendas, a "vibrant" civil society assumed to provide a foundation for democracy and serve as the preferred non-political channel through which to funnel international development aid. This sector thus enjoys international support and funding, and its activities are deployed in two principal directions: development projects in the broadest sense of the term, and advocacy, generally taken to mean the defence of human rights and democracy.

Of course, this change is also particularly relevant in the face of a repressive regime. In a coercive context, commitment of this sort can prove to be relatively less costly to the activist than a political career often punctuated by long periods of imprisonment. The globalization of justice – and even more than the establishment of international tribunals, the widespread legitimacy that the demand for rights now enjoys – are also sources of support.[2] But involvement in the non-profit sector, "which is increasingly disconnected from the established political sphere",[3] is not specific to repressive regimes, but is rather part of a broader trend. This is an example of how local structural factors affecting the organization of the activist sphere combine with international factors linked with opportunities for international support. In fact, civil society has become a repertoire of action in its own right.[4]

Depoliticization?

The move toward the non-profit sphere raises the possibility of depoliticization.[5] The involvement of former leftwing and Arab nationalist activists and new "human rights"[6] activists in civil society offers an activist alternative in this regard, but what are the consequences of such a shift? It is difficult to associate disaffection toward the party system and depoliticization, as clearly these human rights organizations are very involved in the public debate, seeking to influence national agendas and deploying actions that are far from limited to the charity sphere. Even if it would be wrong to talk about true depoliticization, this alternative form of commitment nevertheless uses methods other than party politics to situate itself in the public arena. These differences have repercussions on the ways organizations engage in or refrain from conflict with the regime and the very ways in which the activists perceive themselves. Advocacy groups are often less on the offensive when it comes to national issues, and instead tend to devote their energies to issues in specific sectors. Their legitimization in particular is of a different order. These organizations draw heavily on international legitimacy that makes reference to human rights values and technical, social and humanitarian skills. This gives them access to external resources, funding and new spaces of politicization. But it also carries for them the risk of being "labelled as foreign agents"[7] and winding up in a heteronomous situation.[8] This frame of reference often creates tension within activists who position themselves on a dual front: on the international scene with respect to donors and networks of human rights organizations, and on the local scene, where they seek to act while nevertheless having to justify their "authenticity".

The diversity of the various strands of the Islamist movement partly escapes this tension. First of all, Islamists remain strongly present in the realm of party politics, unlike former Arab leftists and nationalists. The movement has tended to maintain and reinforce a dual positioning, both in party politics and in charity organizations, enabling it to utilize fluctuating modes of integration in these spheres and develop a truly hegemonic strategy. Furthermore, the reference to Islam partly enables them to elude doubts about their "authenticity" and to attack other activists on this point. They also have an alternative international support network. Without eliminating national specificities and competition among various Islamic movements, this common reference places them in support networks and on very active scenes of debate that largely exceed the borders of the Middle East.

Most of the Jordanian Islamic organizational network remains oriented toward classic forms of social work. But that doesn't mean that it is totally removed from the international sphere. In fact, certain Islamic associations are tending to adapt to the agendas of international donors, setting up compatible operating procedures and applying for their programmes. The diversity of donors enables them to find funding niches. Compared to other associations, they have an enormous asset: their social base far outweighs any that Jordanian human rights organizations can claim.

This bipolarization between Islamism and human rights organizations is a major trend in activist reconfigurations in the Middle East. It is particularly perceptible if one analyses public debates where the two movements often confront one another, especially on matters of personal law and women's rights. But nor should it be exaggerated. On such topics as democratization, temporary alliances can be formed between the two movements. In this bipolarized context, the Islamist movement often remains the only standard-bearer of Palestinian nationalism, even when the Palestinian theme is present in human rights associations from the angle of criticizing the living conditions imposed on Palestinians in the Palestinian Territories. The migration of nationalist and leftist activists toward these organizations alters the agendas they promote, which now must be made compatible with international organization agendas. As Kinda, a former communist activist who has become a representative of Amnesty International in Jordan, points out, this is one of their major problems: "our reports on the Israeli–Palestinian conflict are criticized locally because we are accused of placing Israel and the Palestinians on an equal footing, whereas we are praised for our reports on Guantanamo".[9] Thus human rights, women's rights and environmental issues are emphasized while national questions or Arab unity are no longer mentioned.

Leftist forums

With more flexible procedures for joining, forums have proliferated that are halfway between movements and organizations. Forms of participation that are less structured than formal membership have been set up. This more volatile and informal type of activism also makes them more difficult to suppress. Furthermore, forums mobilize around specifically targeted issues in the short term rather than striving to agree on an overall ideology. They advocate reform rather than revolution. An evolution is also palpable in the themes of mobilization. Even if in this regard priorities differ from one group to the next, the influence of international organization agendas as well as alter-globalism is plain to see.

These forums are often founded by former leftwing activists in search of new ideas, new methods of action and new activists. This is the case with Khaled, whose membership in the Communist Party and studies in Romania were mentioned earlier, and who along with others founded the Social Forum in the mid-2000s, having grown weary of the Community Party's many divisions and subdivisions and what he calls its lack of realism:

> It's really a shame about the Communist Party, because that was my life. But they are not part of the modern world, they keep asking for this, wanting that, but I put together precise proposals

and programmes for each ministry! [...] I raised questions that the head of Social Security could not answer. To draw up our programmes, we bring in some thirty experts on the matter, we sit them down at a table, and we take what fits with our political line.

The above testimony indicates the claims of expertise and involvement in a reform effort. The concerns adopted by Khaled's forum have changed focus; the Palestinian cause, Arab unity and anti-imperialism have moved into the background, viewed as somewhat utopian. Defending them, according to Khaled, leads nowhere except for occasional clamorous declarations in the media. On the other hand, it has brought to the forefront an analysis of the social and economic administration of Jordan and made specific proposals for change:

> For instance, one of our present proposals: there is a fund to compensate people who do not work; [...] we want this fund to be devoted to training and for these people to be offered jobs. If they refuse, then they won't get any money, but if they aren't found work, then they get money.

A number of leftist activists admittedly cannot relate to this type of proposal. Above all, the discourse has radically changed levels, no longer referring directly to an ideology and an overall worldview, but striving to be concrete and technical. This doesn't mean that it does not imply normative choices, but that the basis for such choices remains largely implicit. Khaled describes himself as a pragmatist with a Marxist background, no longer talking about social justice, but instead about the fight against poverty. The Social Forum is situated at a sort of intersection between international organizations and alter-globalism – a positioning that is far from exceptional among former activists in the Arab left and beyond Jordan's borders. It is mirrored in the professional careers of activists, some of whom may be officials in an international organization and, as some mention, adopt the position expected of them in the internal reports they write for these organizations while elsewhere questioning the agendas of these same organizations. However, even when they are critical, the ties these activists have with international organizations tend to make them appear as an external, internationalized elite, which compounds the difficulties the Arab left has in finding a social base.

Khaled is thus not out of step with the "expert" turn taken by the regime under King Abdullah II, but on the contrary. It is the repertoire of action that he wants to be involved in, even if he criticizes the new liberals and the Western experts, those "who think they can rule society with *PowerPoint*", that the monarchy relies on. This is reflected in the ambivalent relationship to the regime that illustrates the specificities of authoritarian liberalism and its characteristic dissociation between the social and economic agenda and questions of democracy and freedom of speech. Just as the regime uses both co-optation and repression with forum activists, Khaled hesitates between integration – he was allegedly offered a post as a minister – to set up the measures he recommends, and political opposition through petitions and demonstrations. Activities are thus divided between the officially registered forum itself, which organizes activities of a social, cultural and technical nature, while more specifically political activities, such as organizing tent protests when the Israeli army attacked Gaza, are associated with the Jordanian Social Movement, which is not officially registered. However, members' opinions differ regarding this division of labour. Khaled is convinced that it gives the forum additional room to manoeuvre, as it is not subject to the new law on political parties that requires a minimum of 5,000 members. It also limits interference in internal voting processes – one of the methods the government uses to control advocacy groups and political parties. This procedure involves having masses of new "activists" join just prior to organizations' internal elections in order to place government candidates. But the person in charge of the forum's youth section is much more doubtful.[10] He does not feel he can ask students to join a movement that does not have official status, because the risks are too great for the students, whose enrolment may be rejected or their grants denied. Here again is an illustration of the dilemma of choosing a repertoire of action in a repressive regime that has nevertheless not entirely taken control of the political scene: to opt for head-on opposition, thereby making activism more costly, or to make utmost use of authorized modes of expression.

The Socialist Thought Forum, founded in 1993 by leftwing activists, is situated politically in a more radical perspective closer to the positions of the National Anti-Normalization Committee comprising members from several different professional associations. Here the Palestinian cause and Arab unity remain major issues. The two forums provide a good illustration of the range of positions open to the Arab left, from classic references to Arab nationalism and the Palestinian cause to closer involvement in international organizations using the vocabulary of aid and the defence of rights. In both cases, however, mobilization in the name of alter-globalism is also a preferred channel for access to the international sphere. In both forums, however, international involvement forces them to address the question of the Israeli–Palestinian conflict and their refusal to have anything to do with Israeli organizations.

At the national level, the Socialist Thought Forum is subject to the same methods of repression and co-optation, as Hisham, one of its most active members, recounts. A thirty-five-year-old dentist, he is one of the few members of his generation, most of the Forum activists being older. Hisham is also a member of the National Anti-Normalization Committee:

> Right now we're under pressure: there is a law against gatherings, but the professional associations don't respect it.

They have more room to manoeuvre. But in cultural associations and NGOs, the pressure is more acute. We hold elections to renew the board [...] and the government locates lots of former members, some of whom have become associated with the government, to get them to vote for a pro-government list.[11]

In this regard, forums experience the same tensions as political mobilization in the professional associations. Founded by professional elites, these forums are an integral part of the neopatrimonial system of redistribution, and are in fact close to government bodies even when they challenge them. They encounter the same difficulties of mobilizing beyond the elites, and as in parliamentary elections, logics of patronage are also at work in recruiting activists to the forums. The head of the forum's youth section, not having a university degree, is thus is beholden to Khaled for having found him a job as a tour guide.

Moreover, the divide between Jordanian Palestinians and Transjordanians is clearly present: the Social Forum is made up only of Jordanians. Khaled at first denies it, then explains the fact by a strategy of recruiting locally rather than according to political stance. However, another factor was the presence of Nahed Hattar, a standard-bearer of Jordanian nationalism, in the forum. In the 1990s the expression of exclusively Jordanian nationalism became more vocal – a challenge to the policies of the Hashemite monarchy. The regime is ambivalent toward this form of nationalism, which advocates exclusively Jordanian origins, with means that the Hashemites themselves could be considered foreigners. This nationalism focuses on a leitmotiv: the refusal to integrate post-1948 Jordanian Palestinians, but it is associated with support for Palestinian nationalism – in the Palestinian Territories – as well as opposition to the Jordanian–Israeli peace accords of 1994.[12] In this current, reference to a Palestinian nation is seen as a solution to the problem of the Palestinian refugees who arrived in Jordan in 1948 and 1967, which would thus enable them return to the Palestinian Territories. This divide considerably weakens the Jordanian left by limiting possibilities for joint mobilization.

Activist career changes: old activists, new activism?

For activists in Jordan, the loss of political opportunities for leftwing parties, deprived of funding, international support and an underlying ideology, resulted in career changes that combine disengagement from activism, new forms of commitment and professional reorientation. Just as multiple divisions and shake-ups have affected political parties, leftwing activist careers have gone through a number of shifts and splits. Involvement in the advocacy sector and NGOs under the banner of the fight for human rights in this case corresponds to a structural evolution of this variety of activism.

From communism to human rights

Ahmed A., like his wife, joined Amnesty International, at first alongside his commitment to the Communist Party. However, in 1996, after yet another preventive arrest, he left Jordan and took a job in Cyprus with Amnesty International. More than the harshness of the crackdown during the previous period and the difficulties of semi-secrecy, it was disillusionment with the democratic opening that finally put an end to Ahmed's communist activism. Communist dissent and weaknesses came to light, whereas the new repertoire of action that had opened up in the form of participation in democracy proved illusory. His commitment became devoid of meaning, and the repression was therefore unbearable. When he returned to Jordan four years later, he left the Communist Party for good while maintaining his involvement with Amnesty International, where he worked as a translator. Even though Ahmed A. doesn't put it this way, the position was indeed a professional advancement that ensured him a better income than his former teaching positions, from which he was fired at the behest of the intelligence services. From an activism standpoint, however, for Ahmed it was a reorientation "by default" that did not assuage a gnawing bitterness about the outcome of his commitment. His story thus confirms the analysis of Assia Boutaleb, Jean-Noël Ferrié and Benjamin Rey, who point out to what extent "the switch to civil action for government opponents is a way of making a virtue of necessity – by playing a role only within the realm of legality in the regime [...] and the consequence of a victory for political repression".[13] Ahmed maintains his Marxist convictions, but withdrew from the Communist Party, affected by the lack of international support after the fall of the Soviet Union as well as by changes within the organization and by government crackdowns. Indeed, Ahmed was all the more affected by Communist Party divisions because he was in a mid-level cadre position, caught between the positions held by the leadership, which often sought to appease the situation, and grassroots activists who wanted to continue the fight. When the divisions burst in the open after the democratic opening, this position became all the more intolerable as it crystallized the organization's structural contradictions.

At the same time, Ahmed increasingly experienced the communists' social isolation. When he had joined the Communist Party, he didn't have the feeling of embracing an ideology and lifestyle that would put him at a distance from society, but rather that he was fighting for its cause. It was gradually, as the left lost influence and the consequences of repression were felt, that he noted a progressive marginalization, at first offset by communist solidarity. When this disintegrated in the wake of divisions, he truly began to feel like an outsider, despaired at his fellow citizens, and felt dually sidelined politically by both state repression and Islamist social hegemony. In this situation, involvement with Amnesty International very concretely enabled him to recover the valued references of international support and a network, and reopened opportunities for activism. He thereby partly came out of his political isolation, but nevertheless has not truly regained a national foothold. In fact, he encounters the same tensions that the entire NGO and human rights sector faces, their actors being readily perceived as externalized elites. International support and funding lead to accusations of betrayal and neglect of the Palestinian, Arab and anti-imperialist struggles. These accusations are reinforced by the depoliticization of human rights agendas that redefine the actors as victims.

This is not, however, how Ahmed perceives the evolution in his political ideas. On the contrary, he stresses the continuity of his Marxist convictions and is still prepared to fight for them, even if he no longer wants to be member of a party, as the local and world situation has changed completely. Indeed, the ideology an activist chooses to adhere to gradually acquires a personal meaning over the course of his career, the activist having made considerable sacrifices. The more intense the experience, the slower and more difficult the career reorientation, and the more it is filled with bitterness. This dimension has to be taken into account, and renders the analysis of ideology, often viewed solely in terms of its function of legitimizing a system of power, more complex. By the same token, a political commitment cannot be understood only with respect to a political context and the realm of possibilities it offers. Far from remaining a theoretical framework, ideology truly becomes personalized and embodied through the activist career. It can continue to hold meaning for an activist even when it no longer corresponds to any political offer.

Human rights thus do not appear for Ahmed as an alternative reference to Marxism, but as the only means to continue his political involvement in a general context of marginalization or rejection of the Marxist left in the Arab world. The use of this reference and mobilization in its name do not prevent him from being dissatisfied with the human rights/Islamist bipolarization mentioned above, or from acutely perceiving the limits of human rights movements. Indeed, human rights primarily concern living conditions and identification of victims of human rights violations. Many opponents prefer to define themselves with respect to the political causes they defend. Due to their limits, human rights do not offer an alternative to a comprehensive ideology, and the search continues – implicitly – for an anti-hegemonic movement whose references are international while enjoying national legitimacy. For these activists, the reference to human rights does not meet this requirement and does not constitute a true political cause.

From leftwing politics to Islamism?

Such a context sheds light on the careers of some activists who have switched from leftwing politics to Islamism – a shift that some often find surprising and that remains on the fringe of both tendencies. Beyond obvious divergences, continuity can be detected in the very comprehensive nature of these movements that suggest models of conduct, though their social acceptance is unmatched in the case of Islamism. These activists of course change their lifestyles radically, which forces them to break off ties with former comrades, particularly due to the use of alcohol. Activist social ties and the communist counter-society had already been weakened, however, and slackened due to their political marginalization. Some observers note that Islamists can recruit among those who leave the communist counter-society because their religious movement creates another model of counter-society. As Diane Singerman points out with regard to Egypt: "Islamist movements have framed their agenda around fundamental questions about the meaning of life and how Islamic beliefs and practices should inform daily life, law, morality, the economy and governance."[14]

But above all, they retain two political themes: nationalism and social justice. Pan-Arab nationalism and Palestinian nationalism are among the priorities of the Arab left, even if one strand or the other is emphasized depending on the current. In the Islamist movement, keeping the Palestinian national issue on the agenda goes without saying, even if it is expressed using a different vocabulary and connected with the notion of a Muslim *umma*. Muslim Brotherhood support for this issue contributes considerably to the organization's impact, and the Palestinians continue to perceive its leading figures as their spokesmen. What explains the persistence of this nationalism in Jordan? According to Philippe Droz-Vincent, it is based in a strong sense of "betrayal by the notables".[15] Indeed, for a segment of the population, the Jordanian regime seems bent on implementing Western policies and does not really take into account Jordanian and Arab interests. Added to that is a feeling of injustice fuelled regionally by the Israeli–Palestinian conflict and Western hegemony. Jordanians find maintenance of the status quo unbearable, associating this with a growing sense of being the economic and political losers of history. In this context, reference to nationalism, particularly the Islamist version, represents a last line of defence that might finally ensure a reversal of history. Nationalism in this regard has increasingly become an identity marker. In interviews, nationalism is much more associated with pride and dignity than with a political programme. It is also perceived as a means for marginalized populations to position themselves in a globalized world. The demand for social justice is another common theme shared by leftwing politics and Islamism, although the Islamist version shuns the anti-liberal dimension in favour of the notion of fairness. Islamism is given credit for the attention it pays to this issue, which seems all the more crucial in a society with extremely inegalitarian economic development. The Islamist social programme thus takes on its full meaning, as does its charity network, which virtually offers an alternative to the state system.

In any event, such trajectories remain the exception, and rather than true commitment, former leftwing activists instead express sympathies with only certain aspects of Islamism. The Lebanese Shi'a movement Hezbollah thus garners more votes than the Jordanian Muslim Brotherhood. Moreover, even if the notion of leftist Islam is sometimes mentioned by leftwing activists, it is never used by the Jordanian Muslim Brotherhood. More than local Islamist movements, the alternative represented by Hezbollah exhibits a fascination with Jordan. Former communists do not hesitate to associate Che Guevara with Nasrallah[16] and joke about the common root in Arabic shared by the words Communism and Shi'ism. They place Shi'ism and the figure of Ali and his sons within a tradition of opposition to the dominant authorities they identify with, unlike Sunnism.[17] The Lebanese Islamic nationalist movement is perceived as having successfully opposed Israel since the Israeli withdrawal from South Lebanon in 2000, and even more so since the failure of the Israeli offensive in 2006. But its social achievements also attract considerable interest. Former activists travelled to South Lebanon after late 2006 to observe the situation closely, returning outraged by the destruction wreaked by the Israeli army, but highly impressed by Hezbollah's ability to provide services to the population. Hezbollah thus appeared to them as the real victim of Israel, and as a social and combatant movement. In this regard, it may embody the ideals of Palestinian nationalism for some activists. However, Hezbollah's support for the Syrian regime's brutal crackdown on the opposition movement since 2011 has alienated certain sympathizers, although the Jordanian left remains divided over this issue. For Baathist activists, the Syrian regime continues to represent Arab socialism, and for this reason some of them vandalized an exhibition organized by the Jordanian Muslim Brotherhood in a show of support for the victims of repression at the hands of the Syrian regime. Foreign interference and the militarization of the opposition have also been criticized.[18] Positions toward the Syrian regime have redrawn the lines separating nationalism, Islamism and the left. Part of the Baathist left backs it, whereas other Baathist activists belonging to dissident branches have experienced Syrian prisons. The 2011 and 2012 uprisings rekindled these tensions and divided the activists; a segment of the Jordanian left reduces the Syrian opposition to the Islamists alone and does not support it, while others identify with the protest against an authoritarian regime.

The Arab Spring mobilizations of 2011 and 2012: issues and limits

The Arab Spring mobilizations in Jordan in fact fit on a continuum of opposition. They thus encountered the same structural limits that have weakened the Jordanian opposition, the main one being the division that has built up between Palestinians and Transjordanians, but they also exceed others. These mobilizations drew on pre-existing opposition movements. However, through them the left recovered a form of mobilization that was broader than expert activism, and the Islamists, by taking a stronger confrontational stance, to some extent lost their image of a co-opted opposition. The year 2010 had already been marked by several union mobilizations, and the demonstrations of 2011 and 2012 do not stand out in terms of scale, which remained fairly small, except in the early stages of the movement, despite being continuous. Furthermore, the range of categories of activists mobilized was particularly broad. New actors began taking part, with youths taking front stage, whereas until then few had participated in the opposition, to the point where activist organizations faced problems of generational renewal. Movements also cropped up within the tribes.

The primary demands were economic and social, reinforcing recurrent demands in Jordan. Criticism of government inefficiency and corruption also spread. This issue of protest was not new in Jordan, although it grew in scale, and did not appear particularly revolutionary to the monarchy, which moreover addressed some of the criticisms levelled toward the parliament formed after the elections held in late 2010.

But in addition to these social demands were political claims, expressed largely by the Islamists. They pertained to the establishment of a true constitutional monarchy and the election of the prime minister rather than his appointment by the king. This latter demand indicates a change in tone, although the issue had already been mentioned by certain opposition figures, overstepping the red lines of political censorship that allows criticism of the government, but not of the monarchy. The omnipresence of the intelligence services and widespread corruption have also joined the topics broached by demonstrations. The example set by Tunisia brought into the open in Jordan, in a collective and organized manner, criticisms that were generally made only in private and in subdued terms. Mobilization took on the classic forms of sit-ins and demonstrations. Several communiqués and pamphlets were published, and new movements and coalitions were formed. Among these are the National Front for Reform, formed by figures from the Islamist Action Front (Muslim Brotherhood), leftwing nationalist parties and trade unions, as well as independent opposition figures. It is a common opposition front similar to the coalition formed in 2002 under the banner of anti-imperialism. The National Front for Reform calls for the establishment of a parliamentary monarchy and economic reforms to reduce poverty and inequality (establishment of a minimum wage, a social security system and redistributive tax reform in particular).[19] The Youth and People's Coalition for Change in Jordan grew out of the 24 March Youth Coalition, based on an initiative from one of the first and largest sit-ins in a public square on 24 March 2011, following the Egyptian model of the occupation of Tahrir Square, though the occupation did not last in Jordan. It included young independents as well as sympathizers of various opposition parties and members of Thabahtuna, the

National Campaign for Students' Rights, formed prior to the Arab Springs. It focused on civil liberties and reform of the security apparatus, but fairly quickly ceased its activities under this name and split up in April 2011. Youths have nevertheless continued to mobilize through the appearance of various groups. The largest of these, Hirak[20] ("Movement"), claims to be independent from any political party, while issuing fairly radical criticism of the regime.

Several Transjordanian coalitions have also been formed, such as Jayyin ("we are coming"), made up of students, workers, teachers and pensioners as well as nationalist and leftist groups[21] (especially the Social Forum mentioned above). A group of military veterans, mainly Transjordanian, started to mobilize in 2010, denouncing corruption as well as the fact that Jordan is allegedly becoming an alternative homeland for Palestinians, once again taking up a leitmotif of (Trans)Jordanian nationalism. They joined after the Arab Spring demonstrations and proclaimed their intention to form a party. As for the tribes themselves, they are divided. Some send letters of support to the king, while others demand more extensive reform. This division shows that it is impossible to reliably predict the positions of tribal networks, which are not automatically in line with the king's. Their social composition is diverse. They are currently fraught with serious political tensions and do not represent a united force. In 2011, thirty-six tribal notables issued a statement accusing the queen and her entourage of corruption. The fact that it was the queen and not the king who was the object of criticism is highly significant. She is of Palestinian stock, and advocated new legislation that would enable women to pass on their citizenship more easily. This has been perceived as an open door to the naturalization of new Palestinians and the increase of their demographic weight in the country. Since then, the major tribes in Jordan have held increasing numbers of gatherings as well as meetings with reform movements. Economic issues are central to the demands of Transjordanian movements. Their large numbers in public sector jobs due to affirmative action policies implemented by the monarchy have consequently made the issues of privatization and decreases in subsidies and pensions all the more sensitive for them. They feel that Abdullah II has reneged on the pact they had with the monarchy and their preferential treatment as regards access to state resources. This echoes the idea of a breach of the social contract, also noted in other Arab countries.[22]

Salafi groups also joined the mobilization by holding gatherings. The Salafi movement in Jordan is divided over the question of political violence, mainly between reformist Salafi and Jihadi Salafi factions. While both draw on the same texts,[23] they are strategically opposed, and only the jihadis can be considered as an opposition in the true sense.[24] They are distinguished by their organization as a loose network structure to escape repression and their refusal to co-operate in any way with the regime. They are involved in controversies with the Muslim Brotherhood, and do not hesitate to heap verbal abuse on the movement.[25] Their recruitment base would appear to be among the poorest classes that are hardest hit by the economic crisis. According to Quintan Wiktorowicz, the movement has few actual members, but their sympathizers – a difficult phenomenon to assess – number close to those of the Muslim Brotherhood. During the 2011 and 2012 mobilizations they held rallies and demonstrations, some of which ended in clashes with the police, particularly in Zarqa in April 2011. Sometimes armed with swords and sticks, their form of mobilization differs from other groups, and they were arrested en masse. This type of demonstration, while very rare compared to the rest of the movement, provoked a crisis within the opposition, which makes a point of emphasizing its pacifism even when violently dispersed by security forces. The Salafis have distanced themselves from the movement, and in particular its calls for democracy,[26] demanding above all the release of their jailed leaders. The involvement of Jordanian Jihadi Salafis in the Syrian rebellion has further exacerbated this reluctance. Jordan's Arab Spring was in fact characterized by a reformist rather than revolutionary ideal. Demonstrators did not call for the overthrow of the regime, and stressed a non-violent repertoire of action. There is a degree of convergence among the various tendencies with regard to demands for political liberalization and the fight against corruption, as well as concerning economic and social demands. However, the Jordanian Palestinian/Transjordanian divide remains very apparent, and is reflected in political divergences, especially over reform of an election law that currently favours rural and tribal areas.

The Jordanian monarchy's response to these movements combines several different levels. It has sought at once to renew the economic pact, restore the legitimacy of the monarchy, which has distanced itself from the maligned institutions that critics want to reform, and lastly, to divide and weaken the opposition. Systematic exploitation of divisions between Jordanian Palestinians and Transjordanians as well as among tribes is a hallmark of the regime's strategy to undermine mobilization. In addition to harsh police repression, opposition rallies have regularly been attacked by organized groups claiming to be Transjordanian and royalist. As no investigation has been conducted, it is impossible to identify the assailants, but in any event, the intelligence services certainly allowed them to act with impunity.[27] The aim is to portray the demonstrators as Palestinians, foreign to what lies at the heart of Jordanian identity, thereby depriving the mobilization of any legitimacy. This exercise has proven difficult in Amman, where although Islamists form the bulk of the ranks of mobilization, they are not exclusively Palestinians. It has plainly been impossible in the case of protests on the periphery, particularly in southern Jordan, where Palestinians are virtually absent. There, it is inter-tribal strife and potential clashes that are highlighted instead, and used to sow division.

Repression takes the form of heavy police presence, the violent dispersion of protest rallies, and the arrest and imprisonment of political opponents, often followed by rough treatment. The Jordanian Penal Code of 1960 includes articles that punish "undermining the political regime", "insulting the king" and "inciting resistance", for which the State Security Court can try protesters who have expressed opinions deemed to be offensive. Youth movement leaders in particular have been targeted by these measures, accused of carrying signs, chanting slogans or broadcasting messages over social media such as "O Abdullah, son of Hussein, where has the people's money gone?" or "Monitoring phone calls is a violation of our constitutional rights."[28] Moreover, in addition to the countless laws and measures hampering the work of political parties and associations, censorship persists. The passage of a new law censoring the Internet is the latest episode of repression.

Furthermore, the monarchy played the cards of political reform and social redistribution. There were five changes of prime minister between January 2011 and March 2013. Wage and pension increases were announced, while the king officially asked the new government to implement an effective social policy and made several announcements concerning social issues (waiving of school registration fees, Ramadan bonuses and so on). Some tribes have obtained additional land, which counterbalances prior expropriations. At the same time, a process to revise the constitution was officially announced, along with the establishment of a Constitutional Court and an Independent Election Commission. These reforms were not really implemented, and were considered insufficient by most of the active groups. After parliament was dissolved at the end of 2012, the 2013 elections – boycotted by most of the opposition – did not renew the regime's political legitimacy. However, the strategy implemented by the monarchy turned out to be effective in containing the movement, even though it failed to quell it.

The Arab Springs in fact revived political mobilization in Jordan by creating a synergy among various groups: Islamists, youth, tribes and so on. In particular, as elsewhere in the Arab world, even if existing political organizations – Islamists, trade unions and professional associations, and more on the fringe, nationalist and leftist organizations – have ensured the perpetuation of the movement, in Jordan it was sparked by youths who were not usually mobilized.

Up until recently, youth activism had mainly taken the form of involvement in NGOs and human rights organizations, especially when their orientation is somewhat to the left. For instance, the daughters of Ahmed A., a communist activist mentioned in previous chapters, became involved in the human rights sector even though they admired their father's commitment. Kinda, daughter of Ali, a leftist and trade union activist, had completed a master's degree in refugee rights in England after receiving her BA in journalism. She worked in Jordan for a few months as a journalist, then was hired by the British Council to co-ordinate cultural and social projects aimed particularly at young people:

> For instance, we organize debates: the youths are trained for months to express their opinions in a reasoned manner, drawing on facts and research. And then they also have to defend an opinion that is not their own [...] in order to better understand it. For example, yesterday we held a debate on the one person, one vote law [...]. It's the future. We give them a foundation on which to build creative political engagement.[29]

Kinda, who was jailed for short periods several times while she was at university, thus combines her human rights commitment with her occupation. The sector, heavily funded by international organizations, also offers real career opportunities. Kinda feels in tune with the agendas and organizational processes open to her, in particular the international standardization of these projects that aim to develop "a culture of peace and democracy":[30] "Jordan is a good testing ground, because it's small and you can see results right away [...], so projects are often tried out here and then transplanted elsewhere, Indonesia for instance." Unlike activists of the preceding generation, she is not reluctant to work with the British administration on this basis, despite her father penning vehement articles against imperialist policies. As she talks to him about a new corporate human rights project she has been approached with, her father interrupts her: "A leftwing or rightwing project?" She sighs with exasperation. To her mind, the issues are very different, and her father lives in a world of bygone divisions. At the same time, she was very dismayed that at university, community identities were emphasized to the detriment of political positions:

> At the university, communities suddenly became a central issue. Our professors and everyone else encouraged it [...]. It became very hard to take a stance against it, because all the groups emphasized it. Jordanians would say "Jordan first", Fatah would say "the Palestinian cause first", and if a Jordanian shows support for them, they'll suspect him of being an informer [...]. Now the university is the worst place to be involved in politics.

Kinda situates her commitment wholly with reference to human rights – a sphere that provides her axiological framework and that in her opinion offers an avenue for effective social action, beyond communal divisions as well as political ideologies. She does not belong to any political party. On the other hand, she was involved in the Thabahtuna student campaign. She is an example of how expertise, in her case in law, frames an activist repertoire of action, but also illustrates its elitist nature. Activist collectives based on expertise require specific skills and exclude bringing in people who might have found a role in more common activities that beginning activists engage in: distributing literature, demonstrations and so on.[31]

However, the mobilizations of 2011 and 2012 went beyond this aspect by recruiting more widely through classic activist tactics such as sit-ins and demonstrations. Beyond sector-based matters, they brought national political issues – the constitution, the regime, corruption and so on – back into the spotlight: agreements were reached regarding ad hoc actions rather than all-encompassing ideologies. Forms of activism were renewed with the use of social media, but these remain communication tools, and say nothing about the political opinions the messages convey. It is thus important to be wary of a vision of a "technophile utopia"[32] that confuses the use of these media with certain political positions: spontaneous and leaderless participatory activism, Western sympathies, pacifism and so on. Furthermore, it is once again in the street, through sit-ins, demonstrations and strikes, that pressure has been put on the regime. Until now, these youths – a large majority of them students – have initiated various gatherings and demonstrated their desire to remain independent from established political organizations. However, the various coalitions, co-ordinations and other regroupings that came about during the Jordan Spring proved shifting and ephemeral, and for the most part did not last beyond 2011 or 2012. They fragmented, split or simply vanished, the most stable of them having turned out to be Transjordanian movements. Transforming their mobilizations into formalized political groups that could influence the political scene in a lasting manner is thus a real issue. It is a pressing issue for political mobilization in Jordan, but also a broader issue of generational renewal in political activism.

The end of ideologies? Rise and decline of "grand narratives"

Today's mobilizations highlight a certain generation gap as regards metanarratives. While activist practices are handed down, comprehensive ideologies do not seem to be passed on. They no longer appear to meet any expectations, and on the contrary, all-encompassing discourses arouse distrust, giving way to temporary and specifically targeted mobilizations against such-and-such a reform or plan, or with very general watchwords such as justice or dignity that do not imply a specific interpretation of the political situation. Has activism regained its appeal through the pleasure of acting and working together toward a common cause without necessarily adhering to a long-term political view? Can mobilization do without reliance on alternative utopias? The young activist viewpoint, associating politics with dishonest compromises – or, on the contrary, utopia – and wanting to move beyond old divisions, tends to situate them in a post-ideological or even post-political era. The matter of their more or less clear involvement either in an economically liberal trend or in alter-globalist mobilizations remains an open question. The very term "youth" is in fact somewhat misleading. There is no real political unity among youths who come from a variety of social backgrounds and situations and subscribe to different political lines. Youth coalitions that wish to remain independent from political organizations only include a portion of them, mostly students or activists in advocacy groups, whereas other youths have joined Transjordanian or Islamist organizations.

When the time comes to perpetuate such movements through participation in electoral processes and/or by assuming power, it is clearly classical political organizations with comprehensive programmes that take over, even if they may have incorporated certain demands and watchwords expressed by the new mobilizations. The Muslim Brotherhood is in the front line in this case, and remains the major political force. Even though the left continues to have a strong presence, it has had trouble finding new paradigms to mobilize activism. The whole question of disenchantment affecting nationalist and leftwing activists is posed here, and rests on "the quest for a substitute ideology to take the place of nationalism, the main threads of which – modernism,

Third-Worldism, (relative) secularism – began to show signs of exhaustion in the early 1980s".[33] And that is indeed where Islamism has found its place. Beyond questions of content, it met an enduring expectation of many activists, that of providing a comprehensive worldview that gives coherence and meaning to their experience on the whole. In this regard, it is a long way from post-ideological. The failure of previous ideologies made room for an alternative metanarrative that would reinterpret history and account for political failures while placing them in a new, positive context of expectation. Islamism relies on the promotion of a glorious Arab past, a golden age that it ties in with the permeation of religious fervour. In this perspective, the return of religious considerations in politics and practices, if they in fact ever truly vanished, can only mean a great renaissance, and enable Muslims to return to the forefront, to take control of their countries and challenge internal and external dominant forces. Reference to Islam has thus indeed infused the public space and gained paradigmatic status, being used to legitimize or delegitimize existing regimes. In this regard, the Islamists have been successful, even hegemonic, having won the ability to embody the opposition. But that does not preclude debate within this sphere or great diversity in the ways of belonging to Islam. Moreover, even if Western imperialism is a target for criticism, in economic matters the Islamists do not question the liberalist trend that dominates worldwide. This, together with the shift of nationalist and leftist activism to the field of human rights, has led to the near disappearance of any political force that delivers a structured alternative discourse to economic liberalism.

The relationship of the Arab Spring mobilizations to ideology thus remains an open question. Indeed, new forms of activism claim a post-ideological posture and correspond to a disavowal of politics and existing organizations. They mobilize younger categories of activists hitherto involved in non-profit organizations, However, more long-term involvement in the power struggle with the regime is basically framed around established organizations. Furthermore, the paradigm of Islamism remains dominant. It appears that the perpetuation of the movement cannot dispense with a comprehensive, structured political vision that reaches beyond circumstantial demands. For the moment, only the Islamists are identified as being able to embody such a proposition. This gives them, almost by default, unrivalled political influence that exceeds its numbers of actual members.

CHAPTER 8

Disillusioned Islamists

Islamism has stabilized to some extent, after riding high, at least as far as Jordan's mainstream movement, the Muslim Brotherhood, is concerned. Despite the frequently announced end of political Islam, the currents have diversified, with evolutions in organizational styles and different ways of connecting Islam and politics. The various strands of Salafism have become increasingly serious rivals to the Muslim Brotherhood, especially among the younger generation. A certain post-Islamism[1] – in other words, a rejection of the political interpretation of religion as propounded by Islamist organizations – has also developed. As the following testimonials offered by Youssef, Asma and Ibrahim show, this stance is the product of reflection on what it means to Islamize society, but also, and probably most of all, real disappointment in the way the Muslim Brotherhood functions. Disillusioned Islamists are activists who have had serious disagreements with the movement, especially over the transparency of its policies. But even if they turn away from Islamism, that does not mean they question the reference to Islam. On the contrary, they are actively searching for another way of interpreting and anchoring this reference in their society.

Youssef: a post-Islamist trajectory

Youssef initially became involved in politics by joining the Muslim Brotherhood, having been a sympathizer at a very young age, as many people close to him were members.[2] In that respect, he followed the classic process described earlier in this book of joining the most readily available movement. This process relies on mentors and local hegemony – a phenomenon characteristic of all political movements. Youssef, who was born in 1969, was a serious pupil who liked to learn and rounded out his education from the age of thirteen by attending Quranic school at the mosque. His parents, small-scale farmers in a village in northern Jordan, were very religious and were determined for him to receive religious instruction. Religion also occupied an important place among his group of friends. They conducted their daily prayers, went to the mosque frequently and discussed their religion classes at length. For Youssef, religion was one subject among others to be mastered, and he was determined to excel in the field. During that period he did not make any connection with politics, but religious teaching at this mosque was dispensed by the Muslim Brotherhood. In addition, his older brother, a physician, was also a member of the movement and had climbed the ranks. Graduating at the top of his class with the baccalaureate, Youssef was granted a scholarship to study a prestigious scientific discipline. But he chose not to follow that path, thus marking the first detour in his trajectory. After one semester of physics, he enrolled in Arab literature and developed a passion for poetry. His parents did not learn of his change of course until two years later. It coincided with his political commitment, but cannot be entirely ascribed to the Muslim Brotherhood, which equally values engineering professions. This academic reorientation, however, was part of an identity quest and a desire to deepen his Arab and Muslim culture.

His arrival at Yarmouk University in Irbid in 1987 had coincided with a politically critical moment for the university, following a number of strikes and demonstrations that had been harshly crushed:[3] "Silence and anticipation reigned at the university, [...] the situation was unbearable, [...] the university was broken, unstable. Everyone was waiting in fear." Youssef thus arrived at a university that he described as broken, but where discontent continued to simmer. Communists and leftist movements took the lead. However, Youssef's activist socialization had occurred prior to then, and he remained within the sphere of influence of the Muslim Brotherhood. He nevertheless refused to join the movement officially, preferring to remain a sympathizer, to maintain his independence. The first step he took was to become actively involved in the attempt to create a nationwide Jordanian student union. In 1991 Youssef ran for office in his faculty as an independent Islamist affiliated with the Islamic alliance, and won easily. He became a Yarmouk representative on the preparatory committee for the national student union that met regularly in Amman at the union headquarters. But the attempt was entirely blocked by the Jordanian prime minister in 1992, and failed. Most students involved in the initiative finished their studies and scattered.

From the moment he entered university, his political commitment became more time-consuming, causing him to fall behind in his studies. In 1992 he gained his bachelor's degree in Arabic. Despite his activism, he then landed a teaching position in the public school system. As a sympathizer of the Muslim Brotherhood, which had ministers in the government at that time and was considered an ally of the monarchy, he was not barred from a state job, unlike the communist activists. Despite the failure of the student union initiative, his success in the student elections gave him an important role and stepped up pressure from Islamists for him to join their ranks officially when the party was created in the wake of the democratic opening and the lifting of the ban on political parties. Youssef abandoned being a mere sympathizer and took out membership in 1993. This represented a strengthening of his commitment.

Despite his parents' opinion, worried about government crackdowns, Youssef followed in his brother's footsteps by joining the Islamic Action Front. He felt the political situation had changed and that it was possible to engage in structured political activity. However, the IAF's methods of action were not enough for him. His politicization at Yarmouk University had not only concerned the issue of students' rights and their status. In this university, which had a large Palestinian student body, the first Palestinian Intifada (1987-1993) was followed with intense excitement. Numerous debates and demonstrations of support were held. Support for the Palestinian cause was also a major theme for the Muslim Brotherhood, making it a mainspring of their establishment in Jordan. But its position was more ambivalent, because beyond support for the Palestinian cause, increased fundraising drives and impassioned speeches, it was anxious to preserve its relations with the monarchy and was not opposed to its bargaining positions. This issue was a bone of contention within the movement, with the exacerbation of distinctions between "Transjordanians" and "Jordanian Palestinians" as of the 1970s. Within the Islamist movement there was consensus about the Palestinian cause in the Occupied Territories but tension regarding Jordanian domestic policy: Palestinian nationalism was accused of monopolizing the political issue to the detriment of domestic Jordanian issues, and Palestinian groups were accused of trying to take control of Jordanian politics.

Youssef took a stand within this context. He was particularly disappointed by the outcome of the Oslo Accords of 1993 - the lack of land granted to the Palestinians - and especially Jordan's position on this issue:

After 1994 the government had a position: Palestine for the Palestinians, and Jordan for the Jordanians. We didn't agree with that. We wanted to say no, we were from east of the Jordan River, [Trans]jordanians, and we still wanted to stand up for Palestine [...]. Doing something for Palestine meant that the Jordanians didn't abandon Palestine.

Shrouded in the utmost secrecy, with three Jordanian friends from the university – a graduate student working on his master's like himself, an engineer and a computer scientist – he began to prepare an operation against an Israeli military base on the banks of the Jordan in 1995. Over the course of a year they slowly obtained weapons and explosives and honed their plan. But in 1996 the Jordanian secret services got wind of their project and they were arrested. They were questioned for a month and a half. The intelligence services wanted to know most of all whether the operation had ties with the Islamic Action Front and the Muslim Brotherhood. Both organizations immediately and publicly disavowed the group, and Youssef and his friends insisted that the plan was entirely their own initiative. The profile of the group's members particularly bothered the Jordanian authorities: they were Transjordanians from major tribes and held advanced degrees. In the minds of their interrogators, they should have formed the core of the monarchy's support. The group's political activities seemed all the more subversive because the fact that they were Transjordanian was supposed to induce them naturally to support the monarchy, unlike the Palestinians. This consideration was reflected in a targeted crackdown on Transjordanian communists, as illustrated by the trajectory of Ahmed A. described earlier. In Youssef's case, due to his membership in the Muslim Brotherhood, considered something of an ally of the monarchy, the questioning was not as tough as it would have been if he had belonged to the Communist Party, and his tribal origins protected him to some extent. At first sentenced to death, the punishment was later commuted to life imprisonment due to his clean police record and the mere preparatory nature of his actions.

In prison

Rather than discussing prison conditions, Youssef preferred to talk about the experience of political exchange and debate that his period of imprisonment offered him. Baathists, communists and jihadis all mix there. Discussions and political readings are intense. This is indeed characteristic of political internments that prisoners, when not in solitary confinement, try to transform into opportunities for political education. In Syrian, Jordanian and Israeli prisons, political prisoners withstand incarceration by establishing strict group schedules that allow considerable space for the transmission of knowledge among activists. Without eliminating the differences among the various persuasions, the creation of a collective space can end up producing a common "prisoner" identity that fosters contacts among activists. This proved to be the case for Youssef and his three associates, who thus came into contact with nationalists, leftwing activists and other independent Islamists. On the other hand, relations with certain jihadi Islamists quickly became tense. Youssef distinguishes between two groups in prison, the "Jordanian Afghans" and Zarqawi's group:

> The Jordanian Afghans blew up cinemas in 1994, [...] poor, simple people without much education. Among them there were three or four who had just returned from Afghanistan, so we called them Jordanian Afghans. But most of them didn't know Afghanistan and had never set foot there [...]. They believed that the movies corrupted morals, so they blew up two movie theatres, one in al Zarqa and the other in Amman, and they were of course arrested and thrown in prison, about twenty of them.

But it was not this group, which had a fairly unstructured ideology, that Youssef clashed with, but with the one led by Abu Musab al-Zarqawi (and Abu Muhammad al-Maqdisi):[4]

> They represented that idea that Arab regimes were apostate regimes [...] according to a verse of the Quran, "And whoever does not judge by what Allah has revealed – then it is those who are the disbelievers."[5] They interpret this verse as follows: anyone who does not govern constitutionally according to what "Allah revealed" is an apostate, so they excommunicate regimes, the police, the army and so on [...]. We weren't like that, we fought for a national cause and a Muslim cause.

Here again is evidence of the usual opposition – and competition – between Islamo-nationalism and Jihadi Salafism, a division that runs throughout the Arab world, even if Islamo-nationalist, Sunni and Shi'a movements are the majority (such as Hamas in Palestine or Hezbollah in Lebanon). The Muslim Brotherhood in Jordan is affiliated with the Islamo-nationalists, and Abu Musab al-Zarqawi with the Salafi current. The main difference lies in the deterritorialization of the Jihadi Salafis, who do not defend a specific national cause, but rather an all-out struggle against the enemies of Islam, Western regimes as well as apostates and heretics among Muslims themselves. In this context, areas of conflict such as Israel/Palestine, Chechnya/Russia, Iraq and so on all become de facto proof of this systematic aggression against Muslims. But to Youssef, the difference resides mainly in the relationship to Arab regimes. Dissatisfied with the Muslim Brotherhood's ambivalent position toward the Jordanian monarchy, some activists have found in Jihadi Salafism a means of opposing the regime head-on that justifies the use of violence against regimes considered to be illegitimate (a position that differs from reformist Salafism, which also exists in Jordan, but does not legitimize the use of violence). Youssef is thus at odds with both versions of Salafism. He is intent on sparing the king's person and on making a clear distinction between the policy of the government – regarded as corrupt – and the king (although is important to make allowances for self-censorship in the interview regarding this point). Moreover, he was looking for a "contemporary and modern version of Islam" that he didn't really find in the Muslim Brotherhood, and even less in Salafism.

From activist to political columnist

Youssef was finally released in 1999 during the blanket amnesty that followed the death of King Hussein and Abdullah II's rise to the throne. As soon as he was released from prison, Youssef was able to return to the university and resume his studies, continuing to major in Arabic, which for him was closely linked to his identitarian and political views. He was awarded his PhD in Arabic in 2007. To pay for his education, he went back to teaching in public school, which was allowed by the amnesty (unlike communists, who were banned from the public sector upon release from prison). However, drawn by a higher salary and the prospect of returning to the capital, he soon went over to the private sector, and upon finishing his PhD he was recruited by one of the private universities that had been cropping up in Jordan – less prestigious, but better paying than the state universities.

From a professional standpoint, his stint in prison merely delayed his career without really hampering it. But politically, it turned out to be decisive for his ideological development and his career as an activist. Indeed, he formed a network there that brought together all political persuasions – Islamists, nationalists and the Arab left – which would have been impossible in any other context but prison. This exposure induced a personal evolution, crystallizing lingering doubts he had with regard to the Muslim Brotherhood's view of Islamism, nevertheless without leading him to reject his Muslim heritage. His questioning of Muslim Brotherhood policies now went beyond the Palestinian question, and armed action was no longer an option for him. He was in conflict with not only the Muslim Brotherhood, but also the Salafis, whose ideas he was now very familiar with. What he was seeking was a true renewal of Islamic thought: "Islamic thought is progressive, and needs new tools and methods for its development." His stint in prison gave him legitimacy and relationship skills, and he quickly began publishing articles on these themes, becoming a political columnist specializing in Islamic thought and movements. His time with the Muslim Brotherhood, in which his elder brother still holds a senior position, and especially the time he spent in prison, enable him to combine firsthand knowledge of the inner workings of Islamist movements with the position of outside observer. Like others who become critical of these movements after having been closely involved in them – aside from the social and personal difficulties this distance involves – he has been able to capitalize on this specific position by becoming a sought-after commentator in Jordan as well as internationally.

After prison, Youssef thus ceased his career as activist to engage in a more intellectual commitment and media involvement, working toward an "Islam that embraces a new thought, an enlightened philosophy in tune with our times. Islam has been around for 1,400 years; we can't apply third-century Islam. In our day, there are new interpretations, many new proofs, so Islam should embrace this new thought." He is critical of the type of backward-looking political Islam deployed in Jordan, contrasting it with a critical and historicized religious interpretation rooted in today's world. He draws on scholarly references throughout the Muslim world, and relates to a tradition of interpreting Islam that continually comments on sacred texts and examines them in the light of contemporary issues.

His commitment no longer takes the form of involvement in a party or any other sort of organization. Approached just after his release from prison, he refused to take part in the elections. This distancing is partly explained by the lack of any party representing his conception of a new Islamic reference – in fact, he is much more specific about what he rejects than what he proposes – and by total skepticism about the Jordanian political system, even though he carefully avoids naming the king. Youssef intervenes in the Jordanian public space as an intellectual critic. But his position also indicates the lack of room for a new political and Islamic current in this space, due to the majority held by the Muslim Brotherhood and the locked political system. The careers of other former Muslim Brotherhood activists who share a similar critical political line, but who more or less successfully attempt to work within organizational structures, illustrate this same difficulty.

Asma: politics through satire and reform through education

Asma did not really leave the Muslim Brotherhood of her own free will.[6] In fact, she was expelled. She says her outspokenness and independence made her undesirable to the organization, although she deeply subscribed to its political vision and stills claims affinity with its line of thought, or at least a Muslim curriculum that embraces all aspects of life, public as well as private.

Asma had joined the women's branch of the Muslim Brotherhood after entering university to study English literature and Muslim law. She is from a family of Palestinian refugees living in Jordan since 1948. They are devout Muslims, but not activists. Her father, who holds a PhD from Columbia University, was a teacher before becoming a senior official in the Ministry of Education. Asma, born in 1970, says her life has always been steeped in a political atmosphere associated with the Palestinian situation: "Politics is in the air we breathe!" She was deeply shocked by the massacre in the Sabra and Shatila Palestinian refugee camps in Lebanon in 1982, and was affected by the start of the first Intifada in 1987. She has read the works by Hassan al-Banna, founder of the Muslim Brotherhood in Egypt, and other writings about the repression of the Muslim Brotherhood in Egypt. Like many future activists, she was driven by a sense of injustice, not only the general injustice regarding the treatment of Palestinians, but also regarding her experiences in education. At the university she became involved in the most readily available movement to her, the Islamist movement, to combat injustice and because she found there a way of life and a comprehensive approach:

> What I found particularly interesting with Hassan al-Banna was his refusal to confine himself to a single aspect of religion [...]. To him, Islam was not limited to social welfare organizations. You have to work on all aspects – politics, charity, sports as well – because you have to have a healthy body. Islam is a global approach.

Like many activists of that generation and the preceding one, there is evidence of a search for comprehensive ideologies that offer a worldview and an ethic. For Asma, it goes together with a repertoire of action that primarily involves taking a stance in public debates by writing articles. More than the activities offered by the Muslim Sisterhood, what she was interested in was publishing, mainly about the Muslim religion and its modern interpretation, first in the student newspaper, and later in publications by the Muslim Brotherhood. She was thus able to combine a political commitment, a deepened identity quest into Arab and Muslim culture and her pleasure in writing. The Islamist themes of authenticity and integrity served as a particularly important moral and identity base on which to challenge the treatment of Palestinians, but also inequality and repression in Jordan. Thus she did not compromise in her public stances, which she believed should reflect these aspects that give her cause all its meaning. She points out that already when in school she had refused to read a poem on the occasion of the national holiday that was too slavishly devoted to the king; she wanted to talk about the people in general. Drawing on these aspects, she thus views the Muslim Brotherhood as an open and transparent organization that does not indulge in doublespeak, unlike other organizations, which she says are influenced by foreign agendas (she is referring to the communists in particular).

It is precisely on this point that she would soon become disillusioned, for she joined the movement just after 1987 and the student revolts at Yarmouk University:

> Everyone said we should keep quiet, but I wanted to talk! [...] Everyone was afraid, [...] there was a general atmosphere of obedience [...] the Muslim Brotherhood was also put down, not jailed like the others, but it ran into trouble. I personally know people who lost their jobs [...]. You had to have a "good behaviour certificate" from the intelligence services to work, and everyone was afraid of not getting one.

In this context, the Muslim Brotherhood tried to regain control over its base, and added internal hierarchical pressure to the intimidation of the intelligence services. The Islamist movement adopted a low profile and closely monitored the public stances taken by its members. Asma wound up being expelled from the movement for challenging the leadership and not abiding by orders for political discretion:

> One of the things they held against me was that if I ran into a Brother and he was with someone who wasn't part of the Muslim Brotherhood, I'd talk to him the same way as if I was in the presence only of Muslim Brothers. There was no hidden agenda, so why not talk about it? I wanted to talk. Even the government had to know this, that there was no hidden agenda.

More than ideological issues, it was thus the organization's functioning and ambivalent political stances that put her in a difficult position. She stresses the fact that she has kept up with certain contacts and that she still considers herself a participant in this political strand, but she rejects the way the Muslim Brotherhood in Jordan puts it into practice. She also disagrees with the movement in terms of the application of its own principles, which she believes lacks transparency. This is because in her mind the Muslim Brotherhood had advocated a "renewal of the Muslim way of life", and she wishes to continue in this direction, and even beyond. She is thus against any form of backward-looking nostalgia about a so-called Arab and Muslim golden age:

> I disagree with that nostalgia of the past. We're not at the top because it's not our turn to be at the top, but that's not a reason to be all the way at the bottom. Europe used to be a leader, and now it's the United States, but that doesn't mean Europe's all the way at the bottom. That's what we have to aim for, to stop being nostalgic and find a new role.

Thus, despite her expulsion from the Muslim Brotherhood, she wants to deepen her understanding and her thinking along these lines, combining a strong sense of Muslim identity and culture with a contemporary application. However, she was turned down for the doctoral programme in Islamic studies, since she at first chose Muslim law only as a minor.

Asma had difficulty choosing a curriculum, and gender issues played a role in this regard: at first tempted by studies in engineering, she was told that it would require considerable travel, which was rather incompatible with her status as a woman. She was urged by her father to study medicine, but she lacked faith in her abilities and considered that it would involve too much responsibility toward patients if she did not get perfect grades. She thus enrolled in pharmaceutical studies, but did not feel comfortable there, so switched to English literature and Muslim law. Having been turned down for a PhD, she went into education and teaching, while continuing to write her columns and also taking the initiative to take collections to support the families of Islamist militants in Gaza. Yet, after her marriage and the birth of her four children, she gave up all her professional, social and political activities and followed her husband when he went to work in Dubai.

On her return nine years later, she fully intended to resume these activities and combine political commitment and a professional occupation. And indeed, now with a master's degree in education, it is through education that she hopes to reform Jordanian society. She set out in search of funding to open a private primary school that would reflect her ideals. Asma does not put forward a specifically women's commitment and does not speak about the role assigned to women, unlike Islamist activists in professional associations,[7] but her trajectory mirrors the standard gender divisions that assign children's education to women. In the curriculum she wants to implement, she stresses in a rather ambivalent manner an education "in which the point is not to train parrots who repeat things" and at the same time "learning by heart the Quran, poetry and everything that gives us a strong identity: historic dates, wars and so on." Asma is appalled by what she describes as the new generation's identity vacuum and its depoliticization, and it is at this level that she wants to act, even if she remains fairly pessimistic about the Jordanian system: "It's as if political disappointment and discouragement formed a big black cloud, the economic situation a muddy terrain, and that the flowers of education cannot bloom and experience a very short-lived springtime," she points out figuratively.

She does not wish to remain silent about what she calls "the stupidity of our system" and the deterioration of the economic and political situation. In addition to working in education, she has once again chosen the role of political columnist to voice her criticism. In her column she uses humour and even sarcasm to point out routine absurdities and get her ideas across while distilling a critical viewpoint on subjects ranging from foreign policy to the division of tasks in married couples, or cumbersome bureaucracy. This approach does not draw a distinction between "small" private and family issues and "major" national and international questions: she broaches them by dissecting everyday experiences rather than by making broad political analyses. In that regard, she also engages in a method of commitment that at once illustrates and pushes back gender limits. The modesty of her starting point and her micro-analyses enable her to publish alongside primarily male counterparts without seeming to compete with them or questioning what she herself claims: "men are the ones who have the real political power". Furthermore, she also revalues the private sphere in which women are supposed to operate by demonstrating the social and political issues that are found there.

For Asma, political and social reform can only occur through a commitment such as her own that blends an ability to question things and to voice one's opinion with a strong sense of identity based on thorough knowledge of religion and culture. These activists disenchanted with the Muslim Brotherhood draw on references to a religious and cultural heritage to define a political stance, the content of which, however, is not necessarily very clear. They know what they are against – political authoritarianism and violent repression, foreign domination and imperialism, dishonest compromises and hierarchy in political organizations – and as an antidote invoke a resolutely modern version of Islam. But beyond this, the way it might translate concretely in terms of an organization and a programme remains rather vague. The perspectives are limited by the closed nature of the Jordanian political system and its peripheral status with regard to post-Islamist currents in other Arab countries. The difficulty these critical activists have in finding an appropriate political or organizational structure after moving away from the Muslim Brotherhood is also illustrated by the route taken by Ibrahim, who finally sought answers to his quest in leftist associations and forums.

Ibrahim: from Islamism to the left

Ibrahim[8] joined the Muslim Brotherhood at the age of fifteen through the youth activities offered by its boy scout group. His very devout father is a village sheikh. And like Youssef, Ibrahim has an older brother who became an important cadre in the Muslim Brotherhood. This is another case of an activist signing up for the movement closest at hand, and Ibrahim emphasizes the sociability he found in the movement more than his political positions. However, in 1978 he was particularly influenced by the atmosphere of "Islamic awakening", as he describes it, that focused on the mujahideen's fight in Afghanistan, which was the topic of many articles and speeches. In this context, his meeting with Abdullah Azzam, a Muslim Brotherhood leader at the time, and professor at the University of Jordan, proved to be decisive. Azzam described the feats of the Afghan mujahideen in vivid speeches and insisted that support for them was the duty of all Muslims. Having been expelled from the university of Jordan in 1980, Azzam resumed teaching in Saudi Arabia, where Ibrahim followed him and became a student of journalism. Abdullah Azzam played the role of mentor in terms of Ibrahim's journey to Afghanistan, but Ibrahim's commitment took shape with respect to his studies and areas of interest. He was hired as a researcher in a centre for political and Islamic studies in Islamabad because the head of the Arabic department of this institute was a leader in the Muslim Brotherhood. Ibrahim moreover divides the "Afghan Arabs" into two categories:

> The first group included qualified academics who worked in aid and development institutions set up to help Afghan immigrants and mujahideen. Most of them belonged to the Muslim Brotherhood [...]. The second group included young people who had come to take part in jihad and fight alongside the Afghans. They were young, they hadn't finished their education, had no ties with the Muslim Brotherhood, and their religiosity was recent.[9]

This distinction moreover matches the distinction in economic and social profiles between recruitment into the Muslim Brotherhood and the Salafi movement in Jordan.

This is where Ibrahim started to become disillusioned. He was appalled by the conditions in which young Arabs signed up to fight in Afghanistan, without any preparation or training, in total ignorance of the local political context: "Most of the volunteers had no idea what to do at the front. Exhausted by hunger and fear, they came back after a few days of combat where they had no business and that the Afghans could have avoided." While he was more positive about the social, cultural and humanitarian initiatives set up, he also deplored the media coverage of the young Arabs' involvement, the confusion between these actions and armed struggle, and the numerous arrests and trials upon their return (to Jordan as well as elsewhere):

> These youths, who worked in various areas of development in difficult conditions, would have been prepared to play a role in their own country if they had been allowed to, rather than being the object of suspicion and forced into being enemies of their government and their country.

After this experience in Afghanistan, marked by disillusionment with jihadi action and Islamist speeches of support, Ibrahim secured a teaching position in the Gulf in 1990, which he lost in 1991 in the wake of the Gulf crisis. He returned to Jordan, still a member of the Muslim Brotherhood despite his Afghan experience. He then became further disillusioned due to the trouble he had sharing his Afghan experiences and the questioning it triggered in him. He felt isolated. The Muslim Brothers who remained in Jordan did not understand his experiences, and those who returned from Afghanistan and who were not in Salafi groups adopted a low profile and tended to withdraw from their political commitment, caught between fears of government retaliation and disillusionment with the Muslim Brotherhood itself.

But it was precisely his status as a relative outsider, after countless internal battles and incidences of rivalry among favourites, that led to his enlistment as editor-in-chief of the Islamist movement's first monthly publication. However, upon taking on the job, all the ideological and structural contradictions which he perceived with respect to the movement became clear. Ibrahim was one of those younger Brothers who were ill at ease with the movement's hierarchical structure and its government deals, unlike the elder Brothers who had climbed the ranks. Ibrahim challenged the actions of movement leaders, and more generally their participation in government and parliamentary activity. One of his articles, pointing out the irony of the discrepancy between pressing geopolitical issues and the anecdotal nature of the agenda of the Jordanian parliament (presided over at the time by a Muslim Brotherhood member), sparked off a new crisis. A lawsuit was initiated against him, and he left the magazine's editorial board. He had trouble surmounting the many attacks directed at him and the ensuing setbacks, and so took refuge in the "safer" sector of children's literature, away from politics. Yet fairly quickly he found a new space in the Islamist press and continued to publish articles about Islamist movements. It was another article, in this case dealing with relations between the Jordanian Muslim Brotherhood, Hamas and the government, that triggered new proceedings, this time within the Muslim Brotherhood, which resulted in his being banned from the organization. Ibrahim drew from this the conclusion that the problem does not lie in debate on points of doctrine within the movement or that he dared question the advocacy of an Islamic state, but rather in dealing with the organization's governance and leadership. According to him, there are two subjects that are off limits: relations with Hamas, and corruption and clientelism in the movement's charity work. Regarding the issue of Hamas, Ibrahim finds the same division within the Jordanian Muslim Brotherhood regarding the place of the Palestinian question in Jordan in its political agenda – a division that coincides with differences between Jordanian Palestinians and Transjordanians. Even if these identities and their "ethnological" bases are artificial, the political division is now a reality, although the Muslim Brotherhood officially denies it. The issue is not support for the Palestinian national struggle, about which there is consensus, but the political role of Palestinians in Jordan, which explains the particular sensitivity about the question of Hamas's influence on the Jordanian Muslim Brotherhood. The issue is all the more sensitive because the Jordanian regime regularly uses discoveries of armed Hamas cells as an excuse to suppress the Islamists. In this regard, unlike Youssef, Ibrahim, a Transjordanian, finds himself, like his older brother, siding with the faction that maintains a distance from Palestinian groups. On the other hand, at the same time, and like Youssef, he criticizes the government's influence over the Muslim Brotherhood and its publications, as well as its doublespeak in this regard: "There was no place for me in a press organ that decides whether to publish or not following a phone call from a high government official, whether I was writing about coffee, the Sahara or His Majesty the King's birthday."

Thus, in these three portraits it was internal dissent regarding the organization's governance that proved to be decisive. Asma and Ibrahim began to express their disagreement openly and expose duplicity within their organization, even if they increasingly had trouble tolerating the recriminations directed at them and from which they personally suffered. It was finally the Muslim Brotherhood that banned them, as its way of dealing with dissent within the organization.

The shift to the left

The ending of his membership of the Muslim Brotherhood nevertheless did not cost Ibrahim his job as columnist in the press. On the contrary, like Youssef, he was also able to negotiate a role as an expert in the Islamist movement nationally and internationally, while taking into account the limits of the public space in Jordan.

From a doctrinal standpoint, already while part of the Islamist movement, and especially since his experience in Afghanistan, Ibrahim had been questioning the wisdom of promoting an Islamic state, finding the principles behind it too vague. After he was expelled, his reservations grew stronger. Ibrahim remains a devout Muslim, but he had difficulty with the link the Islamists make between religion and politics, and particularly their justification of certain policies on religious bases. In his mind, Islam upholds certain fundamental values, but the way in which these values are put into practice remains historically grounded:

> Should we say that Islam should not be mixed up with politics? Yes and no. There's no yes-or-no answer to these questions. Islam gives general ideas – justice, freedom, equality, sovereignty – a set of general principles shared by humanity as a whole. So there is no religious state in the religious sense of the term. There are general principles in Islam that guide the state and that serve as references for the state and for governments [...]. The Islamist movement needs to change into a movement somewhat like the Christian Democratic Party or the British or American conservatives. Islamism doesn't have a plan for women's issues, the environment, civil liberties, social justice and economic development. The interpretations it offers are not specific to Islam. Islamists demand elections, reform and a constitution. That is no different from the demands of communists, liberals or other groups. They are contained in Ali Abderraziq's[10] and Khatami's[11] projects [...]. No one can say that these are specifically Islamic aspirations.

Like Asma and Youssef, Ibrahim advocates a resolutely contemporary form of politicization that places Arab political movements within international currents, rather than excluding them by constantly appealing to a glorious past and principles that he considers not to be specifically based in Islam, and at best outmoded. In terms of doctrine, he bases his argument on contemporary Muslim thinkers abroad whose writings and positions he knows well. But in Jordan itself he has few political options left outside mainstream Islamism represented by the Muslim Brotherhood: he rules out the Salafis due to his experience in Afghanistan. In the end, he connected with an anti-globalization association primarily made up of leftwing activists that wanted to join up with the alter-globalist movement. He followed them when the association changed into a leftist forum and expressed stances on Jordanian politics and was fairly involved in the international space. He was also drawn by their Marxist references, the scope of its intellectual framework, and now makes use of Marx's *Capital* to renew his criticism of the Muslim Brotherhood.

It should be pointed out, however, that the forum itself has only Transjordanian members; for a time it included a champion of a variety of Jordanian nationalism that criticized Palestinian influence in Jordan. Ibrahim was not attracted to the forum due to this theme, but the social links that led him there are related to Transjordanian identity. Once again, Ibrahim belonged without belonging, emphasizing his separate status, the rhetoric that amounts to nothing and the lack of a base among younger generations. He supports the political expertise and the advocacy of specific programmes, but regrets the lack of a social foothold. He finds himself at the heart of the dilemmas of political opposition in Jordan, where no political group has managed to form a real political alternative to Islamist movements.

Disillusioned Islamists thus differ from activists that have moved away from the nationalist or leftist currents in that they have deserted a movement that remains dominant and the only one to have a broad social base. In fact, this largely explains why these activists first sought to reform and reorient the movement from within before ultimately being banned. Disappointment in Islamism in this case means first and foremost disappointment in the way the main political organizations representing this current operate internally. In Jordan, this has to do not only with relations with the regime and the Islamist movement's status of co-opted opposition, but also the gap between official positions and the movement's internal strategy. It is thus a matter more of disappointment regarding its realpolitik than a doctrinal disillusion, even if Asma, Ibrahim and Youssef have at the same time pondered the way the reference to Islam should be interpreted politically. Despite being banned or having distanced themselves from the political organization, the reference remains central for them. Like activists from other political persuasions who have diverged or broken away from a movement, they never mention ideological changes of heart. Such a move would be interpreted as personal betrayal, a profound questioning of what had once been their worldview, whatever their itinerary in the political organization. Even Ibrahim, who goes the furthest in this direction, insists politically on the notion of social justice that he finds in both Islamism and the left, as do sympathizers that take the opposite route, from the left to Islamism. And it is in the name of a greater respect for religious values that he wishes to dissociate these from the use political groups make of them, political parties being in his mind too socially and historically situated for their interpretation not to be an oversimplification. In this regard, Islamist organizations are called into question for their way of functioning and their political positions in the very name of the basic principles of Islamism. It is not the principles themselves that are called into question – this almost never occurs in these activist careers. On the contrary, principles serve as the activists' guiding theme, lending their trajectory meaning and coherence, whatever direction their party commitments may take.

Conclusion

In the face of an authoritarian regime, the opportunity to carry on political battles becomes a challenge in itself when the regime seeks to eliminate all forms of politicization. The constitution of political arenas is an objective in itself, even before the matter of the content and goals of protest. The case of Jordan illustrates the possibility of dissociating democratic institutions from political arenas, and the hybrid and ambivalent nature of liberal authoritarianism, which does not rule out the existence of democratic institutions, but depletes them of meaning. That does not mean, however, that such institutions as elections and parliament have no role, but simply that they do not serve to produce a changeover in power or to define public policies in Jordan. They are used by the regime to create co-opted elites and set up frameworks of patronage and clientelism. They are not loci in which political opposition can be forged or expressed. The whole challenge for activists is thus to find or shape other arenas of political opposition, relying on movements or organizations that have sufficient resources to afford a certain political space from which to confront the regime. Thus professional associations, for instance, which constitute an elite that is well integrated into the regime's structure and which play a major role in the country's economy, have partly been able to serve as a base for political protest. The Muslim Brotherhood social movement, with its unique charity network, whose social services partly replace those of the state, has also managed to form a network out of which political challenges and counter-ideologies have emerged.

Advocacy NGOs – a sector to which former leftist activists have massively turned – can rely on international visibility and funds, despite the fact that they do not have a strong social base in Jordan. However, these alternative arenas have their own structural constraints that restrict the type of activism that can develop there. Their field of action can be limited by various forms of repression: direct pressure on activists, restrictive legislation, or entryism and falsification of internal elections. But their structural limits are also associated with the economic and social functions of these arenas. Professional associations, being reserved for the licensed professions, are by nature elitist, and as professional bodies, they preclude class-based activism. While they wield professional skills that are crucial to Jordan's economy, they also hesitate to jeopardize their role as elites by engaging in an overly frontal opposition to the regime. The Muslim Brotherhood, on the other hand, enjoys a social hegemony that it does not necessarily seek to convert into direct political power, which can be more uncertain. Its unique situation shows that a certain form of hegemony can develop outside the spheres of power – for the Muslim Brotherhood is indeed Jordan's primary producer of ideology, despite not having political power or even a monopoly over the opposition.

For NGOs, their methods of action do not easily lend themselves to mass activism; they are also elitist, focused on a brand of expert and pro-reform activism. Often reliant on the agendas of major donors, they can be perceived as externalized elites. When these alternative opposition arenas become too integrated and no longer offer a space in which strong opposition can be expressed, a phenomenon of activist radicalization can be observed, as shown by the case of Jihadi Salafis who challenge the positions of the Muslim Brotherhood in Jordan.

These structural limits lead the Jordanian opposition to occupy shifting and ambivalent positions that waver between the position of challenger and a co-opted force. The arenas of politicization and mobilization are changing. Authoritarianism is not a smooth process, and on the contrary relies on a constant trade-off between repression and co-optation, on a convergence of multiple processes that can make up for one another when one fails. The evolution of authoritarian processes in Jordan, from Hussein to Abdullah II, toward a brand of authoritarian liberalism that combines a democratic façade and economic liberalism is an example of this. At the same time, new arenas can emerge, as shown by the conversion of leftwing activists to causes represented by NGOs, but also more recently the fact that tribal networks, long considered pillars of the regime, sustain protest.

Activist careers illustrate these questions and illustrate the specific difficulties the opposition faces with respect to the ambivalences of liberal authoritarianism. Depending on the period in history as well as the connections between periods and their intrinsic temporality, activists tend to get involved in certain arenas. For these activists, secondary school and university were thus essential loci of politicization. Their youth in the 1960s and 1970s was a period of intense politicization in universities. On the other hand, coming out of university, opportunities for activism became a serious issue. They were made vulnerable paradoxically by a so-called political liberalization in the early 1990s that authorized political parties while preventing them from acting. Although activism turned to alternative arenas such as professional associations and later NGOs, the emergence from underground proved to be a period of serious destabilization for nationalist and leftist activism. Whatever the alternative strategies either of these groups may have chosen, they never recovered the influence they had once enjoyed. Even if they remained politically visible by being involved in international structures and networks, this did not improve their influence on a national level. Leftwing activists were the first to ponder this situation repeatedly since what they consider to be an Islamist takeover of the Arab Springs, despite the significant role the left played in these movements. The field of opposition has split into two poles: the leftist human rights strand and, opposite it, the Islamists. Why does the Arab left constantly have such difficulty securing social support no matter what recognition it enjoys for its involvement in local and sector-wide struggles? What is the origin of the hegemonic syntax the Islamists enjoy? The Arab left has had trouble producing new paradigms that are not immediately identified as being rooted in Western dominance, despite its anti-imperialist political positions. Not only has the failure of Soviet communism and Pan-Arab nationalism left a large part of the Arab left without its core references, but the adoption of socialism by Arab authoritarian regimes has disqualified another segment of it. The left is thus currently caught between galvanizing but very general watchwords, such as the call for dignity, and specific mobilizations where it has real impact, without that enabling it to gain recognition for a promising alternative political project. References to human rights and democracy cannot play this role. These ideals are not specifically associated with the left, as the Islamists recast them with religious meaning. Moreover, these recognized values do not suffice to define a political project, and many opponents refuse to be identified and defended merely as victims of human rights violations, which in their view amounts to depoliticizing their struggle and ignoring their political vision. The difficulty of promoting truly alternative paradigms is not specific to the left in the Arab world, but it is heightened in the region by the issue of Western imperialist domination. At an ideological level, the issue is indeed one of developing a post-colonial approach that is not merely a reversal of orientalism – a particularly difficult exercise in this context. Indeed, drawing on an ahistoric Arab and Muslim identity to offset various political and ideological failures produces what the critic Sadik Jalal al 'Azm calls "reverse orientalism",[1] a tendency characteristic of the Islamists. It contributes to reifying and dehistoricizing the Middle East and the Arabs, as does orientalism, but in this case enhancing it. Debates then revolve around the usual oppositions: authenticity and contemporaneousness, heritage and renewal, secularity and religion. Getting beyond the classic binary oppositions of orientalism or reverse orientalism to devise post-colonial paradigms is a difficult undertaking. The left, when it defines itself as "progressive" for instance, thus does not escape the oppositions between modernity versus tradition and rationality versus irrationality related to the reification of differences between East and West, making it all the more difficult for the left to dissociate itself from Western imperialism. Islamism does not challenge this framework, but simply overturns it by making positive references to the Orient, which enables it to claim authenticity based on this religious and cultural base.

The Arab Springs of 2011 did not fundamentally change the situation on this level, even if they revived activism to some extent. The initial mobilizations indeed combined new actors and a new repertoire of action with renewed inspiration and revived regional circulation. In Jordan, identification and regional solidarity shifted the lines of the power struggle with the regime even without there being any basic change at the national level. Prior to the Arab Springs, sector-based mobilizations, strikes and sit-ins had proliferated throughout the country. These mobilizations served as a breeding ground for a more fundamental challenge to the regime, partly drawing on processes of regional identification that revived the issue of Arab identities, and partly on general watchwords – dignity, freedom and so on – that resonate well beyond mobilizations in the Arab world. And even if the political projects driven by these movements remain vague, the watchwords suggest a vision of emancipation that encourages identification on a global scale. Thus the description of these movements is infused with a vocabulary of emotion that arouses strong empathy. Political emotions are predominant. A re-enchantment with politics has occurred that no longer hinges on a metanarrative promising bright days ahead, but on the action itself, in a dramatized gesture with symbols that circulate worldwide. This is true for the activists taking part, but also beyond them. Political activism in this case has connected local and national struggles with regional references and a projection worldwide, thereby multiplying its impact tenfold.

The use of social media did not radically alter the content of activism, but it fostered horizontal mobilizations that have challenged the usual hierarchies. This is an evolution in terms of form, but also of substance, as new, younger actors mobilize while not identifying with classic structures, rejecting leaders and organizational hierarchies. If the phenomenon lasts, greater youth presence might alter the problem of generation renewal encountered by classic activism. In fact, Jordanian universities are no longer the essential spaces for politicization they once were for previous generations of activists. Depoliticization via the work of tribalization the regime had undertaken has had an obvious effect. However, for most of these youths, it was not the first step in their commitment. Many were often already mobilized on other levels in the non-profit sphere.

However, while the early days of these mobilizations gave evidence of some novelty, the participation of established organizations, with their experienced activists and classic repertoires of action, was required to keep them going. Their originality and their capacity to step up the pressure on the regime thus lay more in the breadth of the mobilization spectrum than their methods of action or their demands. After shows of solidarity with the movements in Tunisia and Egypt, demands made of the Jordanian regime became clearer: in addition to economic and social demands came increasingly political demands due to the lack of delivery on promises of reform. A certain consensus emerged among demonstrators on the issue of a constitutional monarchy, even if the Jordanian opposition remains silently wrought and weakened by the lasting opposition between "Jordanians" and "Palestinians". It should nevertheless be pointed out that the "Palestinians" did not form an advocacy group as such. The Palestinian camps, which remain places of memory, are not actually strong arenas of mobilization and politicization in Jordan, and they scarcely took part in these movements. On the other hand, political groups formed exclusively on the basis of Transjordanian identity had a strong presence, grouped around tribal personalities, but not only them. Their originality is that they no longer throw their support unconditionally behind the king, no matter how the monarchy tries to exploit this political identity.

But although the Islamists were not the instigators of the mobilizations, the movement grew when they joined in the protests. After the initial mobilizations, the left was unable to impose a specific agenda – a situation it had already experienced when forming common opposition fronts with the Islamists. In addition, support for the Syrian regime from part of the Jordanian left did not make its position any easier. It indeed seems to make sense, following Sarah Ben Nefissa's analysis of the movements in Egypt and Tunisia,[2] to distinguish between an open revolutionary moment and an electoral moment focusing on a pragmatic political horizon in which the Islamists have the upper hand. In fact, there was never a true revolutionary moment in Jordan, where the perspective has always been one of regime reform through a constitutional monarchy rather than overthrow.

How do activists now assess their situation, and how do they project themselves into the future? What are their horizons of expectation, to use Koselleck's expression?[3] Have they been profoundly revived by the Arab Springs – which, in this regard, beyond the issue of taking power, can be said to have been truly revolutionary? Has there been more sweeping political involvement that would go beyond merely challenging Arab authoritarian regimes? It would certainly be too hasty to see a direct connection between the various mobilizations today, the Indignants and the Occupy movements in the West, and the Arab Springs, because while a segment of the Arab left is involved in alter-globalism, it remains a marginal phenomenon. However, links do exist, if only in the interplay of identifications and cross-references, when, for instance, Spain's Indignants or 15-M Movement alluded to the Arab revolutions[4] or in Egypt pizzas were ordered on Facebook to back workers in Wisconsin.[5] A cross-comparison of activist revivals can thus be made on a global scale. But the evolution of these mobilizations also sheds a stark light on the obstacles encountered by movements claiming to be post-ideological and loosely structured. Protest in Jordan has not been confronted with the question of taking over power which has rent other similar movements that claimed to be horizontal and leaderless from the start. However, these new forms of protest have also encountered the structural difficulties of a struggle without a precise political vision that strives to dissociate ideological watchwords and methods of action. Disaffection with ideology and grand narratives is obvious, yet it is also because the Islamists have a clearly identifiable political project that they have an impact that goes beyond their actual political support. Few clear political visions have emerged to compete with the religious and cultural authenticity they claim, and there is a sort of expectation of new and alternative paradigms, an expectation that the initial moments of the Arab revolts cast in a stark light, but that has trouble informing a precise political project. Indeed, as the activist careers retraced in this book show, ideologies are also lifestyles, and are rarely disowned, unlike the organizations that represent them. The evacuation of meaning as a function of ideology thus does not describe the activists' experience. The strongly connoted vocabulary of ideology is difficult to use today. The term "ideology" is often reserved for application to the interpretative frameworks of "others", and it is certainly easier to identify peripheral and non-hegemonic ideologies. However, the matter at hand is indeed the construction of political convictions. These connect a commitment to the ongoing need for visions that make sense, that make sense of reality and experience, and deeply affect activists. Involvement in a meaningful political vision explains that the vocabulary of enchantment and the pleasure of action – "the lovely days", as one former activist puts it – remain present among activists, and this despite the harshness of repression. Certainly, activism raises the fundamental question of political power, explaining the search for arenas of mobilization that escape repression, but not only that. As the testimonials of these activists confronted with a coercive regime show, their commitment also reinforces a *Weltanschauung* and a horizon of expectation that closely links a period in the actors' lives and a period of history.

Methodological appendix

Questions of position

At the origin of this study lies a reflection on the conditions and consequences of political commitment over the long term and activists' experience in the face of a coercive regime. It also involved a shift in focus, because I was changing territory after ten years of research in the Palestinian Territories of the West Bank and the Gaza Strip. This switch coincides with a change in my approach to political involvement. The activist experience and the conditions and consequences of becoming involved in activism were already a central aspect of my research in the Palestinian Territories, but I primarily focused on youth activism, whose experience is necessarily over the fairly short term, which by definition leads to a more synchronic than diachronic view, even if generational evolutions can be detected between the first and the second Intifada. But even then, I had come across itineraries – switches from leftwing activism to Islamism in particular – that at first seemed surprising, and the question of activists circulating from one movement to another, their changes of allegiance, disinvolvement and reinvolvement seemed important to explore. The link here was made, beyond cultural areas, with more general evolutions in the sociology of political commitment and the attention paid to the dynamics at work over the long term, to the dialectical relationship with a changing political context and adjustments in private, professional and activist temporalities.

This presented a dual challenge. First, it meant understanding activism diachronically, over the long term, no longer focusing on such-and-such a movement at a given point in time, but examining the paths of activists who made these movements, their destiny, their evolutions, and thus in a way attempting to match the time of the actors and the time of history, or in any case, trying to understand the connections and the powerful moments. The analysis of trajectories and their changes in course is here akin to what Frédéric de Coninck and Francis Godard identify as a "structural model" that focuses on "temporalities that surpass an individual biography and associate this biography with these temporalities".[1] The actors' changes in course in this case are less a matter of unpredictability that needs to be explained within a relatively stable social context[2] than of "fluid political circumstances" characterized by strong structural uncertainty.[3] Like any political activist, these actors are particularly sensitive to geopolitical evolutions in their region and are strongly affected by the successive failures of the various ideologies they have supported and the movements they have participated in: Arab nationalism, Palestinian nationalism, communism and so on. But perhaps more than for others, these evolutions have had significant direct consequences on the everyday life of their society, beyond political involvement. Reintegrating political involvement into this history by examining biographies and conducting a historical sociological analysis also offers a different perspective on areas where the political news is perpetually topical, constantly changing and widely covered in the media, which is difficult to reconcile with the timeframe of research.

Second, turning my attention to these changes in affiliation, some of which may appear paradoxical, as they seem, at least at first, to imply strong variations in political convictions, was also a way of examining the question of the meaning given to conviction and its status in political involvement. This type of example, or rather counter-example, apparently furthest from any ideological coherence, seemed likely to reveal the connections or disconnections between political meaning and activist career. It seemed to me that these extreme cases would shed particular light on the relationship to ideologies. The question of ideologies may seem dated, especially with regard to strands of sociology that tend to reason in terms of career, market and social-cause entrepreneurs. However, it is difficult to disregard the notions of meaning and interpretation to account for the action of these actors. Application of the market metaphor to this field assumes an actor that in a way would remain outside "causes" perceived as undifferentiated products that he or she would consume or market and that would remain all the same to him or her. The relationship, however, is far from distanced. Causes are not objects one handles while maintaining a stance that views them simply in terms of profits and losses. These causes represent real interpretations of the world, and deeply influence convictions and lifestyles. If this aspect, which transpires in the activist discourse, also has to do with justifications and values expounded, the fact remains that the question of political and social meaning is an integral part of the activist experience that cannot be accounted for by evacuating this dimension or by simply falling back on external determinants. Ideologies are thus approached from the standpoint of Paul Ricœur's definition, which views ideological production as one of the aspects of human symbolic activity that serves as a "code of interpretation that secures [social] integration",[4] rather than through the usual questions of ideological distortion (ideology and truth) or even their function of legitimization of power structures. And more than on the subtleties of these ideologies as conceived by their theorists, attention was turned to how they were perceived, assumed, interpreted and experienced by the activists. What did they see in them, and to what extent was it possible or not to connect their trajectories of involvement and disinvolvement?

The aim was thus to articulate these two aspects – duration and political conviction – in an analysis of their trajectories that would not focus solely on their careers, because while the term is used to emphasize a process-oriented analysis, it must be acknowledged that it conveys many other elements that prejudge the activists' experience, or at least reduce it. The approach thus remained within the framework of a rather Weberian-inspired comprehensive sociology in which questions of motivation and legitimization remain central. Although the biographies are not chronicled and analysed by presenting ideal-type trajectories, recurrences and tendencies, key moments and overlapping timeframes have been identified. They emerged as heuristic instruments which, in moving back and forth between an individual itinerary and an evolving context to seek explanations, could describe the situation in Jordan and a field of possibilities, as well as certain general aspects of activism, while preserving the singularity of each trajectory in the presentation.

Questions of methodology

The field investigation that enabled the reconstitution of the life histories per se took place over several years, mainly between 2005 and 2010, with stays of several months each year. Fifty-five life stories were collected through one or more semi-directive interviews in Arabic, with the exception of a few interviews conducted in English. The length of the study made possible a certain longitudinal follow-up with activists I met with each year, and in any case a more in-depth inquiry with recurrent interviews spaced out over time, where variations could appear from one year to the next as positions shifted (for example, an interview with an activist before and after being elected as president of a professional association, who thus no longer presented his itinerary in the same light). The interviews were recorded when the respondent agreed, and then transcribed and translated, or if they didn't agree, notes were taken during the interview. The entire investigation produced about 600 pages of interviews. In addition to individual interviews, three group interviews were conducted in professional associations and the Islamic Action Front, a few written questionnaires were distributed in professional associations, more informal discussions were held, and time was devoted to observation during meetings, rallies and election campaigns.

The target group of interviewees was made up of activists from various political persuasions who were part of a protest scene, with long histories of involvement, and who for that reason were either in leadership positions or were identified by other activists as major figures, even if they had left the organization and converted their commitment into other forms of involvement – in other words, activists who enjoyed a certain visibility and renown. Such recognition by other activists could also be due to the particular harshness of the repression they had suffered.

The field study was constructed through a series of introductions, necessary in order to gain access to anything more than the official discourse of spokespersons I was referred to whenever I tried to make direct contact with political organizations. My early contacts were given to me by Palestinian activists in contact with other activists, particularly members of professional associations in Jordan. Subsequently, I had other introductions into the Islamist movement and in leftwing activist circles. Once the initial contacts had been made, I followed up on them by asking each interviewee to give me names of other activists. While they naturally mentioned people in their closest network first, they also answered my more specific requests with more precise criteria. For instance, having noticed the importance of professional organization activism,

I decided to conduct a specific study on this aspect. Indeed, the political landscape gradually came into sharper focus for me, and it especially took clearer shape as a field with activists from different tendencies that positioned themselves with respect to one another. This being a purposely qualitative study, I was more interested in representing the greatest possible variety of positions than a representative sample. I thus oriented my research toward the blind spots I had managed to identify, devoting particular attention to leftwing activists, not because of their significance within the field, but because it seemed to me that the usual focus on Islamists characteristic of studies on activism in the Middle East tended to ignore this political facet, while the difficulties they had encountered and their reorientation toward human rights NGOs and so on shed a different light on politics and the possibilities open to activists.

I thus followed the different activist networks, but also made a few relational leaps that were likely to prove instructive. For instance, after meeting a long-time communist activist who mentioned the issue of "leftist Islamism", I asked him for a few names along those lines, which he readily provided, even though he was not involved in it. When I contacted these so-called leftwing Islamists, they agreed to the interview, but subsequently rejected the term out of hand and cut the interview short. It was obviously the wrong approach, but it was instructive to see that while leftwing activists hoped to find a few of their themes picked up by Islamist activists, among Islamists the label was unpopular. When I tried once again to investigate leftist Islamism by questioning Islamist sources, they all told me that the current did not exist in Jordan, unlike in Egypt and Lebanon.

Gradually, the famous snowball effect occurred. Contacts multiplied, and the investigation became easier. The circle of activism is a small one: activists know each other and talk among themselves. I used the division into three main political strands – Islamist, nationalist and the left – adopted by the activists themselves, which corresponded to different ideologies, organizations and networks, even if some overlapping did occur. However, they did identify a common arena of protest. Some activists thus encouraged me to go see such-and-such a person in a competing current, asking who I had already talked to, indicating missing figures, eager for me to have an overall picture. For there was not only the question of their position in the Jordanian political space, but also that of the position of the Jordanian political scene in the entire region and the international picture. Some were eager to show that political activism indeed existed in Jordan, to counter recurrent remarks, which they mentioned and I had also heard when I stated the aim of my research: "Activism in Jordan? Is there any?" Toward the end, contacts overlapped, and while of course it is always possible to keep going and a subject can never be exhausted entirely, I began to have the feeling I had a panoramic view of the field. This impression was reinforced by the choice of these visible and long-term activists, who narrowed the field, even if in counterpoint, beyond these major players,[5] and I also wanted to meet younger and grassroots activists. These meetings also sometimes proved difficult to organize, because they had trouble understanding my interest in them and were more afraid than more seasoned activists of the visibility that might ensue, tending to refer me to the official, authorized spokespersons of the organization.

Interviews and activist narratives

The interviews aimed to allow the activist to produce a life history with a dominantly political theme, even if other topics were broached (family, education, profession and so on). In this regard, the biographical narrative was not entirely open to the activist's choice, but instead already oriented. I will not go back over the body of debates surrounding the issue of trajectories, life stories and "the biographical illusion"[6] here, but I will point out certain aspects of it. It is obvious that in reconstructing an itinerary after the fact, an activist tends to seek coherence in this itinerary – a search for coherence encouraged in this case by the sociologist who has predefined a common thread, that of political involvement. The approach by this type of narrative has a specific advantage for studies on activism, which is to contextualize and personalize ideological discourse – not that ideological discourse is false and the activist itinerary true, but that it becomes easier to grasp what is meaningful for the activist who selects and personalizes among the various interpretative frameworks available to him or her, which transpires in the greater variation of responses and stories. Furthermore, reporting via a narrative is often less unambiguous than what is often said, and a certain degree of variability can arise from one interview to the next[7] as well as within a single interview. The interviewees finally handled a certain diversity of responses fairly well, switching registers, emphasizing a specific point here, another one there, sometimes giving various, even contradictory, reasons for acting. Questions about a trajectory indeed tend to transform a life into a life story – in this case, the narrative of a commitment into a story with its various stages: first steps in their activist career, strengthening of the commitment, interweaving and consequences for other aspects of life, disinvolvement, change of course or reinforced conviction. But some narrators seem to be able to vary somewhat the motivation and high points of their narrative, and thus are conducive to a plurality of analyses.

It is thus a reconstruction after the fact, recounting an experience interpreted in retrospect, the value of which is as much in the line of reasoning and justifications offered as in the facts related. When Islamists highlight their academic achievements, for instance, we learn more than anything that academic performance is something that is important to them. This does not mean, however, that the narrative is purely subjective. Other sources exist. The historical and political context is known. There is what the activist says about his or her experience and his or her trajectory, but there is also what other activists say about it.

The narrative is moreover produced in specific circumstances – those of an interview, a context that often turns out to be politically and humanly much more than a mere interaction with a sociologist. When an Islamist leader carefully writes down my questions and I ask him why, and he answers that they provide him with information on the French government's Middle East policy, the framework of the interview is made clear, no matter what explanations I give him about my job and my status. Others constantly made comparisons between what they told me and what they said or omitted during interrogations by the Jordanian intelligence service. Recording then proved troublesome, even when they had at first agreed to it, with guarantees that their remarks would remain anonymous. Agreeing to an interview still represents a form of exposure, on top of revisiting a painful past. They would sometimes ask me to turn off the recording device during the interview to discuss certain points. Others who seemed not to pay any attention to the recorder suddenly resumed the interview after I turned the device off, believing the interview finished. The content moreover didn't change radically, but their language became less formal; the recorder made their speech seem more public to them, which was not always experienced as a problem. Interviewees who demonstrated a desire to bear witness publicly, on the contrary, paused periodically to make sure their words were properly recorded.

The matter of the degree of formalization of the interview is also reflected in the meeting place chosen by the activist: place of work, political venue, public venue or private space. And it is noteworthy that in the case of activists who invested the most in the task of reviewing their experience, using the situation to reflect with the interviewer on their trajectory, they often chose a more personal space, or a variety of places, and were prepared to spend a long time telling their story, alternating subjects and places (at work, with friends, at home with family, in a café and so on) in a personalized approach that broke with the formal aspect of the interview. Perhaps it was also because the interaction itself was a sort of recognition of their activism. As I pointed out in the Introduction, such investments were generally more characteristic of leftist activists, who pondered the failure of their movement and who also enjoy less recognition for their efforts despite the hardships they have endured. On the other hand, the content of discourse was also carefully selected for a Western sociologist – a selection that was sometimes rather comically evident, such as during an interview with an older activist in the company of his son. Whereas the interview took place in Arabic, the activist periodically turned to his son (who found the whole thing very amusing) to tell him, still in Arabic, that he would not talk about this or that incident in front of the foreign lady (they were always issues of internal quarrels in his political organization, which he had published in his memoirs in Arabic, but in his mind the Arab and Western political scenes were entirely separate).

A similar phenomenon occurred when I made a point of giving the interviewee a copy of the interview transcript, with a view to verifying its accuracy that might also lead to another interview and enable me to go back over certain topics. Most activists showed little interest in the document. For them it was a discourse produced for my own benefit in specific circumstances, and not for them. It was more the public aspect – in other words, what I would do with it – that they were interested in. Only two of them, who intended to publish their memoirs at a later time, paid any real attention to it. In those cases, the interviews had played a part in reconstructing a memory and a political identity, and became documents in their own right.

Sociodemographic data on the activists interviewed

Biographical interviews (apart from group interviews and observations) were conducted with fifty-five activists. Below is

METHODOLOGICAL APPENDIX 199

a summary of the sociodemographic and political data on these activists, to provide an overall picture of them, although the breakdown into categories does not necessarily account for changes of allegiance and individual characteristics. These can be found in the presentation of their trajectories earlier in the book.

Returning to the categories of the activists' political affiliation, twenty-two belonged to the Islamist current and were members of the Muslim Brotherhood, some were members of its party, the Islamic Action Front, one of them belonged to another small Islamist party, and others claimed to be independent Islamists or were on Islamist lists for professional organization elections. Twenty activists belonged to the leftist sphere, in which I included Communist Party members, members of the PFLP (or its Jordanian branch) and the DFLP, and the Social Forum, other small leftwing parties and the human rights tendency in its leftist form. Twelve activists belonged to Arab nationalist spheres - Nasserist or Baathist - Palestinian nationalist ones (Fatah and Fatah-Intifada) or Jordanian nationalist ones. One of them declared he was entirely independent, situated between Islamists and the left. Other breakdowns or groupings could of course be made, for instance bringing together those who belonged to the Palestinian organizations the PFLP, DFLP and Fatah (nine altogether). Furthermore, I noted the activists' main affiliation, but some of them switched from the Communist Party or the PFLP over to Fatah, from Islamism to the left, from the Communist Party to human rights organizations, had left the Muslim Brotherhood and so on. Twelve of them were active in professional associations (which does not exclude other forms of activism). Out of all these activists, thirteen were women, ten of them in the Islamist sphere and three of them leftists - a number that reflects their lack of visibility and relative marginality in political bodies on the whole.[8]

The activists belonged to various age groups, with birthdates ranging from 1920 to 1981, but most of them were born between 1945 and 1965 (see the table below). There was, however, a difference in age bracket between the Islamists and the others: most long-term Islamists were born between 1956 and 1965, whereas for the other tendencies, their birthdates were rather between 1946 and 1955.

The notion of a generation group was not, however, used as such. It implies a difficult passage from the birthdates continuum to the generational discontinuum.[9] And most of all, this group is not characterized either by a single founding event[10] or by a clearly expressed generational awareness.[11] Definitions based on exposure to a founding event or a particular social structure often pose a problem when various parties are studied, as is the case here.[12] In fact, a host of outstanding events come into play. Moreover, they may differ from one movement to another (for instance, the relative importance of the fall of the Soviet Union) and because of shifting conditions.

Among these activists, twelve were born in Palestine (in the Gaza Strip, the West Bank[13] or in cities of the Palestine of 1948: Jaffa, Haifa and so on).[14] The others were born in Jordan, fourteen of them in Amman. Seven others came from the northern regions (Irbid, Ajloun, Mafraq, Yarmouk), six of them from the Balqa region and the city of Salt in the northwest, six others from the area of Karak in central Jordan, and the remaining ones from Zarka in the northeast and Madaba. Three came from other Arab countries (Iraq, Egypt and Kuwait). It is worth noting that while most of them worked in Amman, nearly half of them began their lives in small villages, in that regard reflecting the demographic evolution in Jordan, the rural exodus and exponential growth of Amman. In fact, fourteen of the older activists had parents who were small farmers, the others' families being from wealthier socio-occupational categories or local notables. The younger activists had a father whose profession situated him among the first generation of graduates – dentists, engineers and so on – was a schoolteacher or held unskilled white-collar or blue-collar jobs. Apart from families of farmers in which

Distribution of activists by birth date

	1916–1920	1921–1925	1926–1930	1931–1935	1936–1940	1941–1945	1946–1950	1951–1955	1956–1960	1961–1965	1966–1970	1971–1975	1976–1980	1981–1985
Islamists						2			4	6	4	4	2	
Leftists and nationalists	1	2		1	1	2	7	9	4	1	1	1	1	1

mothers were clearly identified as taking part in chores, most mothers were designated as housewives, one female declaring that her mother was a nurse. The activists thus cannot be considered to come from the same social background, the range of their parents' occupations being fairly broad.

On the other hand, the evolution in terms of educational degrees within the family is fairly clear for the older activists, as only two out of the fifty-five interviewees did not embark on a university education. Although five of them never graduated, twelve had a bachelor's degree, fifteen finished studies in engineering and nine in medicine or medical professions, six had a master's degree in other fields, and six were PhDs. Clearly activism attracts and shapes a certain profile, as the respondents are not representative of the Jordanian population.[15] Earlier in the book I discuss the relationship between activism and education. Unsurprisingly, the Islamists had received training as engineers or held PhDs in Islamic law or the Arabic language. The situations were more varied among the leftwing activists and nationalists, although there was a strong presence of medical professions.

Lastly, the activists' occupations more or less reflected their educational level: twelve were teachers at various levels from primary to university, and nine were in a medical profession – doctor, dentist, surgeon and so on. However, only nine were engineers – a fact that indicates the difficulty women (eight of whom had an engineering degree) have in finding a job in relation to their degree. Seven were journalists, three were lawyers (there were law majors among the bachelor's degrees), three worked for NGOs, the others being a business owner, a cultural events organizer, an occasional tour guide, one unemployed, and one of the young activists was still a student. It is especially worth noting that seven of them devoted themselves to political and professional activism full-time, being more meagrely remunerated by their organization, or employed by the administration of their professional associations.

Notes

INTRODUCTION

1. Joseph Massad, *Colonial Effects: The Making of National Identity in Jordan*, New York, Columbia University Press, 2001, p. 274.
2. According to figures for 2003, 18 per cent. Jalal Al Husseini, "La question des réfugiés palestiniens en Jordanie entre droit au retour et réinstallation permanente", *Cahiers de l'Orient*, No. 75, 2003, p. 37.
3. Luigi Achilli, "Fun, Football and Palestinian Nationalism", *Jadaliyya*, February 2013. Online: http://www.jadaliyya.com/pages/index/9983/fun-football-and-palestinian-nationalism.
4. Reinhart Koselleck, "Transformations of Experience and Methodological Change", in *The Practice of Conceptual History: Timing History, Spacing Concepts*, Stanford, CA, Stanford University Press, 2002, pp. 45–83.

CHAPTER 1

1. Jeffrey Goldberg, "The Modern King in the Arab Spring", *The Atlantic*, 18 March 2013. Online: http://www.theatlantic.com/magazine/archive/2013/04/monarch-in-the-middle/309270/.
2. Henry Laurens, *La question de Palestine, I) l'invention de la Terre sainte*, Paris, Fayard, 1999, p. 306.
3. For mental health reasons.
4. Betty Anderson, *Nationalist Voices in Jordan: The Street and the State*. Austin, TX, University of Texas Press, 2005, pp. 147–191.
5. Kathrine Rath, "The Process of Democratization in Jordan", *Middle Eastern Studies*, Vol. 30, No. 3, July 1994, p. 534.

6. Massad, *Colonial Effects*, Chapters 1 and 3.
7. Irène Maffi, "The Creation of Jordanian National Identity: A Short Museographic Story of a Complex Process", in Myriam Ababsa and Rami Daher (eds), *Cities, Urban Practices and Nation Building in Jordan*, Beirut, Presses de l'Ifpo, 2011, pp. 143–160. Online: http://books.openedition.org/ifpo/1737.
8. Betty Anderson, "Writing the Nation: Textbooks of the Hashemite Kingdom of Jordan", *Comparative Studies of South Asia, Africa and the Middle East*, Vol. 21, Nos 1–2, 2001, pp. 5–14.
9. These figures do not take into account the Palestinians deprived of their status as residents of the West Bank by the Israeli administration in the 1970s, when the numbers of displaced persons were counted. Falestin Naïli, "Les déplacés de 1967", in Jalal Al Husseini and Aude Signoles (eds), *Les Palestiniens entre État et diaspora: le temps des incertitudes*, Paris, Karthala/IISMM-EHESS, 2012, p. 80.
10. For a discussion of the political implications of these figures, see Jalal Al Husseini, "La gestion de la question des réfugiés palestiniens dans les pays arabes: à la recherche d'un équilibre incertain", in Françoise de Bel-Air (ed.), *Migrations et politique au Moyen-Orient*, Beirut, IFPO, 2006, pp. 102–125. Géraldine Chatelard, "Les Palestiniens de Jordanie", in Riccardo Bocco and Géraldine Chatelard (eds), *Jordanie: le royaume frontière*, Paris, Autrement, 2001, pp. 92–99, and Vincent Legrand, *Le triangle "Jordanie–Palestine–Israël" et la décision jordanienne de désengagement de Cisjordanie (1988)*, Brussels, Bern, Berlin, Peter Lang, 2009, p. 191.
11. Michel Camau, "Remarques sur la consolidation autoritaire et ses limites", in Assia Boutaleb, Jean-Noël Ferrié and Benjamin Rey (eds), *L'Autoritarisme dans le monde arabe*, Cairo, CEDEJ, 2005, pp. 9–51.
12. Holger Albrecht (ed.), *Contentious Politics in the Middle East: Political Opposition under Authoritarianism*, Gainesville, FL, University of Florida, 2009, p. 2.
13. Géraldine Chatelard, *Briser la mosaïque: les tribus chrétiennes de Madaba, Jordanie XIXe–XXe siècle*, Paris, CNRS éditions, 2004, p. 333.
14. Daniele Cantini, "Understanding Higher Education: An Ethnographic Perspective from Jordan", unpublished communication for the International Conference on Ethnography and Education, Oxford, 16–17 September 2008.
15. See Oliver Wils, *Wirtschaftseliten und Reform in Jordanien. Zur Relevanz von Unternehmer-Bürokraten-Netzwerken in Entwicklungsprozessen*, Hamburg, Deutsches Orient Institut, 2003. Françoise de Bel-Air "Migrations internationales et politiques en Jordanie", *Revue européenne des migrations internationales*, Vol. 19, No. 3, pp. 9–41, and Pénélope

Larzillière, "Research in Context: Scientific Production and Researchers' Experience in Jordan", *Science, Technology and Society*, Vol. 15, No. 2, 2010, pp. 309-338.
16. Eberhard Kienle, "Libéralisation économique et délibéralisation politique: le nouveau visage de l'autoritarisme", in Olivier Dabène, Vincent Geisser and Gilles Massadier (eds), *Autoritarismes démocratiques et démocraties autoritaires: convergences Nord-Sud*, Paris, La Découverte, 2008, pp. 251-266.
17. Approximately 120-240 euros.
18. Interview with Orayb Rantawi, Amman, March 2009.
19. See Janine A. Clark, "Questioning Power, Mobilization, and Strategies of the Islamist Opposition: How Strong is the Muslim Brotherhood in Jordan?", in Albrecht (ed.), *Contentious Politics in the Middle East*, pp. 117-137. Ellen Lust-Okar, "The Decline of Jordanian Political Parties: Myth or Reality?", *International Journal of Middle East Studies*, Vol. 33, 2001, pp. 545-569.
20. Orayb Rantawi, *an-nuwâb wa muwâzana 2009: qirâ'a fi-l-ittijâhât wa-l-'aûlawiyyât* [*The MPs and the 2009 Budget: Reading of the Trends and Priorities*], al-Quds Center for Political Studies, April 2009.
21. Andrew Barwig, "Elites, Elections and Regime Stability: Insights from Jordan and Morocco", communication for the MESA Annual Meeting, 2009, Session P2217, "Electoral Authoritarianism? State Strategies and Political Contestation".
22. Kevin Koehler, "Authoritarian Elections in Egypt: Formal Institutions and Informal Mechanisms of Rule Export", *Democratization*, Vol. 15, No. 15, 2008, pp. 974-990.
23. Gudrun Krämer, "L'intégration des intégristes: une étude comparative de l'Egypte, la Jordanie et la Tunisie", in Ghassan Salame (ed.), *Démocraties sans démocrates*, Paris, Fayard, 1994, p. 278.
24. Michael Robbins and Lawrence Rubin, "The Rise of Official Islam in Jordan", *Politics, Religion and Ideology*, Vol. 14, No. 1, 2013, pp. 59-74.
25. Hamit Bozarslan, *Sociologie politique du Moyen-Orient*, Paris, La Découverte, 2010.
26. However, turnout would have been only 41 per cent if calculated by the number of eligible voters (3.1 million), and not only those registered to vote. See André Bank and Anna Sunik, "Parliamentary Elections in Jordan, January 2013", *Electoral Studies*, No. 34, 2014, pp. 376-379.
27. Agence française de développement, *Macroéconomie et Développement*, No. 10, September 2013.
28. Number of refugees registered by the UNHCR in February 2015. Online: http://data.unhcr.org/syrianrefugees/country.php?id=107.
29. Followed by the United Arab Emirates, the United Nations Relief and

Works Agency (UNRWA) and the European Union, which paid out $141 million in 2012 and $180 million in 2013.
30. See the analysis by Jalal Al Husseini, "La Jordanie face à la crise", in François Burgat and Bruno Paoli (eds), *Pas de printemps pour la Syrie*, Paris, La Découverte, 2013, pp. 282–288.
31. Jeremy M. Sharp, *Jordan: Background and U.S. Relations*, Congressional Research Service Report, January 2014, p. 3.
32. On 9 November 2005 Iraqi jihadists perpetrated three suicide attacks against major hotels in Amman, leaving sixty dead. A Jordanian jihadist operating in Iraq, Abu Musab al-Zarqawi, claimed responsibility for them. The attacks, aimed to demonstrate the group's opposition to the monarchy and its American ally, caused great outcry in Jordan.
33. In the mid-1990s Abu Musab al-Zarqawi and Abu Muhammad al-Maqdisi were jailed for the crimes of lèse-majesté, possession of weapons and participation in an illegal organization. They were released in 1999. Abu Muhammad al-Maqdisi spent several years in Afghanistan in the late 1980s. He returned to Jordan in 1992 and became a Jihadi Salafi leader, recruiting mainly among "Afghan Arabs". He was al-Zarqawi's mentor until they clashed in prison over the leadership position and the use of violence in Jordan and Iraq. When he was released from prison, Abu Musab al-Zarqawi returned to Afghanistan before going to Iraq, where he was killed in 2006. Abu Muhammad al-Maqdisi stayed in Jordan, and was soon imprisoned again. See the interview with Youssef in Chapter 8 about disillusioned Islamists.

CHAPTER 2

1. This does not preclude overlapping and subdivisions, which will be discussed later.
2. See in particular the work of Molly Andrews, *Lifetimes of Commitment: Aging, Politics, Psychology*, Cambridge, Cambridge University Press, 2008 (1st edn 1991); Mounia Bennani-Chraïbi and Olivier Fillieule (eds), *Résistances et protestations dans les sociétés musulmanes*, Paris, Presses de Sciences Po, 2003, and Frédéric Sawicki and Johanna Siméant, "Décloisonner la sociologie de l'engagement militant. Note critique sur quelques tendances récentes des travaux français", *Sociologie du travail*, No. 51, 2009, pp. 97–125.
3. Bernard Pudal, "La vocation communiste et ses récits", in Jacques Lagroye (ed.), *La Politisation*, Paris, Belin, 2003, p. 152.
4. It is essential to preserve the respondents' anonymity: last names are not given, first names have sometimes been changed, and only selected biographical data are provided. The interviews were recorded and

transcribed if respondents gave their consent. Fifty-eight interviews were conducted in Arabic (covering fifty-five individual trajectories through one or more interviews and three group interviews), thus quotations are always translated from Arabic unless otherwise specified for the two interviews conducted in English. See the details in the Methodological Appendix.

5. *Umma* means "nation" or "community" in Arabic. The word was used in particular by Nasser to refer to an Arab nation in the context of pan-Arabism, but today it is more often used to refer to a Muslim community that extends beyond national borders.

Throughout this book, Arabic words, names and titles have been transcribed in a simplified fashion: neither the emphatics nor the hamza are indicated. The 'ayn is noted by an opening quotation mark, and the qâf by a q. The plurals have been partly anglicized.

6. Hamzeh, an activist with the Islamist Action Front (Muslim Brotherhood). Interviews, Amman, June 2006 and February 2009.
7. Interview, Amman, March 2007.
8. A literal translation of *shebâb al fun*, a colourful expression used by the speaker, meaning "privileged youth that has fun".
9. Interviews, Amman, June 2006, March 2007 and 2008.
10. Interview with Ahmed A., former communist leader, May 2006.
11. Interview in English, Amman, March 2007.
12. In this regard, the hypothesis that people join movements because of an "identity/movement linkage" which Doug McAdam mentions would be an oversimplification here. Doug McAdam, "Pour dépasser l'analyse structurale de l'engagement militant", in Olivier Fillieule (ed.), *Le désengagement militant*, Paris, Belin, 2005, p. 63.
13. Founder of the Syrian social nationalist party in 1932, who propounded the idea of Greater Syria.
14. The Baath Party, a Syrian pan-Arabian nationalist movement (and the only party in Syria since 1966), was founded in 1944 by Michel Aflaq and Salah Bitar, and from the start had a branch in Jordan. Other Baathist groups in Jordan later had ties with the Iraqi Baath Party (the single party there between 1968 and 2003).
15. Regarding sociability in Karak, see Christine Jungen, *Politique de l'hospitalité dans le sud jordanien*, Paris, Karthala, 2009.
16. This Palestinian organization was founded in 1959 by Yasser Arafat and was present in Jordan. It grew after the Arab defeat of 1967. At the time it advocated armed struggle against Israel.
17. Mounia Bennani-Chraïbi has noted the same features for activists in Morocco: Mounia Bennani-Chraïbi, "Militantismes partisans au Maroc, 2008. Online: https://applicationspub.unil.ch/interpub/noauth/php/Un/

UnPers.php?PerNum=39533&LanCode=37&menu=rech&smenu=proj, p. 12.
12. Molly Andrews, who studied the biographies of fifteen lifelong activists in England, talks about "identifiable individuals" who had an influence on their careers: Andrews, *Lifetimes of Commitment*, p 113. Frédéric Sawicki and Johanna Siméant describe these as among their transversal findings in the sociology of activism: Sawicki and Siméant, "Décloisonner la sociologie de l'engagement militant", pp. 104–105.
18. Doug McAdam, "Recruitment of High-risk Activism: The Case of Freedom Summer", *American Journal of Sociology*, Vol. 92, 1986, pp. 64–90.
19. Bennani-Chraïbi, *Militantismes partisans au Maroc*, p. 12.
20. It was made up of activists who had left the Communist Party of Palestine in 1943 following a clash with party Zionists. They sought to build a left wing of the Palestinian national liberation movement.
21. Gamal Abdel Nasser came to power in Egypt after the Free Officers Movement overthrew the monarchy in 1952. Nasserism combines pan-Arab nationalism and Arab socialism. While his pan-Arab nationalism has often been doubted, many viewing it as a desire for Egyptian hegemony, he has nevertheless continued to embody it for the people. See Olivier Carré, *Le nationalisme arabe*, Paris, Payot, 2004 (1st edn 1993), p. 100.
22. Interviews, Amman, April and May 2006 and March 2007.
23. Sayyid Qutb (1906–1966), an Egyptian essayist and theorist of the Muslim Brotherhood. His ideas became more radical in prison in the second half of the 1950s. His later political writings are used as a reference by Jihadi Salafists. See in particular François Burgat, *Islamism in the Shadow of al-Qaeda*, Austin, TX, University of Texas Press, 2008.
24. Interviews, Amman, April, May and June 2006, March 2007 and November 2009.
25. Vincent Romani makes the same observation regarding the trajectory of leftwing sociologists from Palestine: "They [the Marxists] promised to free people from the weight of religious, clan and family tradition, and collective liberation from the Israeli occupation." He quotes one of them: "I'm from a very Muslim family in Gaza. For me, the Palestinian left was a total liberation, from the family, from religion, from senseless traditions; it was a liberation struggle, the plan for a fairer society, the freedom to talk to girls on campus, in meetings and so on. I have to say, activist meetings were a space of freedom outside the family to meet girls without needing the elders' approval." Vincent Romani, "Sciences sociales et coercition: Les social scientists des Territoires palestiniens entre lutte nationale et indépendance scientifique", Université Aix-Marseille III, Institut d'études politiques d'Aix-en-Provence, dissertation for PhD in political science, 2008, p. 258.
26. Interview in English, Amman, December 2005.
27. Interview, Amman, April 2007.

NOTES

CHAPTER 3

1. Elisabeth Longuenesse, *Professions et société au Proche-Orient: déclin des élites, crise des classes moyennes*, Rennes, Presses Universitaires de Rennes, 2007, p. 139.
2. Since then more universities have opened, especially private ones starting in the 1990s. Jordan currently has twenty-two universities, ten of them state-funded.
3. See Chapter 6 on the activism of professional associations.
4. Al Husseini, "La gestion de la question des réfugiés palestiniens dans les pays arabes", p. 112.
5. In 1958.
6. Interviews, Amman, March 2007 and March 2009. Betty Anderson also shows how Arab nationalists in Jordan were affected by this unique atmosphere. See Anderson, *Nationalist Voices in Jordan*.
7. Affiliated with the Iraqi Baath Party.
8. Approximately half of university admissions are by "royal privilege", partly circumventing the official criteria of grades required for the secondary school diploma. This affirmative action policy in particular enables Transjordanians to matriculate at university with lower grades than Palestinians, and has led to a decline in the number of Palestinians in universities. The proportion is estimated to have decreased from 95 per cent in the 1970s to 50 per cent today. See Yitzhak Reiter, "Higher Education and Sociopolitical Transformation in Jordan", *British Journal of Middle Eastern Studies*, Vol. 29, No. 2, 2002, p. 152.
9. Founded in 1964 on an initiative of the Arab League and Egyptian President Nasser, it included Fatah and the PFLP. After the Jordanian army offensive against the Palestinian camps in Jordan in September 1970, it had to leave Jordan for Lebanon during that period.
10. One of the founders of the Jordanian-Palestinian Communist Party in 1951. After its secretary-general Fouad Nassar went into exile in 1957 following the declaration of martial law, al-Salfiti became acting secretary-general in Amman.
11. Interview, Amman, March 2007.
12. The term *Mukhabarat*, "intelligence" in Arabic, is widely used to refer to the all-pervasive secret services.
13. Criticism of the Communist Party that could later be published in the newspapers.
14. This dividing line is not specific to the Jordanian Communist Party. It is also found, for instance, in the Lebanese Communist Party. Karim Mroué uses the term "Euro-communism" to define this tendency. See Karim Mroué, "Réflexions sur le marxisme aujourd'hui et le communisme

arabe du XXe siècle", interview by Anne Jollet, *Cahiers d'Histoire, revue d'histoire critique*, No. 101, April–May–June 2007, p. 137, and Karim Mroué and Samir Amin, *Communistes dans le monde arabe*, Pantin, Le Temps des Cerises, 2006.
15. Interview, Amman, February 2009.
16. Samir Kharinu, *Al-Harakah al-tullâbîyah al-urdunîyah, 1948–1998* [*The Jordanian Student Movement, 1948–1998*], Amman, Al-Urdun Al-Jadid Research Center, 2000, p. 76.
17. Other political tendencies also employ the notion of *intimâ* ("membership"), but also political commitment in the strong sense.
18. Interview, Madaba, April 2007.
19. *Harâm*, forbidden in the religious sense.
20. See in particular Pierre-Nicolas Baussand, who talks about a bottleneck in engineering professions that dates back to 1976, even before the mass return of skilled Jordanians migrants in the 1990s in the wake of the Gulf War. Pierre-Nicolas Baussand, "L'utilisation de l'immigration pour stabiliser une économie post rentière en crise", *Revue Tiers Monde*, Vol. 41, No. 163, 2000, p. 646.

CHAPTER 4

1. For the lifelong activists discussed in this volume. Rejection by the activists' family circle further reinforces the disconnect with their environment and increases the likelihood of disengagement.
2. Christians make up about 4 per cent of the population.
3. Interview with 'Abdel 'Azîz el 'Utî, one of the founders of the Jordanian Communist Party.
4. As Frédéric Sawicki and Johanna Siméant point out: "The adjustment, or on the contrary the lack of adjustment, between the family circle, the circle of friends, professional life and activism condition the chances of remaining committed or not, or even of stepping up one's level of commitment. Identity tensions, role conflicts and practical impossibilities between expectations and values specific to each of theses spheres can thus lead to calling into question one's activist commitment. On the contrary, approval (or mere acceptance) of activism in family and affective circles, its compatibility or even its connection with a person's professional career are highly likely to strengthen activist involvement." Sawicki and Siméant, "Décloisonner la sociologie de l'engagement militant", p. 9.
5. Interview, Amman, March 2009.
6. Stéphanie Latte-Abdallah, "Vers un féminisme politique hors frontières au Proche-Orient. Regard sur les mobilisations in Jordan (années 1950–années 2000)", *Vingtième siècle*, Vol. 3, No. 103, 2009, p. 179.

7. As Faleh Jabar terms them in *Post Marxism and the Middle East*, London, Saqi Books, 1997, p. 8.
8. See Maher Charif, "From Marxism to Liberal Nationalism: A Transformation in Palestinian Marxism", in Jabar (ed.), *Post Marxism and the Middle East*, pp. 69–77, and *Falestîn fi-l-archîv es-sirrî lil-Komintern* [*Palestine in the Secret Komintern Archives*], Damascus, Dar al-Mada, 2004.
9. Latte-Abdallah, "Vers un féminisme politique hors frontières au Proche-Orient", p. 182.
10. His joining the Muslim Brotherhood in 1966 was described in Chapter 2: he was one of the founding members of the Islamic Action Front in 1992, at a time when political parties were allowed.
11. Group interview with six young activists from the Islamic Action Front, Amman, April 2007.
12. Interview, Amman, March 2009.
13. See Diane Singerman, "Réseaux, cadres culturels et structures des opportunités politiques. Le mouvement islamiste en Égypte", in Mounia Bennani-Chraïbi and Olivier Fillieule (eds), *Résistances et protestations dans les sociétés musulmanes*, Paris, Presses de Sciences Po, 2003, pp. 219–242.
14. Religious tax, one of the five pillars of Islam.
15. See Aude Signoles (ed.), "Les municipalités islamistes", *Critique internationale*, No. 42, 2009/1.
16. This is true of the main strand of Islamism, the Muslim Brotherhood. The situation is different for the Jihadi Salafists, who are actively hunted down.
17. A young woman activist from the Islamic Action Front. Group interview, Amman, April 2007.
18. Group interview, Amman, April 2007.
19. Sadik Jalal al 'Azm "Orientalism and Orientalism in Reverse", in Alexander L. Macfie (ed.), *Orientalism: A Reader*, New York University Press, 2000, pp. 217–238. For a discussion of reverse or "backward" orientalism, see also Gilbert Achcar, "L'Orientalisme à rebours: de certaines tendances de l'orientalisme français après 1979", *Mouvements*, No. 54, 2008/2, pp. 127–144.
20. Young Islamic Action Front activist. Group interview, Amman, March 2009.
21. He has studied this tendency in Egypt: Patrick Haenni, *L'Islam de marché: l'autre révolution conservatrice*, Paris, Seuil, 2005, p. 72.
22. Patrick Haenni draws a parallel with the Protestant ethic in ibid., pp. 60 ff.

23. "To speak of activist capital is to emphasize a dimension of the commitment that political capital does not adequately convey. In fact, political capital can be considered as a form of symbolic capital, an asset based on countless credit operations by which agents confer upon a socially designated creditworthy person the very powers that they recognize in him." Frédérique Matonti and Franck Poupeau, "Le capital militant. Essai de définition", *Actes de la recherche en sciences sociales*, No. 155, 2004/5, p. 8.
24. A public university in Mafraq, 70 kilometres north of Amman, founded by decree in 1992 by King Hussein.
25. Founded in 1994.
26. His studies in economics were interrupted by a stint in prison in 1981. He is now a journalist and caricaturist.
27. Due to his Communist Party affiliation.
28. Interview, Amman, April 2007.

CHAPTER 5

1. In 1995, the United Nations High Commissioner for Human Rights Committee against Torture published the following: "The Committee is further concerned that during 1993 and 1994 political detainees were sentenced to death or imprisonment in trials before the State Security Court on the basis of confessions allegedly extracted after torture"; CAT UNHCR Jordan, 26 July 1995, A/50/44, §167. Human Rights Watch, which has documented the use of torture in Jordan prisons since 2006, calls torture "widespread and routine", especially for prisoners accused of crimes against national security: Human Rights Watch, *Torture and Impunity in Jordan's Prisons*, April 2008. Online: https://www.hrw.org/report/2008/10/08/torture-and-impunity-jordans-prisons/reforms-fail-tackle-widespread-abuse.
2. Tarek was not very clear about the date of his birth, which varied between 1942 and 1946 during the interview. It was maybe important for him to have left Palestine when he was old enough to allow him to have memories of the green Jaffa and the huge house with an inside orangery that he likes to talk about: "a dream that was real", he said.
3. These Palestinian organizations have branches in Jordan. The PFLP, founded in 1967 by Georges Habache and Ahmed Jibril, is a communist and pan-Arabic organization. The DFLP stemmed from a split of the latter group in 1969, with a Marxist-Maoist platform.
4. The Jordanian opening up took place in 1989, but political parties were not allowed until 1992. Therefore the first elections took place without parties being able to campaign officially.

5. The Ministry of Awqaf and Muslim Affairs appoints imams (except for the minority of private mosques). A *waqf* (pl. *awqaf*) in Islamic law is an endowment for religious and charitable purposes, and in general a religious or state-approved institution.
6. In 2005, new repressive legislation targeted in particular the Muslim Brotherhood and the Islamic Action Front (the party that stemmed from the Brotherhood) by forbidding the use of mosques for political activities and by increasing control over private mosques. Several imams were arrested.

CHAPTER 6

1. Part of this chapter was published earlier as an article: Pénélope Larzillière, "Political Commitment under an Authoritarian Regime: Professional Associations and Islamist Movement as Alternative Arenas in Jordan", *International Journal of Conflict and Violence*, Vol. 6, No. 1, 2012, pp. 11–25.
2. Robert Bianchi, *Unruly Corporatism: Associational Life in Twentieth Century Egypt*, Oxford, Oxford University Press, 1989; Philippe C. Schmitter, "Still the Century of Corporatism?", *Review of Politics*, No. 36, 1974, pp. 85–131; Nazih N. Ayubi, *Over-stating the Arab State: Politics and Society in the Middle East*, London, I.B. Tauris, 1995.
3. Éric Gobe, "Corporatismes, syndicalisme et dépolitisation", in Élizabeth Picard (ed.), *La politique dans le monde arabe*, Paris, Armand Colin, 2006, p. 185; François Burgat, "Egypte 1990: les refuges du politique", *Annuaire de l'Afrique du Nord*, Vol. XXIX, 1990, p. 540.
4. In order better to render the Jordanian context, I will use the term "professional association" in this specific sense, which excludes labour unions.
5. Umar Hamayil, "Institutional Characteristics of the Jordanian Professional Associations", in Hussein Abu Rumman and Hani Hourani (eds), *Professional Associations and the Challenges of Democratic Transformation in Jordan*, Amman, Al-Urdun Al-Jadid Research Center, 2000, p. 74.
6. Haydar Rasheed, "Labor Unions, Labor Disputes and Industrial Relations", in Abu Rumman and Hourani (eds), *Professional Associations and the Challenges of Democratic Transformation in Jordan*, p. 187.
7. Fida Adely, "The Emergence of a New Labor Movement in Jordan", *Middle East Report*, No. 264, 2012, pp. 34–37.
8. Éric Gobe, "Les syndicalismes arabes au prisme de l'autoritarisme et du corporatisme", in Olivier Dabène, Vincent Geisser and Gilles Massardier (eds), *Autoritarismes démocratiques et démocraties autoritaires au XXIe siècle: convergences Nord–Sud*, Paris, La Découverte, 2008, p. 269.

9. Longuenesse, *Professions et société au Proche-Orient*, p. 109.
10. Nilüfer Göle, "Entre le 'gauchisme' et 'l'islamisme': l'émergence de l'idéologie techniciste en Turquie", in Elisabeth Longuenesse (ed.), *Bâtisseurs et bureaucrates: ingénieurs et société au Maghreb et au Moyen-Orient*, Lyon, Maison de L'Orient, 1990, p. 309.
11. Bernard Botiveau, "The Egyptian Judiciary: A Profession Unveiled by Politics", *Knowledge, Work and Society*, Vol. 5, No. 1, 2008, pp. 119 and 123.
12. Egbert Harmsen, *Islam, Civil Society and Social Work: Muslim Voluntary Welfare Associations in Jordan between Patronage and Empowerment*, Leyde, ISIM/Amsterdam University Press, 2008, p. 121.
13. Source: the Professional Associations Council, January 2011. The teachers' association established in 2012 added 105,000 members; *Jordan Times*, 30 March 2012.
14. Lawyers 1950, dentists 1952, journalists 1953, doctors 1954, pharmacists 1957, engineers 1958, agronomists 1966, veterinarians, geologists, nurses and midwives 1972, entrepreneurs 1982, artists 1997. See Hussein Abu Rumman, "Internal Democracy in the Professional Associations", in Abu Rumman and Hourani (eds), *Professional Associations and the Challenges of Democratic Transformation in Jordan*, p. 93.
15. Longuenesse, *Professions et société au Proche-Orient*, p. 137.
16. Renate Dieterich, *Transformation oder Stagnation? Die jordanische Demokratisierungspolitik seit 1989*, Hamburg, Deutsches Orient-Institut, 1999, p. 315. According to one of the engineers interviewed, out of the 70,000 members claimed by the association, only 15,000 are actually in the country.
17. Source: engineers' association, October 2009.
18. Hamayil, "Institutional Characteristics of the Jordanian Professional Associations", p. 74.
19. Interviews, Amman, November 2007 and November 2009. This activist is a regular speaker at the Professional Associations Complex. He runs a civil engineering office. Aude Signoles describes a rather similar process when she shows how Palestinian engineers become key political actors by gaining technical control over all building permits. Aude Signoles "Les ingénieurs palestiniens entre restructuration interne et accession au pouvoir politique: enjeux nouveaux de la phase de construction étatique", in Institut national d'aménagement et d'urbanisme, *Les métiers de la ville*, Paris, L'Harmattan, 2003, pp. 141–169.
20. Elisabeth Longuenesse, "Les syndicats professionnels en Jordanie: enjeux de société et lutte nationale", 2000. Online: http://halshs.archives-ouvertes.fr/halshs-00111075/.

21. Source: interviews with three members of the committee in Amman, April and November 2007, March 2008, and February and November 2009.
22. Layth Shubeilat comes from an influential tribe in the south of Jordan. He is an engineer, the head of a company and the former leader of the engineers' association. He is particularly known for his anti-normalization positions and for being in favour of a constitutional monarchy. He has been imprisoned several times, and has complained of numerous anonymous acts of aggression, interpreted as attempts at intimidation.
23. Dieterich, *Transformation oder Stagnation?*, p. 312.
24. Hani Hourani, "The Development of the Political Role of the Professional Associations: A Historical Survey 1950–1989", in Abu Rumman and Hourani (eds), *Professional Associations and the Challenges of Democratic Transformation in Jordan*, p. 57.
25. Even though there are no founding laws due to the paralysis of the Palestinian legislative council.
26. Longuenesse, *Professions et société au Proche-Orient*, p. 317.
27. Interviews with the public relations director, Amman, March 2009. Close to the Islamists, this former secretary of the professional associations' Anti-Normalization Committee was arrested in 2003 after the committee criticized the Israeli–Jordanian agreements.
28. Close to a million people gathered in King Hussein Sports City in Amman during the first demonstrations: André Bank and Morten Valbjørn, "Regierung, Opposition in Jordanien und der Gazakrieg", *INAMO*, No. 59, Autumn 2009, p. 8.
29. Interview with the president of the engineers' association, Amman, March 2009.
30. Interviews, Amman, February and October 2009.
31. Longuenesse, *Professions et société au Proche-Orient*, p. 122.
32. "One person, one vote", as it is called in Jordan. The bill was officially withdrawn in January 2008.
33. Frédéric Vairel, "L'opposition en situation autoritaire: statut et modes d'action", in Dabène, Geisser and Massardier (eds), *Autoritarismes démocratiques et démocraties autoritaires au XXIe siècle: convergences Nord–Sud*, p. 231.
34. Interview with Ali (cited above), Amman, November, 2009.
35. Dieterich, *Transformation oder Stagnation?*, p. 316.
36. Interview, Amman, March, 2009.
37. Hourani, "The Development of the Political Role of the Professional Associations", p. 58.
38. Longuenesse, *Professions et société au Proche-Orient*, p. 139.

39. This cannot be explained by enrolment rates in university, which in 2005 were 22 per cent for Palestinians from Jordanian camps (unfortunately, these statistics are not available for the master's degree). Jalal Al Husseini, *Education Profile of the Palestinian Refugees in the Near East*, UNRWA/IUED/UCL, 2007, p. 22.
40. Mahmoud (mentioned earlier), who has a master's in History, was imprisoned again for a year when he returned to Jordan in 1982. When he got out, he joined the engineers' association and was a member of the inter-committee organization.
41. There is no general student union; lifting this ban is one of their recurrent demands. The student movement for defending student rights, Thabahtuna, which was launched in April 2007, made it one of its priorities.
42. Interviews, Amman, March 2007 and March 2009.
43. Interview, Amman, February 2009.
44. Hamayil, "Institutional Characteristics of the Jordan Professional Associations", p. 77.
45. In 1997 women represented 18 per cent of the members of professional associations, 13 per cent if the nurses' and midwives' association is excluded: Suleiman Arabiyat, "Women and Professional Associations", in Abu Rumman and Hourani (eds), *Professional Associations and the Challenges of Democratic Transformation in Jordan*, p. 153.
46. Mahasin al-Imam, "Women and Professional Associations", in Abu Rumman and Hourani (eds), *Professional Associations and the Challenges of Democratic Transformation in Jordan*, p. 161.
47. Questionnaire answered by seven women's association activists, Amman, April 2007.
48. Sawicki and Siméant, "Décloisonner la sociologie de l'engagement militant", p. 110.
49. Yannick Le Quentrec and Annie Rieu, *Femmes: engagements publics et vie privée*, Paris, Syllepse, 2003, pp. 17–51.
50. Vairel, "Opposition en situation autoritaire".
51. See also Anne-Catherine Wagner, "Syndicalistes européens. Les conditions sociales et institutionnelles de l'internationalisation des militants syndicaux", *Actes de la recherche en sciences sociales*, No. 155, 2004–2005, pp. 12–33.

CHAPTER 7

1. Vincent Geisser, Karam Karam and Frédéric Vairel, "Espaces du politique. Mobilisations et protestations", in Picard (ed.), *La politique dans le monde arabe*, p. 212.

2. Bernard Botiveau, "Le droit et la justice comme métaphores et mise en forme du politique", in Picard (ed.), *La politique dans le monde arabe*, p. 119.
3. Stéphanie Latte-Abdallah, "Les frontières intérieures: enjeu palestinien et métamorphoses de l'engagement féminin en Jordanie", in Al Husseini and Signoles (eds), *Les Palestiniens entre État et diaspora*, p. 252.
4. Sarah Ben Néfissa and Blandine Destremau (eds), "Protestations sociales, révolutions civiles", *Revue Tiers Monde*, special issue, May 2011.
5. Picard, *La politique dans le monde arabe*, p. 9, and Pénélope Larzillière, "Sociologie de l'engagement à partir du Proche-Orient", in Al Husseini and Signoles (eds), *Les Palestiniens entre État et diaspora*, pp. 179–188 and 299–301.
6. The term "human rights" is used here in the generic sense to refer to a movement that also includes among its themes the environment and women's rights.
7. Geisser, Karam and Vairel, "Espaces du politique", p. 200.
8. As Benoît Challand notes with regard to the Palestinian context: Benoît Challand, *The Exclusionary Power of Civil Society: International Aid to Palestinian NGOs*, Florence, European University Institute, 2005.
9. Interview, Amman, March 2008.
10. Interview, Amman, November 2009.
11. Interviews, Amman, April 2007, March 2008 and March 2009.
12. Interview with Nahed Hattar, May 2006.
13. Boutaleb, Ferrié and Rey (eds), *L'Autoritarisme dans le monde arabe*, p. 6.
14. Diane Singerman, "The Networked World of Islamist Social Movements", in Quintan Wiktorowicz (ed.), *Islamic Activism: A Social Movement Theory Approach*, Bloomington, IN, Indiana University Press, 2004, pp. 143–163.
15. Philippe Droz-Vincent, *Moyen-Orient: pouvoirs autoritaires, sociétés bloquées*, Paris, PUF, 2004, p. XIII.
16. Hassan Nasrallah has led Hezbollah since 1991.
17. In that Shi'ism is a minority sect born out of the schism with Sunnism over the issue of Muhammad's succession and only recognizes Ali, Muhammad's son-in-law, and his descendents.
18. See also Nicolas Dot-Pouillard, "Syria Divides the Arab Left", *Le Monde diplomatique*, August 2012, p. 11.
19. Their communiqués are available at http://www.jordanreform.org.
20. This generic term is highly ambiguous. In the current political context in Jordan, it can refer either to a Jordanian youth movement that maintains a Facebook page under this name (https://www.facebook.com/7erak), or more generally to all the new movements formed in conjunction with the Jordan Spring.

21. Jayyin, while it does not explicitly claim to be a Transjordanian coalition, puts forward the notion of a Jordanian national movement. See Jamal al Shalabi, Jimena Montaldo Mancilla and Vincent Legrand, "Jordanie: un 'printemps arabe' circonscrit ou en germe?", in Bichara Khader (ed.), "Le printemps arabe: un premier bilan", *Alternatives Sud*, special issue, Vol. 19, 2012, pp. 171–188.
22. Sarah Ben Néfissa, "Mobilisations et révolutions dans les pays de la Méditerranée arabe à l'heure de 'l'hybridation' du politique. Égypte, Liban, Maroc, Tunisie", *Revue Tiers Monde*, special issue, 2011, p. 18.
23. Quintan Wiktorowicz, "The Salafi Movement in Jordan", *International Journal of Middle East Studies*, Vol. 32, No. 2, 2000, pp. 223–224. For a more general study of Salafism in the Arab world, see Bernard Rougier (ed.), *Qu'est-ce que le salafisme?*, Paris, PUF, 2008.
24. Romain Caillet, "A Brief Account of Salafist Use of Public Space in Jordan", in Ababsa and Daher (eds), *Cities, Urban Practices and Nation Building in Jordan*, pp. 307–327.
25. Ibid.
26. Which a major figure of the Jordanian Salafist movement, Mohammed al-Shalabi (Abu Sayyaf), again did explicitly in a telephone interview with the *As-Safir* newspaper on 7 March 2014.
27. International Crisis Group, "Popular Protest in North Africa and the Middle East (IX): Dallying with Reform in a Divided Jordan", *Middle East/North Africa Report*, No. 118, March 2012.
28. Human Rights Watch, "Jordan: End Trials of Protesters for 'Undermining Regime'", news release, 28 October 2013.
29. Interview, Amman, November 2009.
30. Development priorities as seen by international organizations have become increasingly cultural, with themes such as "empowerment", "peace culture" and so on. This can be seen as a "radicalization of aid" because it increases the degree of intrusion of international policies in the recipient societies and seeks to alter behaviours and values, not solely to improve agricultural production, for example. See Mark Duffield, "Social Reconstruction and the Radicalization of Development: Aid as a Relation of Global Liberal Governance", *Development and Change*, Vol. 33, No. 3, 2002, pp. 1,049–1,071, and Pénélope Larzillière, "Production of Norms and Securitization in Development Policies: From 'Human Security' to 'Security Sector Reform'", American University of Beirut, Issam Fares Institute, Working Paper Series 13, December 2012.
31. See Sandrine Nicourd (ed.), *Le travail militant*, Rennes, Presses Universitaires de Rennes, 2008.
32. See Michaël Bechir Ayari's analysis of Tunisia and Egypt in this regard: Michaël Bechir Ayari, "Non, les révolutions tunisienne et égyptienne ne

sont pas des révolutions 2.0", *Mouvements*, Vol. 66, Summer 2011, pp. 56–61; and for a general analysis of the use of social media in the Arab revolts, see Yves Gonzales-Qijano, *Arabités numériques: le printemps du Web arabe*, Paris, Actes Sud-Sindbad, 2012.
33. Alain Roussillon, *La pensée islamique contemporaine: acteurs et enjeux*, Paris, Téraèdre, 2005, p. 67.

CHAPTER 8

1. Regarding the debates on post-Islamism, see in particular Malika Zeghal (ed.), "Intellectuels de l'islam contemporain: nouvelles générations, nouveaux débats", *REMM*, No. 123, July 2008, pp. 32–201.
2. Interview, Amman, November 2009.
3. See Chapter 3 on student activism.
4. See note 33 in Chapter 1. Abu Musab al-Zarqawi and Abu Muhammad al-Maqdisi were released in 1999, unlike the former group that blew up movie theatres. See also International Crisis Group, "Jordan's 9/11: Dealing with Jihadi Islamism", *Middle East Report*, No. 47, 23 November 2005.
5. Surah V, verse 44.
6. Interview, Amman, November 2009.
7. See Chapter 6 on professional activism.
8. His political path was pieced together through four interviews conducted in Amman in 2006, 2007, 2009 and 2010, as well as two essays the respondent drafted for this purpose regarding his experiences in Afghanistan and with the Muslim Brotherhood.
9. Aside from one group of jihadists, Jamaat al-Jihad, whose members were often students.
10. Egyptian theologian and legal scholar. In 1925 he published *Islam and the Foundations of Political Power*, in which he emphasized separation between religious beliefs and historical processes.
11. Mohammad Khatami represents a reformist trend, and was president of Iran from 1997 to 2005.

CONCLUSION

1. Sadik Jalal al 'Azm, *Ces interdits qui nous hantent: Islam, censure, orientalisme*, Marseille, Parenthèses/MMSH/IFPO, 2008.
2. Sarah Ben Néfissa, "Révolution civile et politique en Egypte. La démocratie et son double", *Mouvements*, Vol. 66, Summer 2011, pp. 48–55.

3. Reinhart Koselleck, "'Erfahrungsraum' und 'Erwartungshorizont' – zwei historische Kategorien", in *Vergangene Zukunft*, Frankfurt, Suhrkamp Taschenbuch, 1989 (1st edn 1979), pp. 349–375. English trans. Keith Tribe, "'Spaces of Experience' and 'Horizon of Expectation': Two Historical Categories", in *Futures Past*, New York, Columbia University Press, 2004, pp. 255–275.
4. Jérôme Ferret, "Des devenirs minoritaires. Retour sur l'expérience politique des 'indignés' espagnols", *Mouvements*, No. 75, November 2013, pp. 86–98.
5. Geoffrey Pleyers and Marlies Glasius, "La dimension globale des mouvements de 2011", in Pénélope Larzillière and Boris Petric (eds), "Révolutions, contestations, indignations", *Socio*, No. 2, December 2013, pp. 59–79.

METHODOLOGICAL APPENDIX

1. Frédéric de Coninck and Francis Godard, "L'approche biographique à l'épreuve de l'interprétation: les formes temporelles de la causalité", *Revue française de sociologie*, Vol. XXXI, 1989, pp. 30 and 41.
2. Michel Grossetti, "L'imprévisibilité dans les parcours sociaux", *Cahiers internationaux de sociologie*, Vol. CXX, 2006, pp. 5–28.
3. Michel Dobry, *Sociologie des crises politiques*, Paris, Presses de la Fondation Nationale de Sciences Po, 1992. It should be noted, however, that coercive processes are far more present here than in the examples Dobry studies.
4. Paul Ricœur, *L'idéologie et l'utopie*, Paris, Seuil, 1997, p. 32. Trans. *Lectures on Ideology and Utopia*, ed. George H. Taylor, New York, Cambridge University Press, 1981.
5. An expression coined by Dominique Schnapper, quoted by Michaël Bechir-Ayari, "Exploiter les données d'entretiens biographiques en sociologie. Le cas des trajectoires socioprofessionnelles et militantes tunisiennes", *Alfa*, 2005, pp. 33–44.
6. Pierre Bourdieu, "The Biographical Illusion", in R.J. Parmentier and G. Urban (eds), *Working Papers and Proceedings of the Center for Psychosocial Studies* (Chicago, IL), No. 14, 1987, pp. 1–7.
7. Bernard Lahire, *Portraits sociologiques: dispositions et variations individuelles*, 2002, Paris, Nathan.
8. For a specific study on female activism in Jordan, see Latte-Abdallah, "Les frontières intérieures", pp. 235–262.
9. Pierre Favre, "De la question sociologique des générations et de la difficulté à la résoudre dans le cas de la France", in J. Crête and P. Favre,

Générations et politique, Paris/Laval, Economica/Presses universitaires de Laval, 1989, pp. 283–319.
10. Koselleck, "'Spaces of Experience' and 'Horizon of Expectation'".
11. Karl Mannheim, "The Sociological Problem of Generations", in P. Kecskemeti (ed.), *Essays on the Sociology of Knowledge*, New York, Routledge and Kegan Paul, 1952, pp. 276–322.
12. Favre, "De la question sociologique des générations et de la difficulté à la résoudre dans le cas de la France".
13. The West Bank was under Jordanian jurisdiction as of 1950. It was occupied by Israel in 1967, but administrative ties with Jordan lasted until 1988.
14. These activists were born before 1948.
15. The tertiary enrolment rate was 15 per cent in the 1980s. It has continued to rise, reaching 47 per cent in 2012. Source: UNESCO Institute for Statistics.

Bibliography

Ababsa, Myriam and Rami Daher (eds), *Cities, Urban Practices and Nation Building in Jordan*, Beirut, Presses de l'Ifpo, 2011.

Abu Rumman, Hussein, "Internal Democracy in the Professional Associations", in Hussein Abu Rumman and Hani Hourani (eds), *Professional Associations and the Challenges of Democratic Transformation in Jordan*, Amman, Al-Urdun Al-Jadid Research Center, 2000, pp. 93–110.

Abu Rumman, Hussein and Hani Hourani (eds), *Professional Associations and the Challenges of Democratic Transformation in Jordan*, Amman, Al-Urdun Al-Jadid Research Center, 2000.

Achcar, Gilbert, "L'Orientalisme à rebours: de certaines tendances de l'orientalisme français après 1979", *Mouvements*, No. 54, 2008/2, pp. 127–144.

Achilli, Luigi, "Étiqueter dans un espace incertain: le cas des camps de réfugiés palestiniens en Jordanie", *Migrations sociétés*, Vol. 22, No. 18, 2010, pp. 111–129.

Achilli, Luigi, "Fun, Football and Palestinian Nationalism", *Jadaliyya*, February 2013. Online: http://www.jadaliyya.com/pages/index/9983/fun-football-and-palestinian-nationalism.

Adely, Fida. "The Emergence of a New Labor Movement in Jordan", *Middle East Report*, No. 264, 2012, pp. 34–37.

Al 'Azm, Sadik Jalal, *Ces interdits qui nous hantent: Islam, censure, orientalisme*, Marseille, Parenthèses/MMSH/IFPO, 2008.

Al 'Azm, Sadik Jalal, "Orientalism and Orientalism in Reverse", in Alexander L. Macfie (ed.), *Orientalism: A Reader*, New York University Press, 2000, pp. 217–238.

Al Husseini, Jalal, *Education Profile of the Palestinian Refugees in the Near East*, UNRWA/IUED/UCL, 2007.

Al Husseini, Jalal, "La gestion de la question des réfugiés palestiniens dans les pays arabes: à la recherche d'un équilibre incertain", in Françoise de Bel-Air (ed.), *Migrations et politique au Moyen-Orient*, Beirut, IFPO, 2006, pp. 102–125.

Al Husseini, Jalal, "La Jordanie face à la crise", in François Burgat and Bruno Paoli (eds), *Pas de printemps pour la Syrie*, Paris, La Découverte, 2013, pp. 282–288.

Al Husseini, Jalal, "La question des réfugiés palestiniens en Jordanie entre droit au retour et réinstallation permanente", *Cahiers de l'Orient*, No. 75, 2003, pp. 31–50.

Al Husseini, Jalal and Aude Signoles (eds), *Les Palestiniens entre État et diaspora: le temps des incertitudes*, Paris, Karthala/IISMM-EHESS, 2012.

Al-Imam, Mahasin, "Women and Professional Associations", in Hussein Abu Rumman and Hani Hourani (eds), *Professional Associations and the Challenges of Democratic Transformation in Jordan*, Amman, Al-Urdun Al-Jadid Research Center, 2000, pp. 157–162.

Al Shalabi, Jamal, Jimena Montaldo Mancilla and Vincent Legrand, "Jordanie: un 'printemps arabe' circonscrit ou en germe?", in Bichara Khader (ed.), "Le printemps arabe: un premier bilan", *Alternatives Sud*, special issue, Vol. 19, 2012, pp. 171–188.

Albrecht, Holger (ed.), *Contentious Politics in the Middle East: Political Opposition under Authoritarianism*, Gainesville, FL, University of Florida, 2009.

Anderson, Betty, *Nationalist Voices in Jordan: The Street and the State* . Austin, TX, University of Texas Press, 2005.

Anderson, Betty, "Writing the Nation: Textbooks of the Hashemite Kingdom of Jordan", *Comparative Studies of South Asia, Africa and the Middle East*, Vol. 21, Nos 1–2, 2001, pp. 5–14.

Andrews, Molly, *Lifetimes of Commitment: Aging, Politics, Psychology*, Cambridge, Cambridge University Press, 2008 (1st edn 1991).

Arabiyat, Suleiman, "Women and Professional Associations", in Hussein Abu Rumman and Hani Hourani (eds), *Professional Associations and the Challenges of Democratic Transformation in Jordan*, Amman, Al-Urdun Al-Jadid Research Center, 2000, pp. 151–156.

Ayubi, Nazih N., *Over-stating the Arab State: Politics and Society in the Middle East*, London, I.B. Tauris, 1995.

Bank, André and Anna Sunik, "Parliamentary Elections in Jordan, January 2013", *Electoral Studies*, No. 34, 2014, pp. 376–379.

Bank, André and Morten Valbjørn, "Regierung, Opposition in Jordanien und der Gazakrieg", *INAMO*, No. 59, Autumn 2009, p. 8.

Barwig, Andrew, "Elites, Elections and Regime Stability: Insights from Jordan and Morocco", communication for the MESA Annual Meeting 2009, Session P2217, "Electoral Authoritarianism? State Strategies and Political Contestation".

Baussand, Pierre-Nicolas, "L'utilisation de l'immigration pour stabiliser une économie post rentière en crise", *Revue Tiers Monde*, Vol. 41, No. 163, 2000, pp. 645–667.

Bechir Ayari, Michaël, "Exploiter les données d'entretiens biographiques en sociologie. Le cas des trajectoires socioprofessionnelles et militantes tunisiennes", *Alfa*, 2005, pp. 33–44.

Bechir Ayari, Michaël, "Non, les révolutions tunisienne et égyptienne ne sont pas des révolutions 2.0", *Mouvements*, Vol. 66, Summer 2011, pp. 56–61.

Ben Nefissa, Sarah, "Mobilisations et révolutions dans les pays de la Méditerranée arabe à l'heure de 'l'hybridation' du politique. Égypte, Liban, Maroc, Tunisie", *Revue Tiers Monde*, special issue, 2011, pp. 5–24.

Ben Nefissa, Sarah, "Révolution civile et politique en Egypte. La démocratie et son double", *Mouvements*, Vol. 66, Summer 2011, pp. 48–55.

Ben Néfissa, Sarah and Blandine Destremau (eds), "Protestations sociales, révolutions civiles", *Revue Tiers Monde*, special issue, May 2011.

Bennani-Chraïbi, Mounia, "Militantismes partisans au Maroc", 2008. Online: https://applicationspub.unil.ch/interpub/noauth/php/Un/UnPers.php?PerNum=39533&LanCode=37&menu=rech&smenu=proj.

Bennani-Chraïbi, Mounia and Olivier Fillieule (eds), *Résistances et protestations dans les sociétés musulmanes*, Paris, Presses de Sciences Po, 2003.

Bianchi, Robert, *Unruly Corporatism: Associational Life in Twentieth Century Egypt*, Oxford, Oxford University Press, 1989.

Bocco, Riccardo and Géraldine Chatelard, *Jordanie: le royaume frontière*, Paris, Autrement, 2001.

Botiveau, Bernard, "Le droit et la justice comme métaphores et mise en forme du politique", in Élizabeth Picard (ed.), *La politique dans le monde arabe*, Paris, Armand Colin, 2006, pp. 101–127.

Botiveau, Bernard, "The Egyptian Judiciary: A Profession Unveiled by Politics", *Knowledge, Work and Society*, Vol. 5, No. 1, 2008, pp. 105–125.

Bourdieu, Pierre, "The Biographical Illusion", in R.J. Parmentier and G. Urban (eds), *Working Papers and Proceedings of the Center for Psychosocial Studies* (Chicago, IL), No. 14, 1987, pp. 1–7.

Boutaleb, Assia, Jean-Noël Ferrié and Benjamin Rey (eds), *L'Autoritarisme dans le monde arabe*, Cairo, CEDEJ, 2005.

Bozarslan, Hamit, *Sociologie politique du Moyen-Orient*, Paris, La Découverte, 2010.

Bozarslan, Hamit, *Une histoire de la violence au Moyen-Orient*, Paris, La Découverte, 2008.

Burgat, François, "Egypte 1990: les refuges du politique", *Annuaire de l'Afrique du Nord*, Vol. XXIX, 1990, pp. 535–552.

Burgat, François, *Islamism in the Shadow of al-Qaeda*, Austin, TX, University of Texas Press, 2008.

Caillet, Romain, "A Brief Account of Salafist Use of Public Space in Jordan", in Myriam Ababsa and Rami Daher (eds), *Cities, Urban Practices and Nation Building in Jordan*, Beirut, Presses de l'Ifpo, 2011, pp. 307–327.

Agence française de développement, *Macroéconomie et Développement*, No. 10, September 2013.

Camau, Michel, "Remarques sur la consolidation autoritaire et ses limites", in Assia Boutaleb, Jean-Noël Ferrié and Benjamin Rey (eds), *L'Autoritarisme dans le monde arabe*, Cairo, CEDEJ, 2005, pp. 9–51.

Cantini, Daniele, "Understanding Higher Education: An Ethnographic Perspective from Jordan", unpublished communication for the International Conference on Ethnography and Education, Oxford, 16–17 September 2008.

Carré, Olivier, *Le nationalisme arabe*, Paris, Payot, 2004 (1st edn 1993).

Challand, Benoît, *The Exclusionary Power of Civil Society: International Aid to Palestinian NGOs*, Florence, European University Institute, 2005.

Charif, Maher, *Falestîn fi-l-archîv es-sirrî lil-Komintern [Palestine in the Secret Komintern Archives]*, Damas, Dar al-Mada, 2004.

Charif, Maher, "From Marxism to Liberal Nationalism: A Transformation in Palestinian Marxism", in Faleh Jabar (ed.), *Post Marxism and the Middle East*, London, Saqi Books, 1997, pp. 69–77.

Chatelard, Géraldine, *Briser la mosaïque: les tribus chrétiennes de Madaba, Jordanie XIXe–XXe siècle*, Paris, CNRS éditions, 2004.

Chatelard, Géraldine, "Les Palestiniens de Jordanie", in Riccardo Bocco and Géraldine Chatelard (eds), *Jordanie: le royaume frontière*, Paris, Autrement, 2001, pp. 92–99.

Clark, Janine A., "Questioning Power, Mobilization, and Strategies of the Islamist Opposition: How Strong is the Muslim Brotherhood in Jordan?", in Holger Albrecht (ed.), *Contentious Politics in the Middle East: Political Opposition under Authoritarianism*, Gainesville, FL, University of Florida Press, pp. 117–137.

Dabene, Olivier, Vincent Geisser and Gilles Massadier (eds), *Autoritarismes démocratiques et démocraties autoritaires: convergences Nord–Sud*, Paris, La Découverte, 2008.

De Bel-Air, Françoise (ed.), *Migrations et politique au Moyen-Orient*, Beirut, IFPO, 2006.

De Bel-Air, Françoise, "Migrations internationales et politiques en Jordanie", *Revue européenne des migrations internationales*, Vol. 19, No. 3, pp. 9–41.

De Coninck, Frédéric and Francis Godard, "L'approche biographique à l'épreuve de l'interprétation: les formes temporelles de la causalité", *Revue française de sociologie*, Vol. XXXI, 1989, pp. 25–53.

Dieterich, Renate, *Transformation oder Stagnation? Die jordanische Demokratisierungspolitik seit 1989*, Hamburg, Deutsches Orient-Institut, 1999.

Dobry, Michel, *Sociologie des crises politiques*, Paris, Presses de la Fondation Nationale de Sciences Po, 1992.

Dot-Pouillard, Nicolas, "Syria divides the Arab left", *Le Monde diplomatique*, August 2012, p. 11.

Droz-Vincent, Philippe, *Moyen-Orient: pouvoirs autoritaires, sociétés bloquées*, Paris, PUF, 2004.

Duffield, Mark, "Social Reconstruction and the Radicalization of Development: Aid as a Relation of Global Liberal Governance", *Development and Change*, Vol. 33, No. 3, 2002, pp. 1,049-1,071.

Favre, Pierre, "De la question sociologique des générations et de la difficulté à la résoudre dans le cas de la France", in J. Crête and P. Favre, *Générations et politique*, Paris/Laval, Economica/Presses universitaires de Laval, 1989, pp. 283-319.

Ferret, Jérôme, "Des devenirs minoritaires. Retour sur l'expérience politique des 'indignés' espagnols", *Mouvements*, No. 75, November 2013, pp. 86-98.

Fillieule, Olivier (ed.), *Le désengagement militant*, Paris, Belin, 2005.

Geisser, Vincent, Karam Karam and Frédéric Vairel, "Espaces du politique. Mobilisations et protestations", in Élizabeth Picard (ed.), *La politique dans le monde arabe*, Paris, Armand Colin, 2006, pp. 193-212.

Gobe, Éric, "Corporatismes, syndicalisme et dépolitisation", in Élizabeth Picard (ed.), *La politique dans le monde arabe*, Paris, Armand Colin, 2006, pp. 171-192.

Gobe, Éric, "Les syndicalismes arabes au prisme de l'autoritarisme et du corporatisme", in Olivier Dabène, Vincent Geisser and Gilles Massardier (eds), *Autoritarismes démocratiques et démocraties autoritaires au XXIe siècle: convergences Nord-Sud*, Paris, La Découverte, 2008, pp. 267-284.

Göle, Nilüfer, "Entre le 'gauchisme' et 'l'islamisme': l'émergence de l'idéologie techniciste en Turquie", in Elisabeth Longuenesse (ed.), *Bâtisseurs et bureaucrates: ingénieurs et société au Maghreb et au Moyen-Orient*, Lyon, Maison de L'Orient, 1990, pp. 309-320.

Gonzales-Qijano, Yves, *Arabités numériques: le printemps du Web arabe*, Paris, Actes Sud-Sindbad, 2012.

Grossetti, Michel, "L'imprévisibilité dans les parcours sociaux", *Cahiers internationaux de sociologie*, Vol. CXX, 2006, pp. 5-28.

Haenni, Patrick, *L'Islam de marché: l'autre révolution conservatrice*, Paris, Seuil, 2005.

Hamayil, Umar, "Institutional Characteristics of the Jordanian Professional Associations", in Hussein Abu Rumman and Hani Hourani (eds), *Professional Associations and the Challenges of Democratic Transformation in Jordan*, Amman, Al-Urdun Al-Jadid Research Center, 2000, pp. 63-92.

Harmsen, Egbert, *Islam, Civil Society and Social Work: Muslim Voluntary Welfare*

Associations in Jordan between Patronage and Empowerment, Leyde, ISIM/ Amsterdam University Press, 2008.

Hourani, Hani, "The Development of the Political Role of the Professional Associations: A Historical Survey 1950–1989", in Hussein Abu Rumman and Hani Hourani (eds), *Professional Associations and the Challenges of Democratic Transformation in Jordan*, Amman, Al-Urdun Al-Jadid Research Center, 2000, pp. 17–62.

Human Rights Watch, *Torture and Impunity in Jordan's Prisons*, April 2008. Online: https://www.hrw.org/report/2008/10/08/torture-and-impunity-jordans-prisons/reforms-fail-tackle-widespread-abuse.

Jabar, Faleh (ed.), *Post Marxism and the Middle East*, London, Saqi Books, 1997.

Jungen, Christine, *Politique de l'hospitalité dans le sud jordanien*, Paris, Karthala, 2009.

Kharinu, Samir, *Al-Harakah al-tullâbîah al-urdunîyah, 1948–1998* [*The Jordanian Student Movement, 1948–1998*], Amman, Al-Urdun Al-Jadid Research Center, 2000.

Kienle, Eberhard, "Libéralisation économique et délibéralisation politique: le nouveau visage de l'autoritarisme", in Olivier Dabène, Vincent Geisser and Gilles Massadier (eds), *Autoritarismes démocratiques et démocraties autoritaires: convergences Nord-Sud*, Paris, La Découverte, 2008, pp. 251–266.

Koehler, Kevin, "Authoritarian Elections in Egypt: Formal Institutions and Informal Mechanisms of Rule Export", *Democratization*, Vol. 15, No. 15, 2008, pp. 974–990.

Koselleck, Reinhart, "'Erfahrungsraum' und 'Erwartungshorizont' – zwei historische Kategorien", in *Vergangene Zukunft*, Frankfurt, Suhrkamp Taschenbuch, 1989 (1st edn 1979), pp. 349–375. English trans. Keith Tribe, "'Spaces of Experience' and 'Horizon of Expectation': Two Historical Categories", in *Futures Past*, New York: Columbia University Press, 2004, pp. 255–275.

Koselleck, Reinhart, "Transformations of Experience and Methodological Change", in *The Practice of Conceptual History: Timing History, Spacing Concepts*, Stanford, CA Stanford University Press, 2002, pp. 45–83.

Krämer, Gudrun, "L'intégration des intégristes: une étude comparative de l'Egypte, la Jordanie et la Tunisie", in Ghassan Salame (ed.), *Démocraties sans démocrates*, Paris, Fayard, 1994, pp. 277–312.

Lagroye, Jacques (ed.), *La Politisation*, Paris, Belin, 2003.

Lahire, Bernard, *Portraits sociologiques: dispositions et variations individuelles*, 2002, Paris, Nathan.

Larzillière, Pénélope, "Political Commitment under an Authoritarian Regime: Professional Associations and the Islamist Movement as Alternative Arenas in Jordan", *International Journal of Conflict and Violence*, Vol. 6, No. 1, 2012, pp. 11–25.

Larzillière, Pénélope, "Production of Norms and Securitization in Development Policies: From 'Human Security' to 'Security Sector Reform'", American University of Beirut, Issam Fares Institute, Working Paper Series No. 13, December 2012.

Larzillière, Pénélope, "Research in Context: Scientific Production and Researchers' Experience in Jordan", *Science, Technology and Society*, Vol. 15, No. 2, 2010, pp. 309-338.

Larzilliere, Pénélope, "Sociologie de l'engagement à partir du Proche-Orient", in Jalal Al Husseini and Aude Signoles (eds), *Les Palestiniens entre État et diaspora: le temps des incertitudes*, Paris, Karthala/IISMM-EHESS, 2012, pp. 179-188 and 299-301.

Larzilliere, Pénélope and Boris Petric (eds), "Révolutions, contestations, indignations", *Socio*, No. 2, December 2013, pp. 7-23.

Latte-Abdallah, Stéphanie, "Les frontières intérieures: enjeu palestinien et métamorphoses de l'engagement féminin en Jordanie", in Jalal Al Husseini and Aude Signoles (eds), *Les Palestiniens entre État et diaspora: le temps des incertitudes*, Paris, Karthala/IISMM-EHESS, 2012, pp. 235-262.

Latte-Abdallah, Stéphanie, "Vers un féminisme politique hors frontières au Proche-Orient. Regard sur les mobilisations en Jordanie (années 1950-années 2000)", *Vingtième siècle*, Vol. 3, No. 103, 2009, pp. 177-195.

Laurens, Henry, *La question de Palestine, I) l'invention de la Terre sainte*, Paris, Fayard, 1999.

Le Quentrec, Yannick and Annie Rieu, *Femmes: engagements publics et vie privée*, Paris, Syllepse, 2003.

Legrand, Vincent, *Le triangle "Jordanie-Palestine-Israël" et la décision jordanienne de désengagement de Cisjordanie (1988)*, Brussels, Bern, Berlin, Peter Lang, 2009.

Longuenesse, Élisabeth (ed.), *Bâtisseurs et bureaucrates: ingénieurs et société au Maghreb et au Moyen-Orient*, Lyon, Maison de l'Orient, 1990.

Longuenesse, Élisabeth, "Les syndicats professionnels en Jordanie: enjeux de société et lutte nationale", 2000. Online: http://halshs.archives-ouvertes.fr/halshs-00111075/.

Longuenesse, Élisabeth, *Professions et société au Proche-Orient: déclin des élites, crise des classes moyennes*, Rennes, Presses Universitaires de Rennes, 2007.

Lust-Okar, Ellen, "The Decline of Jordanian Political Parties: Myth or Reality?", *International Journal of Middle East Studies*, Vol. 33, 2001, pp. 545-569.

Maffi, Irène, "The Creation of Jordanian National Identity: A Short Museographic Story of a Complex Process", in Myriam Ababsa and Rami Daher (eds), *Cities, Urban Practices and Nation Building in Jordan*, Beirut, Presses de l'Ifpo, 2011, pp. 143-160. Online: http://books.openedition.org/ifpo/1737.

Mannheim, Karl, "Das Problem der Generationen", *Kölner Vierteljahrsheft für*

BIBLIOGRAPHY 229

Soziologie, Munich, Duncker & Humblot, Jahrgang VII, Heft 3, 1928. Trans. *The Sociological Problem of Generations*, in P. Kecskemeti (ed.), *Essays on the Sociology of Knowledge*, New York, Routledge and Kegan Paul, 1952, pp. 276–232.

Massad, Joseph, *Colonial Effects: The Making of National Identity in Jordan*, New York, Columbia University Press, 2001.

Matonti, Frédérique and Franck Poupeau, "Le capital militant. Essai de définition", *Actes de la recherche en sciences sociales*, No. 155, 2004/5, pp. 5–11.

McAdam, Doug, "Pour dépasser l'analyse structurale de l'engagement militant", in Olivier Fillieule (ed.), *Le désengagement militant*, Paris, Belin, 2005, pp. 49–74.

McAdam, Doug, "Recruitment of High-risk Activism: The Case of Freedom Summer", *American Journal of Sociology*, Vol. 92, 1986, pp. 64–90.

Mroué, Karim, "Réflexions sur le marxisme aujourd'hui et le communisme arabe du XXe siècle", interview by Anne Jollet, *Cahiers d'Histoire, revue d'histoire critique*, No. 101, April–May–June 2007, pp. 131–143.

Mroué, Karim and Samir Amin, *Communistes dans le monde arabe*, Pantin, Le Temps des Cerises, 2006.

Naïli, Falestin, "Les déplacés de 1967", in Jalal Al Husseini and Aude Signoles (eds), *Les Palestiniens entre État et diaspora: le temps des incertitudes*, Paris, Karthala/IISMM-EHESS, 2012, pp. 67–94.

Nicourd, Sandrine (ed.), *Le Travail militant*, Rennes, Presses Universitaires de Rennes, 2008.

Picard, Élizabeth (ed.), *La Politique dans le monde arabe*, Paris, Armand Colin, 2006.

Pleyers, Geoffrey and Glasius Marlies, "La dimension globale des mouvements de 2011", in Pénélope Larzillière and Boris Petric (eds), "Révolutions, contestations, indignations", *Socio*, No. 2, December 2013, pp. 59–79.

Pudal, Bernard, "La vocation communiste et ses récits", in Jacques Lagroye (ed.), *La Politisation*, Paris, Belin, 2003, pp. 147–161.

Rantawi, Orayb, *an-nuwâb wa muwâzana 2009: qirâ'a fi-l-ittijâhât wa-l-'aûlawiyyât* [*The MPs and the 2009 Budget: Reading of the Trends and Priorities*], al-Quds Center for Political Studies, April 2009.

Rasheed, Haydar, "Labor Unions, Labor Disputes and Industrial Relations", in Hussein Abu Rumman and Hani Hourani (eds), *Professional Associations and the Challenges of Democratic Transformation in Jordan*, Amman, Al-Urdun Al-Jadid Research Center, 2000, pp. 181–188.

Rath, Kathrine, "The Process of Democratization in Jordan", *Middle Eastern Studies*, Vol. 30, No. 3, July 1994, pp. 530–557.

Reiter, Yitzhak "Higher Education and Sociopolitical Transformation in Jordan", *British Journal of Middle Eastern Studies*, Vol. 29, No. 2, 2002, pp. 137–164.

Ricœur, Paul, *Lectures on Ideology and Utopia*, ed. George H. Taylor, New York, Cambridge University Press, 1981.

Robbins, Michael and Lawrence Rubin, "The Rise of Official Islam in Jordan", *Politics, Religion and Ideology*, Vol. 14, No. 1, 2013, pp. 59-74.

Robinson, Glenn E., "Defensive Democratization in Jordan", *International Journal of Middle East Studies*, Vol. 30, August 1998, pp. 387-410.

Romani, Vincent, "Sciences sociales et coercition: Les *social scientists* des Territoires palestiniens entre lutte nationale et indépendance scientifique", Université d'Aix-Marseille-III, Institut d' études politiques d'Aix-en-Provence, dissertation for PhD in political science, 2008.

Rougier, Bernard (ed.), *Qu'est-ce que le salafisme?*, Paris, PUF, 2008.

Roussillon, Alain, *La pensée islamique contemporaine: acteurs et enjeux*, Paris, Téraèdre, 2005.

Sawicki, Frédéric and Johanna Siméant, "Décloisonner la sociologie de l'engagement militant. Note critique sur quelques tendances récentes des travaux français", *Sociologie du travail*, No. 51, 2009, pp. 97-125.

Schmitter, Philippe C., "Still the Century of Corporatism?", *Review of Politics*, No. 36, 1974, pp. 85-131.

Schwedler, Jillian, "The Political Geography of Protest in Neoliberal Jordan", *Middle East Critique*, Vol. 21, No. 3, 2012, pp. 259-270.

Sharp, Jeremy M., *Jordan: Background and U.S. Relations*, Congressional Research Service Report, January 2014, p. 3.

Signoles, Aude, "Les ingénieurs palestiniens entre restructuration interne et accession au pouvoir politique: enjeux nouveaux de la phase de construction étatique", in Institut national d'aménagement et d'urbanisme, *Les métiers de la ville*, Paris, L'Harmattan, 2003, pp. 141-169.

Signoles, Aude (ed.), "Les municipalités islamistes", *Critique internationale*, No. 42, 2009/1.

Singerman, Diane, "Réseaux, cadres culturels et structures des opportunités politiques. Le mouvement islamiste en Égypte", in Mounia Bennani-Chraïbi and Olivier Fillieule (eds), *Résistances et protestations dans les sociétés musulmanes*, Paris, Presses de Sciences Po, 2003, pp. 219-242.

Singerman, Diane, "The Networked World of Islamist Social Movements", in Quintan Wiktorowicz (ed.), *Islamic Activism: A Social Movement Theory Approach*, Bloomington, IN, Indiana University Press, 2004, pp. 143-163.

Vairel, Frédéric, "L'opposition en situation autoritaire: statut et modes d'action", in Olivier Dabène, Vincent Geisser and Gilles Massardier (eds), *Autoritarismes démocratiques et démocraties autoritaires au XXIe siècle: convergences Nord-Sud*, Paris, La Découverte, 2008, pp. 213-232.

Wagner, Anne-Catherine, "Syndicalistes européens. Les conditions sociales et institutionnelles de l'internationalisation des militants syndicaux", *Actes de la recherche en sciences sociales*, No. 155, 2004-2005, pp. 12-33.

Wiktorowicz, Quintan, "The Salafi Movement in Jordan", *International Journal of Middle East Studies*, Vol. 32, No. 2, 2000, pp. 219-240.

Wils, Oliver, *Wirtschaftseliten und Reform in Jordanien. Zur Relevanz von Unternehmer-Bürokraten-Netzwerken in Entwicklungsprozessen*, Hamburg, Deutsches Orient Institut, 2003.

Zeghal, Malika (ed.), "Intellectuels de l'islam contemporain: nouvelles générations, nouveaux débats", *REMM*, No. 123, July 2008, pp. 32-201.

Index

Note: *n* following a page number denotes a footnote with the relevant number.

Abdullah I, King, 12
Abdullah II, King, 5, 11, 18, 22
activist capital, 88–9, 212*n23*
activists: and biographical availability, 40–41; biographical bias/illusion, 40–41, 195–6; by age, 199–200, *201*; family background, 200–2; horizon of expectation, 186–7, 188; influences, 2–3; political affiliation, 199; problem of generation renewal, 185; and professional associations, 5–6; professionalization, 87; region of birth, 200; regional role models, 42–4; trajectories, 182; *see also* Arab nationalist activists; Communist activists; Muslim Brotherhood activists; Palestinian nationalist activists
advocacy NGOs: alternative arena, 7–8; and human rights, 140–3, 152–3; international legitimacy, 132, 133, 181; and Islamism, 134, 143–6; new forums, 135–40, 178; reorientation by default for activists, 141–2
Afghanistan, mujahideen, 173–4

age, of activists, 54, 199–200, *201*
alter-globalism, 135, 138, 155, 178, 187
Amman, hotel attacks (2005), 27, 206*n32*
Amnesty International, 135, 140–1
Arab Liberation Front, 57
Arab nationalism: and Hussein, 12–13; membership trends, 54; and Nasser, 42–3; spheres, 199
Arab nationalist activists: armed struggle, 56–60; study abroad, 31, 53, 55–6, 57–8; underground activities, 46; *see also* Palestinian nationalist activists
armed forces, 14, 58, 148
armed struggle, 56–60, 162
artistic creativity, 47–8, 52
authoritarian liberalism, 18–20, 28–9, 180, 182
authoritarianism, 1–2, 5, 17; *see also* repression
Azzam, Abdullah, 173

Baath Party, 38, 57, 207*n14*
Al-Banna, Hassan, 93, 168
Bedouins, 14, 63

INDEX   233

biographical availability, 40–1
biographical bias/illusion, 40–1,
    195–8
Black September (1970), 15, 34, 36
British Council, 152–3

civil society, 132; see also advocacy
    NGOs
commitment: and activism, 210n4;
    Communist, 33, 34, 76–8; early
    determination, 2–3; educated
    women, 128–9; and ideology, 8–10,
    30–2; Islamist (*iltizâm*), 8–10, 69,
    85; long-term, 76–8
Communism: atheism linked to
    immorality, 46, 74–6; banned
    (1953), 13, 62; education valued,
    65; internal divisions, 60, 63–4,
    80–1; Jordanian Communist Party,
    42; membership trends, 54–5; and
    personal emancipation, 46–7; post-
    1989 disillusionment, 9–10, 79–81,
    102–4, 135–6, 140–1; repression, 46;
    way of life, 3
Communist activists: artistic
    creativity and freedom, 47–8,
    52; closed circle, 77–9, 81;
    commitment, 33, 34, 76–8; and
    danger, 76; emergence from
    underground, 80, 81, 102, 103–4,
    182–3; employment experiences,
    88, 90, 91, 93–4; and the family,
    74–6, 78; marginality, 74–7;
    marriage a political issue, 77–8;
    Muslim Jordanians, 102–3; political
    repression, 62–5, 90, 96–9, 101,
    102–4; study abroad, 31, 37,
    51–3, 61–2, 64–5; switch to human
    rights activism, 140–3; switch to
    Islamism, 99, 143; underground
    activities, 62, 63, 77, 95, 96, 96–7;
    university experience, 31, 37, 51–2,
    53, 60–5; Yarmouk University
    activism, 62–3, 64, 74–5; youth
    centres, 3, 32, 33, 36, 45, 55
cross-border families, 35

Democratic Front for the Liberation of
    Palestine (DFLP), 78, 102, 212n3
demonstrations: against Israel's Gaza
    Strip attack (2008–9), 117–19; Fatah,
    59; political repression, 18, 62–3;
    Yarmouk University, 62–3; see also
    Jordan Spring
depoliticization, 4, 18, 122, 133–5, 185
development aid, 25, 25–6, 218n30
disillusionment: Islamist, 159–72; post-
    1989 Communism, 9–10, 79–81,
    102–4, 135–6, 140–1
donors, 7, 25–6, 129

economic liberalism, 19, 29
education: and reform of society, 171;
    valued by activists and families, 33,
    40, 45–6, 65, 69–70, 202
elections: 1989, 17, 104; 1993, 104–5;
    2007, 19, 22; 2013, 23–4; boycotts,
    22, 23, 151; political tribalization,
    17–18; professional association
    leaders, 114–15; vote buying, 19;
    voting reform, 17–18
employment: and activism, 6, 88–95,
    202; Communist experiences, 88,
    90, 91, 93–4; engineering, 51–2, 69,
    71, 127; medical profession, 90–1,
    98–9, 118, 119; Muslim Brotherhood
    experiences, 89, 90–3, 160; public
    sector career limitations, 89, 90,
    106; women's opportunities, 127,
    152–3, 171–2
energy prices, 24
engineering profession, 51–2, 69, 71, 127
engineers' association, 112, 117, 118,
    123–4, 128
expertise: and activism, 7, 153;
    engineering, 112; and leadership, 87;
    professional associations, 113–14;
    Western experts, 137

family: activism hidden from, 37, 38;
    activism as means of escape from,
    39; background of activists, 52,
    200–2; choice of marriage partner

family (*cont.*):
  a political issue, 77–8; Communist activists, 74–6, 78; women and activism, 78, 128–9
Fatah, 39, 59–60, 99, 101, 207n16
Fatah-Intifada, 98, 99

Gaza Strip, 117–19
generation: first-generation students, 91; generational renewal, 7–8, 154, 185; ideology and age, 54, 199–200, 201
Gulf states, migrant labour, 18, 174
Gulf War (1990–91), 18

Hamas, 175–6
Hattar, Nahed, 139
hegemony: Islamic, 9, 21, 84, 181; local, 53–5
Hezbollah, 145
Hirak (Movement), 148, 218n20
horizon of expectation, 186–8
human rights, 6–7, 133, 140–3, 152–3; Islamist/human rights bipolarization, 133–5, 142–3
Hussein, King, 12–14, 16–17

identity, Transjordanian/Jordanian Palestinian differentiation, 4, 8, 13–14, 34–6, 139, 150, 161
ideology: all-encompassing nature, 73–4, 94–5, 191; choice, 2–3; and commitment, 8–10, 30–2; later consolidation, 48–9; local hegemonies, 53–5; post-ideology circumstances, 141–3, 154–6
injustice, 32, 33–4, 168
Iraq, Gulf War (1990–91) and refugees, 18
Iraq War (2003–), Jordan's support for US, 18
Iraqi refugees, 18
ISIL (Islamic State in Iraq and the Levant), 26–8
Islam: Islamist/human rights bipolarization, 133–5, 142–3; religion and politics, 177, 179; and religious instruction, 159; Shi'ism, 145, 217n17; and the *umma*, 32, 207n5
Islamic Action Front (IAF), 19, 82, 119; anti-corruption commission, 86
Islamism: commitment, 8–10, 69, 85; continuity between religion and politics, 85–6; criticism, 163–7; leftist Islamism, 194; post-Islamism, 158; rejection, 165–7; social hegemony, 9, 21, 84, 181; way of life, 3; *see also* Muslim Brotherhood; Muslim Brotherhood activists; Salafism
Islamo-nationalism, 164
Israel: Gaza Strip attack (2008–9), 117–19; Jordan-Israel peace accord (1994), 139; and Lebanon, 59, 145; operations against, 38, 162–3; Six Day War (1967), 56–7; West Bank occupation, 34, 38, 116–17

Jayyin, 148, 219n21
Jihadi Salafism, 149, 164–5
Jordan Spring, 146–54; demands, 24, 147, 185–6; early mobilizations, 184; monarchy's response, 150–1; and non-political actors, 7–8; political reforms incomplete, 23–4, 147, 151; Queen Rania accused of corruption, 148; range of activists, 146; repression, 150–1; sit-ins and demonstrations, 147; and social media, 154; social movements and coalitions, 147–8, 154
Jordanian identity, 13
Jordanian nationalism, 139–40
Jordanian Palestinians: 1970 attack by monarchy, 15; numbers, 14; and Palestinian nationalism, 15–16, 139–40; and Transjordanian divisions, 4, 8, 13–14, 34–6, 139, 150, 161
Jordanian Social Movement, 137
journalism, 166, 168, 171–2
judiciary, 107–8, 151

knowledge, value of, 33, 40, 65, 69–70
Koselleck, Reinhart, 10, 186

labour unions, 110, 111
lawyer-activists, 107–8
leadership: charismatic leaders, 42–4; and early membership, 51; Muslim Brotherhood goal, 70–1; and personal rewards, 87
Lebanon: Hezbollah, 145; and Israel, 59, 145; Sabra and Shatila massacre, 167
leftwing activism, 6–7, 183–4, 199; leftist Islamism, 194; *see also* advocacy NGOs; Communism; Communist activists
liberal authoritarianism, 18–20, 28–9, 180, 182
local hegemonies, 53–5

al-Maqdisi, Abu Muhammad, 27, 164, 206n33
martial law, 13
martyrdom, 43–4
Marxism, 41, 46–7, 59, 73, 142, 178
medical profession, 90–1, 98–9, 118, 119
mentors, 36–41, 38, 42, 173
migrants, 18, 24
Muslim Brotherhood: and 1989 riots, 16; 2007 elections, 22; 2013 election boycott, 23; and academic excellence, 45–6, 69–70; ambivalent opposition status, 20, 21–2, 118; charity and social work, 20, 83–4, 134, 181; criticism, 168–72, 175–9; expulsion from, 167, 169–70, 175; and Hamas, 175–6; Hussein and, 13; ideological strength, 8–9, 21; increase in support, 42; independent funding, 83; internal divisions, 22–3, 28; international support, 134; and ISIL, 27, 28; Islamic Action Front (IAF), 19, 82, 86, 119; and Islamo-nationalism, 164; leadership goal, 70–1; major political force, 155, 157; membership trends, 54; and personal ambition, 86–7; religious instruction, 159; repression, 18–19, 21, 67–8, 106–9, 213n6; social justice and integrity, 86–7; support for Palestinian cause, 161
Muslim Brotherhood activists: employment experiences, 89, 90–3, 160; marriage and family, 82–3; professionalization, 87; university experience, 31, 50–1, 53, 65–9; and youth centres, 45, 173

Nassar, Fouad, 60
Nasser, Gamal Abdel, 42–3
National Anti-Normalization Committee, 138–9
National Front for Reform, 147
National Liberation League, 42
nationalism, 41–2; *see also* Arab nationalism; Palestinian nationalism
NGOs *see* advocacy NGOs
Nsour, Abdallah, 24

Obama, Barack, 24
orientalism, 184

Palestinian camps, 4, 32, 51, 99, 122, 216n39; Black September (1970), 15, 34, 36
Palestinian Intifada (1987–93), 42, 161, 167
Palestinian nationalism, 3–4, 15–16, 115–19, 134–5, 144; *see also* Fatah
Palestinian nationalist activists: armed struggle, 56–60; *see also* Arab nationalist activists
Palestinian refugees, 14, 18, 32, 33–4
parliament, locus for patronage, 105
political emotions, 32, 42, 44, 185
political parties: ban, 13, 17, 55–6, 62; restrictions, 5, 113, 137–8
political reform, 23–4, 147, 151
political repression *see* repression
Popular Front for the Liberation of Palestine (PFLP), 102, 212n3

poverty, 32–6, 57
prison/prisoners: Arab activists, 57, 59, 98; Communist activists, 62–3, 78–9, 80, 97–8; effect on career, 165, 165–7; family support, 78, 98; Fatah dissenter, 99–101; in Israel, 58; knowledge transmission, 163–4, 165; Muslim Brotherhood, 106, 107; prisoner exchanges, 58; psychological effects, 98; sentence duration shortened, 97–8
professional associations, 110–30; ambiguous relations with government, 110, 125–6, 180–1; anti-normalization committee, 116; background of university activism, 122–4; expertise, 113–14; finance, 113; Islamist predominance, 115; and Israel's Gaza Strip attack, 117–19; key role for activism, 5–6; leadership elections, 114–15, 120; limited activism, 112; limited social base, 120–2; membership, 110–11, 113; rallies, 120; support for Palestinian nationalism, 115–19; women and, 126–9, 216n45
professions, 88–9; *see also* engineering profession; medical profession
public sector, 89, 90, 106, 149

Qutb, Sayyid, 44

Rania, Queen of Jordan, 148
reformist Salafis, 149, 164
refugees: Gulf War refugees, 18; Iraqi, 18; Palestinian, 14, 18, 32, 33–4; Palestinian camps, 4, 32, 51, 99, 122, 216n39; Syrian, 25, 28
repertoire of action: armed struggle, 56–60, 162; election boycotts, 22, 23, 151; journalism, 166, 168, 171–2; judiciary, 107–8; non-violence in Jordan Spring, 149, 150, 153–4; social media, 151, 185; writing, 169; *see also* advocacy NGOs; demonstrations

repression, 96–109; Arab nationalists, 57–8; Communists, 62–5, 90, 96–9, 101, 102–4; Hussein, 12–13, 17; Jordan Spring, 150–1; legitimacy derived from, 107–8; Muslim Brotherhood, 18–19, 67–8, 106–9, 213n6

Salafism, 87, 149, 164–5
Saudi Arabia, 25–6, 89
schools, 38, 171
security service (*Mukhabarat*), 62–3, 97, 101
Shi'ism, 145, 217n17
Shubeilat, Layth, 116, 124, 215n22
Social Forum, 135–8, 139
social hegemony, Islamists, 9, 21, 84, 181
social justice, 86–7, 104, 144
social media, 151, 154
social networks, 36–41, 44–9
Socialist Thought Forum, 138
Soviet Union, collapse, 79–81
State Security Court, 107–8, 151
strikes, 24, 66
student associations, 66–7, 71, 123; Thabahtuna (National Campaign for Students' Rights), 147–8, 153, 216n41
student union, 62, 66, 160, 216n41
Sykes-Picot Agreement (1916), 12
Syria, 20, 25–6, 56, 145–6
Syrian refugees, 25, 28

Talal, King, 12
teachers' association, 119–20
teaching profession, 37–8, 92, 160, 165, 171
terrorism, Amman hotel attacks (2005), 27, 206n32
Thabahtuna (National Campaign for Students' Rights), 147–8, 153, 216n41
torture, 97, 100–1, 212n1
tourism, 24
Transjordan, British mandate, 12

INDEX 237

Transjordanians: academic scholarships, 58, 217n8; and Jordan Spring, 148–9; and Jordanian Palestinian divisions, 4, 8, 13–14, 34–6, 139, 150, 161; and Palestinian nationalism, 15–16; plot against Israeli military base, 162–3; tribal identity, 13–14
tribes: Abdullah II and, 18; and Baath Party, 57; and Communist Party, 103; Hussein and, 13–14; identity and activism, 38–9; and Islamism, 84–5; Jordan Spring divisions, 148; political importance, 17–18

underground activities: Communist, 62, 63, 77, 95, 96–7; Communist and nationalist, 46; emergence from underground, 80, 81, 102, 103–4, 182–3
unemployment, 94, 115, 127
United States, aid to Jordan, 24, 25–6
universities, 50–72; and activism, 5; Arab nationalists, 31, 53, 55–60; Communist students, 60–5; gender and curriculum choice, 170–1; General Union of Arab Students, 56; influence on political commitment, 37, 160–1; Islamic students, 31, 50–1, 53, 65–9; negative effect of activism, 57–8, 60, 64–5; and Palestinian camps, 51, 216n39; PhD doctorates, 50, 58, 68, 69; political repression, 57–8, 62–5, 67–8; scholarships, 58; strike (1973), 66; student associations, 66–7, 71, 123; student choice, 31, 51–3; student politicization, 50–1; student union disbanded (1975), 66; student union initiative, 62, 160, 216n41; University of Jordan, 50, 65–6, 68; Yarmouk, 50, 58–9, 62–3, 64, 74–5, 160, 161, 169

water resources, 25
West Bank, 116–17
women: employment opportunities, 127, 152–3, 171–2; engineers, 127; family and professional commitments, 78, 128–9; gender and curriculum choice, 170–1; marginality, 190; and professional associations, 123–9, 216n45; Union of Jordanian Women, 78
work *see* employment

Yarmouk University, 50, 58–9, 62–3, 64, 74–5, 160, 161, 169
young people: Communist youth centres, 3, 32, 33, 36, 45, 55; early influences, 2–3; and Jordan Spring, 147–8, 152–4; lack of political unity, 155; mentors, 36–41, 38, 42, 173; Muslim youth centres, 37, 173; political organizations, 44–9; poverty and the Palestinian cause, 32–6; *see also* mentors; universities
Youth and People's Coalition for Change in Jordan, 147–8

Zaatari camp, 25
al Zarqa University, 89
al-Zarqawi, Abu Musab, 164, 206n32, 206n33

www.ingramcontent.com/pod-product-compliance
Ingram Content Group UK Ltd.
Pitfield, Milton Keynes, MK11 3LW, UK
UKHW020820240326
469204UK00019B/97